# Sexual Assault Experiences in the Active-Component Army

Variation by Year, Gender, Sexual Orientation, and Installation Risk Level

AVERY CALKINS, MATTHEW CEFALU, TERRY L. SCHELL, LINDA COTTRELL, SARAH O. MEADOWS, REBECCA L. COLLINS

Prepared for the United States Army
Approved for public release; distribution unlimited

RAND ARROYO CENTER

For more information on this publication, visit **www.rand.org/t/RRA1385-2**.

**About RAND**

The RAND Corporation is a research organization that develops solutions to public policy challenges to help make communities throughout the world safer and more secure, healthier and more prosperous. RAND is nonprofit, nonpartisan, and committed to the public interest. To learn more about RAND, visit www.rand.org.

**Research Integrity**

Our mission to help improve policy and decisionmaking through research and analysis is enabled through our core values of quality and objectivity and our unwavering commitment to the highest level of integrity and ethical behavior. To help ensure our research and analysis are rigorous, objective, and nonpartisan, we subject our research publications to a robust and exacting quality-assurance process; avoid both the appearance and reality of financial and other conflicts of interest through staff training, project screening, and a policy of mandatory disclosure; and pursue transparency in our research engagements through our commitment to the open publication of our research findings and recommendations, disclosure of the source of funding of published research, and policies to ensure intellectual independence. For more information, visit www.rand.org/about/research-integrity.

RAND's publications do not necessarily reflect the opinions of its research clients and sponsors.

Published by the RAND Corporation, Santa Monica, Calif.
© 2022 RAND Corporation
**RAND®** is a registered trademark.

Library of Congress Control Number: 2022917793
ISBN: 978-1-9774-1012-2

# About This Report

This report documents research and analysis conducted as part of a project entitled *Timely Monitoring of Sexual Harassment and Gender Discrimination Within the U.S. Army*, sponsored by the Office of the Deputy Chief of Staff, G-1, U.S. Army. The purpose of the project was to develop and execute a survey infrastructure to ensure ongoing, timely access to data for monitoring and responding to experiences with sexual harassment and gender discrimination by specific subgroups within the U.S. Army, and to provide additional analysis of secondary data to understand the circumstances surrounding sexual assault and sexual harassment.

This research was conducted within RAND Arroyo Center's Personnel, Training, and Health Program. RAND Arroyo Center, part of the RAND Corporation, is a federally funded research and development center (FFRDC) sponsored by the United States Army.

RAND operates under a "Federal-Wide Assurance" (FWA00003425) and complies with the *Code of Federal Regulations for the Protection of Human Subjects Under United States Law* (45 CFR 46), also known as "the Common Rule," as well as with the implementation guidance set forth in U.S. Department of Defense (DoD) Instruction 3216.02. As applicable, this compliance includes reviews and approvals by RAND's Institutional Review Board (the Human Subjects Protection Committee) and by the U.S. Army. The views of sources utilized in this report are solely their own and do not represent the official policy or position of DoD or the U.S. government.

## Acknowledgments

The research team would like to thank our study action officer, Jenna Newman, Army Resilience Directorate, for her support and guidance throughout the study. We also want to thank our RAND colleagues Lisa Wagner for her input, insights, and project management skills and Deborah Zajdman for her assistance with document preparation. We are grateful to Heather Krull, Maria Lytell, and Craig Bond for their guidance throughout the study and review of this report. Finally, we thank our peer reviewers, Coreen Farris of RAND and Amy Street of Boston University, for their helpful and constructive comments on an earlier draft of this report.

# Summary

In February 2021, U.S. Secretary of Defense Lloyd Austin ordered the military services to take "immediate" action to address sexual harassment and sexual assault in the military, which included both a focus of efforts on "high-risk" military installations and the creation of a 90-day independent review commission to conduct an "immediate, impartial assessment" of the U.S. Department of Defense's (DoD's) efforts to prevent sexual harassment and assault (U.S. Secretary of Defense, 2021).[1] To guide its sexual assault prevention and response efforts, the U.S. Army asked RAND Arroyo Center to create descriptions of soldiers' experiences of sexual assault in the active-component Army.

In this report, we provide the results of an exploratory, descriptive analysis of active-component soldiers' sexual assault experiences. The analysis was conducted using the 2016 and 2018 Workplace and Gender Relations Survey of Active Duty Members (WGRA) (Breslin et al., 2019; Davis et al., 2017). All statistics presented in the findings are conditional on respondents being categorized as having experienced a sexual assault in the year prior to survey administration. This report is a companion to Calkins et al., 2021, which provides similar information on soldiers' experiences of sexual harassment and gender discrimination in the active-component Army.

We provide information on

- the types of sexual assault behaviors experienced by sexual assault victims over the year prior to survey administration, during *all* sexual assault experiences
- perceived perpetrator intent and method of coercion involved in *all* sexual assault experiences over the year prior to survey administration
- the types of sexual assault behaviors involved in victims' *self-identified most serious experience* of sexual assault over the year prior to survey administration
- characteristics (number, military status, gender, and relationship to the victim) of the perpetrator(s) of victims' *self-identified most serious experience* of sexual assault over the year prior to survey administration
- time and place of victims' *self-identified most serious experience* of sexual assault over the year prior to survey administration
- alcohol and drug involvement in victims' *self-identified most serious experience* of sexual assault over the year prior to survey administration
- co-occurrence of victims' *self-identified most serious sexual assault experience* with hazing, bullying, sexual harassment, and stalking over the year prior to survey administration.

---

[1] *High-risk* was not defined in the memo.

Throughout the remainder of this summary, unless otherwise specified, references to *types of sexual assault behaviors, perceived perpetrator intent,*[2] or *method of coercion* refer to the types of sexual assault behaviors involved in *all* sexual assault experiences over the year prior to survey administration, and references to any other characteristics of sexual assault experiences refer to characteristics of victims' *self-identified most serious experience.*

We also compare the sexual assault experiences of the following groups of soldiers:

- sexual assault victims in the 2016 versus 2018 WGRA samples
- female sexual assault victims versus male sexual assault victims
- sexual assault victims who identify as heterosexual versus those of other sexual orientations
- sexual assault victims assigned to installations where they face a high risk of sexual assault versus sexual assault victims assigned to installations where they do not face a high risk of sexual assault, where *high risk* is defined as above-average risk of sexual assault for either male or female soldiers.

## Findings

### *Sexual Assault Experiences Across the Active-Component Army*

The most common type of sexual assault behavior, both for all sexual assault experiences and for victims' self-assessed most serious experiences, is that someone intentionally touched private areas of the victim's body. Penetrative sexual assaults with a penis were the second most common type of sexual assault but were substantially less common than intentional touching of private parts. Nearly 90 percent of victims believed that the assault was committed for a sexual reason, and more than half indicated that the assault was meant to be abusive or humiliating (which can co-occur).

The typical perpetrator of victims' most serious sexual assault experiences is a male enlisted member of the military acting alone. The perpetrator was most often a military peer of the victim, but slightly more than 40 percent of victims indicated that at least one perpetrator was the victim's supervisor or another higher-ranked service member. Slightly more than half of victims indicated that the perpetrator was a friend or acquaintance. Perpetrators who were strangers to the victim were uncommon, and assaults by spouses, significant others, or family members were comparatively rare.

Approximately two-thirds of victims' most serious experience of sexual assault occurred at a military installation. Slightly more than half of victims indicated that their most serious experience occurred during a required military activity, the most common of which was while at

---

[2] Because perpetrator intent is defined using questions about respondents' beliefs about their intent, references to *perpetrator intent* should be interpreted as *perceived* perpetrator intent.

work during duty hours. Victims were approximately equally likely to be assaulted while at work, while in their or someone else's home or quarters, and while out with friends or at a party. Forty percent of victims indicated that they were drinking alcohol during their most serious sexual assault experience, and 42 percent indicated that the perpetrator was drinking alcohol during their most serious sexual assault experience, with 25 percent of victims indicating that the perpetrator either bought or gave them alcohol.

Sexual assaults often co-occur with sexual harassment—and, less often, with stalking—by the same perpetrators. Measures of co-occurrence with hazing and bullying are not comparable across years, but in 2018, 17 percent of victims described their most serious experience as hazing and 24 percent described their most serious experience as bullying.

Table S.1 provides a high-level overview of the findings for respondents' most serious sexual assault experience, focusing on broad categories of characteristics of these assaults (e.g., personal relationship between the perpetrator and victim, time and place of the assault). For each characteristic category and group of soldiers being compared (e.g., men versus women) the table indicates whether we observed statistically significant differences across groups with a solid circle in the appropriate table cell. Blank cells in the table indicate that no significant differences were found. In the sections that follow, we focus only on those categories where we observed differences that may be of practical importance for policy or prevention efforts. Importantly, there may be other differences in different groups of soldiers' sexual assault experiences that we cannot identify because of small sample sizes; this is often true of the comparisons for sexual orientation, especially for men.

# Table S.1. Summary of Findings by Characteristics: Categories and Comparison Group

| Characteristics | Year: 2016 versus 2018 | Gender: Men versus Women | Sexual Orientation Among Men[a] | Sexual Orientation Among Women[b] |
|---|---|---|---|---|
| Perpetrator(s) intended to abuse or humiliate[c] | | ● | | ● |
| Perpetrator(s) threatened or used physical force | | | ● | |
| Victim was unconscious, asleep, drunk, high, or drugged | | ● | | |
| Number of perpetrators | | ● | ● | |
| Perpetrator(s) in the military | | ● | ● | |
| Gender of perpetrator(s) | | ● | ● | ● |
| Rank of perpetrator (if at least one was in the military) | | ● | ● | |
| Perpetrator(s) professional relationship with victim | ● | ● | ● | |
| Perpetrator(s) personal relationship to victim | ● | ● | ● | ● |
| Place assault occurred | ● | ● | ● | ● |
| Time assault occurred | | ● | | ● |
| Alcohol or drug use by victim or perpetrator | ● | ● | ● | |
| Victim described assault as hazing[d] | | ● | ● | |
| Victim described assault as bullying[d] | ● | | ● | ● |
| Victim sexually harassed before or after assault by same perpetrator(s) | | | | |
| Victim was stalked before or after assault by same perpetrator(s) | | | ● | |

NOTES: ● = statistically significant differences across groups ($p \leq 0.05$). Blank cells indicate no statistically significant differences acros gay, bisexual, other. NR = no response. PNA = prefer not to answer.

[a] For men, the comparison is between heterosexual men and men who responded LGBO, NR, or PNA.

[b] For women, the comparisons are among heterosexual women, LGBO women, and women who responded NR or PNA.

were not asked of respondents who qualified as having been sexually assaulted under the first sexual assault behavior (someone put
s anus, mouth, or vagina) because the Uniform Code of Military Justice does not require abusive, humiliating, or sexual intent for this
sexual assault; these percentages, therefore, have the denominator as individuals who qualified as having been sexually assaulted
. See Chapter 2 for further details.
azing changed substantially between survey years. See Chapter 2 for further details.

## Differences by Survey Year

There were few statistically significant changes in the circumstances surrounding sexual assault across survey years. Of the few statistically significant differences across survey years, none are of substantive importance for policymaking (i.e., indicate a needed change in the primary focus of current prevention efforts).

## Differences by Gender

Male and female sexual assault victims in the active-component Army tend to have experienced different types of sexual assault behaviors during all sexual assault experiences over the 12 months prior to the survey date, and there were differences in perceived perpetrator intent and methods of coercion as well. Among soldiers who were sexually assaulted during the year prior to survey administration, and among all sexual assault experiences over the 12 months prior to the survey date, female victims were more likely than male victims to experience completed sexual assaults, where they were penetrated by someone else, or attempted penetrative sexual assaults. Male victims were more likely than female victims to experience sexual assaults where they were made to penetrate someone else. Among soldiers who had been sexually assaulted, nonpenetrative sexual assaults were equally common for male and female victims. Male victims were more likely than female victims to indicate that they believed that the perpetrator intended to abuse or humiliate them, whereas female victims were more likely than male victims to indicate that they believed that the perpetrator had a sexual reason for their actions. Female victims were also more likely than male victims to indicate that they were sexually assaulted while asleep, unconscious, or incapacitated by drugs or alcohol.

The typical perpetrator of soldiers' most serious sexual assault experience was similar for both male and female victims: a male enlisted member of the military acting alone. However, men were more likely to indicate multiple perpetrators; at least one female perpetrator; nonmilitary perpetrators; and, among military perpetrators, perpetrators who were commissioned officers. There were also gender differences in the relationships between victims and perpetrators. Although the typical perpetrator for both male and female victims was a military peer, male victims were more likely than female victims to indicate that at least one perpetrator was their subordinate or someone they managed. Female victims were more likely than male victims to describe the perpetrator as a friend or acquaintance, whereas male victims were more likely than female victims to indicate "none of the above" (i.e., someone they knew other than a family member, current or former spouse or significant other, or friend or acquaintance) on the personal relationships item—a category that might include some military coworkers. Men were also more likely to indicate "not sure" on the personal relationship item.

Male victims were more likely than female victims to indicate that their most serious sexual assault experience occurred during required military activities, particularly while on temporary duty (TDY), during official military functions, during military combat training other than basic training, and while at work during duty hours. Female victims were more likely than male victims to indicate that their most serious sexual assault experience occurred while in their or someone else's home or quarters. Female victims were more likely than male victims to indicate that they and/or the perpetrator were drinking alcohol during their most serious sexual assault experience, and male victims were more likely than female victims to describe their most serious experience as hazing.

## Differences by Sexual Orientation

Sexual minorities (i.e., those who did not identify as heterosexual) in the Army are more often female than male, so an examination of experiences by sexual orientation only would likely be biased because of the different gender balance of individuals in the two groups. We therefore present results regarding sexual orientation separately by gender of the victims. Because of small sample sizes, we had to aggregate active-component soldiers who were sexual minorities into relatively large groups according to their response to the WGRA's sexual orientation question. For women, these groups are (1) heterosexual; (2) lesbian, gay, bisexual, or other (LGBO); and (3) no response (NR) and prefer not to answer (PNA). For men, these groups are (1) heterosexual and (2) all others (LGBO, NR, and PNA).

### Differences by Sexual Orientation for Active-Component Women

We found few differences between heterosexual and LGBO female victims' sexual assault experiences, but we found several differences between the sexual assault experiences of (1) NR and PNA female victims and (2) heterosexual and LGBO female victims.

Heterosexual female victims were more likely than LGBO female victims, who were more likely than NR/PNA female victims, to indicate that they experienced a nonpenetrative sexual assault where they were made to touch private areas of someone else's body during any of their sexual assault experiences in the year prior to the survey. Furthermore, heterosexual female victims were more likely than LGBO female victims and less likely than NR/PNA female victims to indicate that they believed that the perpetrator intended to abuse or humiliate them.

Female sexual assault victims who did not or preferred not to respond to the sexual orientation question (i.e., NR/PNA victims) were more likely than heterosexual or LGBO female victims to indicate that the perpetrator(s) of their most serious sexual assault experience fell into the personal relationship category of "none of the above" (i.e., someone the victim knew, but not a family member, current or former spouse or significant other, or friend or acquaintance). We believe that this category includes military coworkers who the victims did not consider friends. A similar pattern exists for whether the victim would describe their most serious experience as bullying. Additionally, LGBO and NR/PNA female victims were more likely than heterosexual female victims to indicate that their most serious sexual assault experience occurred at a military installation, and LGBO women were statistically significantly more likely than heterosexual and

NR/PNA women to indicate that their most serious experience occurred while being intimate with the other person.

These results indicate that the female sexual assault victims who most often experienced assaults that were meant to abuse, humiliate, or bully were not the LGBO female victims, but NR/PNA female victims. Although this seems important, we cannot say definitively who the NR/PNA female victims are (in particular, whether they are sexual minorities), which makes it difficult to determine the actual policy implications.

## Differences by Sexual Orientation for Active-Component Men

We found several important differences by sexual orientation in male victims' sexual assault experiences. Because of the very small sample of LGBO male victims in particular, there may be some important differences by sexual orientation in male victims' experiences that we are unable to identify.

LGBO, NR, and PNA male victims were more likely than heterosexual male victims to indicate that they experienced all penetrative or attempted penetrative sexual assault behaviors during any sexual assault over the year prior to survey administration, and they were less likely to indicate that they experienced having someone touch private areas of their body. LGBO, NR, and PNA male victims were also statistically significantly more likely to indicate that the perpetrator used or threatened them with violence to make them comply.

We found several differences in the characteristics of perpetrators. LGBO, NR, and PNA male victims were more likely than heterosexual male victims to indicate that the perpetrators were a mixed-gender group; that at least one perpetrator was their supervisor, another higher-ranked member of their chain of command, or a stranger; and that they were not sure of the number, gender, military status, pay grade, and/or their personal relationship with the perpetrator(s) of their most serious experience. LGBO, NR, and PNA male victims were less likely to indicate that all perpetrators were female and that at least one perpetrator was a military member, and they were as likely as heterosexual male victims to indicate that all perpetrators were male.

LGBO, NR, and PNA male victims were more likely than heterosexual male victims to indicate that their most serious experience occurred during basic, officer, or technical training; official military functions; and while on TDY.

LGBO, NR, and PNA male victims were more likely than heterosexual male victims to indicate that they were drinking alcohol or did not know whether they were drinking alcohol at the time of their most serious sexual assault experience. They were also more than twice as likely as heterosexual male victims to indicate that they believed they had been drugged and more than three times as likely to indicate that they did not know whether they had been drugged. Finally, LGBO, NR, and PNA male victims were twice as likely to indicate that they were stalked both before and after their most serious sexual assault experience by the same perpetrator(s) and more likely to describe their most serious experience as hazing and/or bullying.

*Differences by Installation Risk Level*

*Installation risk level* is defined as an installation's average rate of sexual assault (separately for women and men), where installations with rates above the overall Army average (excluding the Pentagon and military academies) are designated as "high risk." Like the results for survey year, few significant differences were observed between high-risk and non–high-risk installations, and of those differences that do exist, none are of substantive importance for policymaking (i.e., none indicate a needed change in the primary focus of current prevention efforts).

## Policy Implications

*Sexual Assault Prevention Training Should Be Aligned with Victims' Experiences*

The first major policy implication of our research is that **sexual assault prevention training materials should emphasize the most common behaviors and scenarios outlined in this report, as we previously recommended for sexual harassment and gender discrimination prevention training.** The approach to sexual assault prevention in the Army is, in many ways, geared toward addressing the sexual assault of heterosexual women. However, our findings show that there are large differences in the circumstances surrounding sexual assault in the Army by gender and sexual orientation. **Sexual assault prevention training materials should be expanded to incorporate the experiences of men, sexual minorities, and others whose sexual assault experiences differ from those of heterosexual women.**

We found that the sexual assault experiences of soldiers at high-risk and non–high-risk installations are broadly similar. We therefore conclude that **there is no need to tailor the content of training materials to individual installations.** For example, a program that uses vignettes as discussion prompts does not need to generate different vignettes for low- and high-risk installations. However, our results are not meant to imply that the overall prevention approach at high-risk installations should look exactly like the approach at non–high-risk installations. For example, a high-risk installation might decide to invest proportionately more prevention resources than a lower-risk installation.

*More Data Are Needed on the Experiences of Sexual Minorities in the Army*

The second major policy implication of our research is that **there is a crucial lack of data on the sexual assault experiences of sexual minorities in the Army.** We found suggestive evidence that sexual minority male victims experienced more penetrative sexual assaults, more violent sexual assaults, and more assaults meant to haze or bully than heterosexual male victims. We also found some evidence that NR/PNA women experienced more assaults meant to abuse, humiliate, or bully than heterosexual women or LGBO women. However, given the relatively small number of soldiers who identified with a sexual orientation other than heterosexual in the combined 2016 and 2018 WGRAs, and our resulting need to aggregate soldiers of differing sexual orientations, it is difficult for us to truly examine these soldiers' experiences in depth. This lack of detailed information on the unique sexual assault experiences of sexual minorities hampers the effort to prevent and respond to sexual assault in the Army.

**The Army should further investigate the sexual assault and other potentially discriminatory experiences of sexual minority soldiers by including sexual orientation as a sociodemographic variable in existing administrative data and in survey data collected in the future.** If sexual orientation were treated as other sociodemographic characteristics (e.g., gender, race/ethnicity) are in administrative data, it might be possible to use that information as part of analyses and as a sampling and weighting variable in future data-collection efforts. **Such treatment of sexual orientation data will require a change in DoD-level policy, and the Army alone may not be able to implement the recommendation.** Such a change would also require a thoughtful examination of how to protect sexual orientation data and the confidentiality of service members' identities. Sexual minorities are not a monolithic group, and if the current restrictions on collecting sexual orientation data remain in place, both DoD and the Army will continue to be limited in their ability to determine whether there are differences between the experiences of sexual minority soldiers and their majority peers. Also, if these restrictions remain, it will ultimately limit the Army's ability to learn about the best way to prevent sexual assaults and serve victims' needs.

# Contents

# Figures and Tables

## Figures

# Tables

# Chapter 1. Introduction

In February 2021, U.S. Secretary of Defense Lloyd Austin ordered the military services to take "immediate" action to address sexual harassment and assault in the military, which included both a focus of efforts on "high-risk" military installations and the creation of a 90-day independent review commission to conduct an "immediate, impartial assessment" of the U.S. Department of Defense's (DoD's) efforts to prevent sexual harassment and assault (U.S. Secretary of Defense, 2021).[3] The report of the independent review commission noted that discussions with junior enlisted service members revealed that "outdated training" on sexual harassment and assault "seemed to reinforce rape myths, rather than address misinformation," and that junior enlisted service members, especially men, lacked understanding on what types of behaviors qualify as sexual harassment or assault (Independent Review Commission on Sexual Assault in the Military, 2021, p. 30). To correct this problem, the independent review commission recommended that DoD and the services update training on sexual harassment and assault to reflect service members' experiences and improve data collection on sexual assault to better reflect the experiences of service members who might be at higher risk for sexual assault because of their race, ethnicity, gender, sexual orientation, gender identity, or some combination of these characteristics (a construct known as *intersectionality*).[4] Furthermore, the independent review commission noted a lack of available data on perpetration, which is key to the prevention of sexual assault (Independent Review Commission on Sexual Assault in the Military, 2021).[5]

Prior RAND Corporation research has examined rates of, risk factors for, and consequences of sexual assault in the military (see, e.g., National Defense Research Institute, 2014; Matthews et al., 2021; Morral et al., 2021; and Schell, Morral, et al., 2021). Although the Defense

---

[3] *High-risk* was not defined in the memo.

[4] Specifically, we are referring to Line of Effort 2: Prevention, Recommendation 2.4, "Modernize prevention education and skill-building to reflect today's generation of Service members" (Independent Review Commission on Sexual Assault in the Military, 2021, pp. 33–34) and a cross-cutting recommendation: "DoD needs to improve data collection, including qualitative research and quantitative survey tools, to better reflect the experiences of Service members whose intersecting identities, such as race, ethnicity, sexual orientation, gender and gender identity, may place them at higher risk for sexual harassment and sexual assault" (Independent Review Commission on Sexual Assault in the Military, 2021, p. 32). Our analysis is a first step toward understanding whether individuals with different risk levels have different sexual assault experiences. We do not focus on race and ethnicity because they are not predictors of sexual assault risk on their own (Schell, Morral, et al., 2021). Gender identity was not included in the 2018 Workplace and Gender Relations Survey of Active Duty Members (WGRA) (Breslin et al., 2019), which precludes studying differences in experience. Our sample is not large enough to examine intersectionality, but the addition of the 2021 WGRA data may make such an examination possible for future studies.

[5] Specifically, we are referring to Line of Effort 2: Prevention, Recommendation 2.6 a: "DoD should establish a dedicated research center for the primary prevention of interpersonal and self-directed violence" (Independent Review Commission on Sexual Assault in the Military, 2021, p. 34).

Manpower Data Center (DMDC) reports top-line characteristics of sexual assault experiences by service branch, there is limited information available on whether sexual assault victims in various groups according to military and demographic characteristics have different sexual assault experiences.[6] Such information is helpful for understanding what types of behaviors and contexts the Army's sexual assault prevention effort should target.

To guide its sexual assault prevention efforts, beginning in December 2020, the Army asked RAND Arroyo Center to create descriptions of soldiers' experiences of sexual assault in the active-component Army, including the information described earlier, with a particular focus on high-risk Army installations. In this report, we compare the experiences of different groups of sexual assault victims in the active-component Army to determine whether sexual assault education materials should be tailored to the experiences of different groups of victims. Prior research suggests that male and female service members' experiences of sexual assault differ in ways that require different prevention approaches (Farrell, 2015); for this reason, we examine differences in sexual assault experiences by gender. We also examine changes in the sexual assault experiences in data collected in 2016 and 2018, because the prevalence of sexual assault in the Army rose from 2016 to 2018 (Breslin et al., 2019; Davis et al., 2017). In addition, we examine differences by sexual orientation because service members who do not identify as heterosexual face an elevated risk of sexual assault (Morral and Schell, 2021; Trump-Steele et al., 2021). Finally, as requested by the Army, we examine whether sexual assault experiences at high-risk installations differ from those at non–high-risk installations.

The analyses presented in this report are descriptions of the experiences of different groups of sexual assault victims based on survey data about different types of behaviors that are likely to line up with the legal definitions of sex crimes under the Uniform Code of Military Justice (UCMJ). They are not drawn from official reports of sexual assault to the Army. These analyses also are not an assessment of different risk levels or the causes of sexual assault in the Army. Finally, the survey data provide general information about perpetrators (e.g., gender, pay grade, relationship with the respondent) but do not provide detail on the risk factors for perpetration.

This report is a companion to Calkins et al., 2021, which provides similar information on soldiers' experiences of sexual harassment and gender discrimination in the active-component Army. Sexual harassment in the military is highly correlated with sexual assault: Army installations that are high risk for sexual harassment also tend to be high risk for sexual assault,

---

[6] The overview reports for DoD's WGRA (Breslin et al., 2019; Davis et al., 2017) provide overall descriptions of which types of sexual assaults soldiers most often experience; the typical characteristics of perpetrators; the times and places sexual assaults most often occur; and other contextual information, such as alcohol and drug involvement and co-occurrence with bullying, hazing, sexual harassment, and stalking. However, these descriptions lack confidence intervals, comparisons across sexual orientation and installation risk level, and some comparisons across survey year. Trump-Steele et al. (2021) provided a comparison of sexual assault experiences across sexual orientations but did not provide Army-specific information.

and across the military, the level of ambient sexual harassment at the installation to which a service member is assigned (that is, sexual harassment of others at that installation) is correlated with that service member's risk of sexual assault (Matthews et al., 2021; Schell, Cefalu, et al., 2021). This evidence suggests that, as the U.S. government often notes, sexual harassment and sexual assault "exist on a continuum of harm" and therefore should be treated as part of the same problem (see, e.g., Independent Review Commission on Sexual Assault in the Military, 2021, p. 4; Farrell, 2017, p. 1; Department of Defense Instruction 1020.03, 2020; and Breslin, Klahr, and Neria, 2020). This report focuses on the end of the continuum that encompasses sexual assault.

## Organization of This Report

Chapter 2 details our data and methods for constructing experience descriptions. In Chapter 3, we provide experience descriptions for all active-component soldiers across the two survey years who were sexually assaulted and discuss differences between the two survey years. In Chapter 4, we discuss gender differences in sexual assault experiences; in Chapter 5, we discuss differences in sexual assault experiences by sexual orientation; and in Chapter 6, we discuss differences in experiences at high-risk versus non–high-risk installations. In Chapter 7, we conclude the report and discuss the policy implications of this work. This report also contains five appendixes: Appendix A provides details on WGRA data preparation, Appendix B provides details on the method used to create sexual assault descriptions, Appendix C provides tabular results for Chapters 3 through 7, Appendix D provides tabular results by gender and survey year, and Appendix E provides tabular results by gender and installation risk level.

# Chapter 2. Construction of Experience Descriptions

In this chapter, we provide details about the method used to describe sexual assault experiences among active-component soldiers who were sexually assaulted over the 12 months prior to the WGRA survey dates. Portions of this chapter are reproduced from Calkins et al., 2021; those portions are noted in the text.

## Data Sources

### Workplace and Gender Relations Survey of Active Duty Members

The data for this report were drawn from the 2016 and 2018 WGRA. The WGRA collects information about service members' experiences with sexual assault, sexual harassment, and gender discrimination (Breslin et al., 2019; Davis et al., 2017).

The analysis draws from the personnel in the active-component Army who responded to the 2016 or the 2018 WGRA. It is possible that some respondents participated in both surveys, although in such cases, respondents would be referring to two different periods (i.e., the year prior to each survey). The survey includes a series of screener questions (which we describe in more detail in the next section) that determine whether the victim was sexually assaulted during the year prior to survey administration.[7] Individuals who were sexually assaulted were asked a series of follow-up questions on their self-identified "most serious" experience over the prior year. Our experience descriptions draw from responses to both the screener questions and the follow-up questions. The analysis uses analytic weights provided by DoD's Office of People Analytics (OPA) to reduce the risk of bias from the survey sampling design and nonresponse.[8] We limited our analytic sample to the 1,022 individuals (776 women and 246 men) who have nonzero weights and who were sexually assaulted in the 12 months prior to their survey date.[9]

---

[7] The 2016 survey data were collected between July 22 and October 14, 2016, and, therefore, cover sexual assaults that occurred between July 22, 2015, and October 14, 2016 (Davis et al., 2017). The 2018 survey data were collected between August 24 and November 5, 2018, and, therefore, cover sexual assaults that occurred between August 24, 2017, and November 5, 2018 (Breslin et al., 2019).

[8] Detailed information on the WGRA survey methodology is available in reports produced by OPA (Davis et al., 2017; Breslin et al., 2019; OPA, 2019).

[9] The 2016 sample comprises 523 soldiers (381 women and 142 men), and the 2018 sample comprises 499 soldiers (395 women and 104 men).

## Determining Whether Respondents Were Sexually Assaulted

The legal definitions of *rape, sexual assault, aggravated sexual contact*, and *abusive sexual contact* in the U.S. military are laid out under Article 120 of the UCMJ (10 U.S.C. § 920). The legal definitions of *rape* and *sexual assault* that were in place during the administration of the 2016 and 2018 WGRA required that an individual commit a "sexual act upon another person" using threats, bodily harm, or fraud, or when the other person does not or cannot consent (10 U.S.C. § 920). The legal definitions of *aggravated sexual contact* or *abusive sexual contact* require that an individual commit "sexual contact upon another person" with similar conditions regarding the other person's consent. *Sexual act* and *sexual contact* are defined using precise, anatomical language, and sexual contact and some types of sexual acts require that the perpetrator's intent be "to abuse, humiliate, harass, or degrade any person or to arouse or gratify the sexual desire of any person" (DoD, 2019, pp. A22-1–A22-12). *Sexual assault* is defined in the WGRA using several questions that determine whether a respondent experienced an event which would likely qualify as rape, sexual assault, aggravated sexual contact, abusive sexual contact, or attempted rape or sexual assault as defined by Article 120 of the UCMJ in the event of an official investigation (Morral, Gore, and Schell, 2014). We refer to these offenses collectively as *sexual assault* throughout this report.[10]

An individual in the WGRA is coded as having been sexually assaulted using a series of responses to questions about whether the individual had experienced any of six types of sexual assault behaviors, which are defined using precise anatomical language that corresponds to the definitions of *sexual acts* or *sexual contact* under the UCMJ, during the 12 months prior to the survey date. Individuals who experienced one of these unwanted behaviors were then asked a series of follow-up questions to determine (1) whether they believed that the perpetrator's intent was either to abuse or humiliate them or whether they believed that the perpetrator committed the act for a sexual reason ("perceived perpetrator intent"),[11] and (2) whether and how their consent was violated ("type of coercion"). The list of questions used to code whether an individual was sexually assaulted is presented in Table 2.1. For the first type of behavior ("someone put his penis into your anus or mouth [or vagina, if you are a woman]"), respondents had to indicate that they experienced the behavior and at least one of the types of coercion to qualify as having been sexually assaulted.[12] For the other types of sexual assault behaviors, respondents had to indicate that they experienced the behavior, indicate at least one of the two

---

[10] Our data were drawn from survey questions about respondents' experiences rather than from the results of an official investigation. Sexual assaults described in this report therefore do not necessarily line up exactly with the legal definitions because they were not found to be sexual assaults by a court of law.

[11] Later references to *perpetrator intent* should be interpreted as *perceived perpetrator intent* because perpetrator intent is assessed from survey questions on respondents' beliefs about the perpetrator's or perpetrators' intentions rather than questions asked of the perpetrator(s) themselves.

[12] This is because this type of behavior qualifies as a sexual act under the UCMJ regardless of perpetrator intent.

perpetrator intent questions, and indicate at least one of the types of coercion questions to qualify as having been sexually assaulted. Once the respondent qualified as having experienced sexual assault, they were asked the remaining questions about types of sexual assault behaviors, but they were *not* asked any further perpetrator intent or type of coercion questions. Because the types of behaviors are separate questions in the WGRA, respondents could indicate that they experienced multiple types of behaviors.

**Table 2.1. Sexual Assault Screening Questions, 2016 and 2018 WGRA**

| Category | Survey Measure |
|---|---|
| Type of sexual assault behavior | Since [date 12 months prior to survey administration], did you have any <u>unwanted</u> experiences in which someone put his penis <u>into your</u> anus or mouth (or vagina, if you are a woman)? (Answer choices: Yes, No) |
| | Since [date 12 months prior to survey administration], did you have any <u>unwanted</u> experiences in which someone put any object or any body part <u>other than a penis</u> into your anus or mouth (or vagina, if you are a woman)? The body part could include a finger, tongue, or testicles. (Answer choices: Yes, No) |
| | Since [date 12 months prior to survey administration], did anyone <u>make you put</u> any part of your body or any object into someone's mouth, vagina, or anus when you did not want to? A part of the body could include your tongue or fingers (or penis or testicles, if you are a man). (Answer choices: Yes, No) |
| | Since [date 12 months prior to survey administration], did you have any <u>unwanted</u> experiences in which someone <u>intentionally touched</u> private areas of your body (either directly or through clothing)? Private areas include buttocks, inner thigh, breasts, groin, anus, vagina, penis, or testicles. (Answer choices: Yes, No) |
| | Since [date 12 months prior to survey administration], did you have any <u>unwanted</u> experiences in which someone <u>made you touch</u> private areas of their body or someone else's body (either directly or through clothing)? This could involve the person putting their private areas on you. Private areas include buttocks, inner thigh, breasts, groin, anus, vagina, penis, or testicles. (Answer choices: Yes, No) |
| | Since [date 12 months prior to survey administration], did you have any <u>unwanted</u> experiences in which someone <u>attempted to</u> put a penis, an object, or any body part into your anus or mouth (or vagina, if you are a woman), <u>but no penetration actually occurred</u>? (Answer choices: Yes, No) |
| Perceived perpetrator intent[a] | Was this unwanted experience (or any experiences like this if you had more than one) abusive or humiliating, or intended to be abusive or humiliating? If you are not sure, choose the best answer. (Answer choices: Yes, No) |
| | Do you believe the person did it for a sexual reason? For example, they did it because they were sexually aroused or to get sexually aroused. If you are not sure, choose the best answer. (Answer choices: Yes, No) |
| Type of coercion | They used or threatened to use physical force to make you comply. For example, use or threats of physical injury, use of a weapon, or threats of kidnapping. (Answer choices: Yes, No) |
| | They threatened you (or someone else) in some other way. For example, by using their position of authority, by spreading lies about you, or by getting you in trouble with authorities. (Answer choices: Yes, No) |

6

| Category | Survey Measure |
|---|---|
| | They did it while you were passed out, asleep, unconscious, or so drunk, high, or drugged that you could not understand what was happening or could not show them that you were unwilling. (Answer choices: Yes, No) |
| | It happened without your consent. For example, they continued even when you told or showed them that you were unwilling, you were so afraid that you froze, they tricked you into thinking they were someone else such as pretending to be a doctor, or some other means where you did not or could not consent. (Answer choices: Yes, No) |
| Number of assaults | Thinking about the past 12 months, please give your best estimate of how many <u>separate occasions</u> you had these unwanted experiences. |

SOURCE: Data are reproduced from the 2018 WGRA survey instrument provided in Breslin et al., 2019. Identical questions were asked in the 2016 WGRA (Davis et al., 2017).
[a] This set of follow-up questions was not asked after the first screener question (i.e., someone put his penis into your anus or mouth [or vagina, if you are a woman]), as the UCMJ does not require either abusive/humiliating or sexual intent for this act to qualify as rape or sexual assault.

When we include the questions on perpetrator intent and type of coercion in our experience descriptions, we use the answer to the question on which the individual qualified as having been sexually assaulted—that is, the first behavior endorsed where the respondent also endorsed at least one of the intent questions (if required) and at least one of the consent questions. Information on perpetrator intent in our experience descriptions therefore includes only the answers of respondents who qualified on a behavior requiring abusive, humiliating, or sexual intent under the UCMJ. This coding creates an implied hierarchy of sexual assault behaviors, where the ordering corresponds to the order in which behaviors are presented in Table 2.1. Perpetrator intent and type of coercion apply to the behavior that a respondent experienced that is highest in that hierarchy.

## Most Serious Experience of Sexual Assault

The WGRA does not provide detailed follow-up information on perpetrator characteristics; time and place; alcohol and drug involvement; or association with bullying, hazing, sexual harassment and sexual assault for *all* sexual assault experiences over the prior year. Instead, the WGRA provides that information on victims' *self-assessed most serious experiences*. Individuals who experienced at least one sexual assault were asked follow-up questions describing the experience that "had the biggest effect on them" and that they deemed to be the "worst or most serious" sexual assault event they had experienced in the year prior to the survey date (Davis et al., 2017; Breslin et al., 2019). The follow-up questions include which type of sexual assault behavior the respondent experienced,[13] characteristics of the perpetrator(s), the time and place the situation occurred, the involvement of alcohol, whether the respondent would describe the

---

[13] Respondents are able to designate only behaviors that they indicated having experienced on the screener questions.

behavior as either bullying or hazing, and whether the respondent was sexually harassed or stalked by the same perpetrator(s) either before or after the sexual assault. A list of the follow-up questions on respondents' most serious experience of sexual assault is provided in Table 2.2. Some questions (noted either as "mark all that apply" or "mark yes or no for each item") may have multiple answers for each respondent.

**Table 2.2. Follow-Up Questions on Most Serious Experience of Sexual Assault**

| Category | Survey Measure |
|---|---|
| Type of sexual assault behavior | Which of the following experiences happened during the event you chose as the worst or most serious? *Mark "Yes" or "No" for each item:* Put their penis into your anus, mouth, or vagina; Put any object or any body part <u>other than a penis</u> into your anus, mouth, or vagina; Made you put any part of your body or any object into someone's mouth, vagina, or anus; <u>Intentionally</u> touched private areas of your body;[a] <u>Intentionally</u> touched ANY area of your body;[a] Made you touch private areas of their body or someone else's body; Made you touch ANY areas of their body or someone else's body;[a] <u>Attempted</u> to put a penis, an object, or any body part into your anus, mouth, or vagina, <u>but no penetration actually occurred</u> |
| Characteristics of perpetrator(s) | How many people did this to you? (Choose one answer: one person; more than one person; not sure) |
| | [In 2016] Please indicate the gender(s) of this person(s). [In 2018] Was/were the person(s) involved . . . ? (Choose one answer: all men; all women; a mix of men and women; not sure) |
| | Was/were any of the person(s) who did this to you a military member? (Choose one answer: yes, they all were; yes, some were, but not all; no, none were military; not sure)[b] |
| | [Asked only of individuals who responded "yes, they all were" or "yes, some were, but not all" to the previous question] At the time of the event, what paygrade was/were the military member(s) who did this to you? *Mark all that apply.* (Answer choices include each pay grade and "not sure.") |
| | At the time of the event, was/were any of the person(s) who did this to you . . . ? *Mark all that apply:* Your immediate supervisor; Someone else in your chain of command (excluding your immediate supervisor); Some other higher ranking military member not listed above; Military peer(s) of about the same rank as you;[c] Subordinate(s) or someone you manage as part of your military duties; DoD/Government civilian(s) working for the military; Contractor(s) working for the military; Not sure |
| | At the time of the event, was/were any of the person(s) who did this to you . . . ? *Mark all that apply:* Your current or former spouse; Someone you have a child with (your child's mother or father); Your significant other (boyfriend or girlfriend) who you <u>live</u> with; Your significant other (boyfriend or girlfriend) who you <u>do/did not</u> live with; A friend or acquaintance; A family member or relative; A stranger; None of the above; Not sure |
| Where event took place | Did the unwanted event occur . . . ? *Mark "Yes" or "No" for each item. If you have not visited these locations or performed these activities since [date one year prior to survey administration], please mark "No."* Response options: At a military installation/ship (for example, on base, on shore duty, etc.); While you were on TDY/TAD, at sea, or during field exercises/alerts; While you were deployed to a combat zone or to an area where you drew imminent danger pay or hostile fire pay; During an overseas port visit while deployed; While transitioning between operational theaters (for example, going to or returning from forward deployment); While you were in a delayed entry program (DEP) or delayed training program (DTP);[d] While you were in recruit training/basic training; While you were in any other type of military combat training; While you were in Officer Candidate or Training School/Basic or Advanced Officer Course; While you were attending military occupational specialty |

| Category | Survey Measure |
|---|---|
| | school/technical training/advanced individual training/professional military education; While at an official military function (either on or off base); While you were at a location off base (for example, in temporary lodging/hotel room, a restaurant, bar, nightclub, etc.) |
| When event took place | Which of the following best describe[s] the situation when this unwanted event occurred? *Mark all that apply:* You were out with friends or at a party that was <u>not</u> an official military function; You were on a date; You were at work during duty hours; You were on approved leave; You were being intimate with the other person;[e] You were in your or someone else's home or quarters; None of the above; Do not recall |
| Bullying and hazing | [Definitions of hazing and bullying, which are different between 2016 and 2018] Based on the definitions above, would you describe this unwanted event as . . . ? *Mark "Yes" or "No" for each item:* Hazing; Bullying |
| Sexual harassment and stalking | Did the offender(s) . . . ? *Mark "Yes" or "No" for each item:* Sexually harass you <u>before</u> the situation; Stalk you <u>before</u> the situation; Sexually harass you <u>after</u> the situation; Stalk you <u>after</u> the situation |
| Alcohol involvement | At the time of the unwanted event, had you been drinking alcohol? Even if you had been drinking, it does not mean that you are to blame for what happened. (Choose one answer: Yes; No; Not sure)<br><br>Just prior to this unwanted event . . .<br>• Did the person(s) who did this to you buy or give you alcohol to drink? (Choose one answer: Yes; No; Not sure)<br>• Do you think that you might have been given a drug without your knowledge or consent? (Choose one answer: Yes; No; Not sure)<br><br>At the time of this unwanted event, had the person(s) who did it been drinking alcohol? (Choose one answer: Yes; No; Not sure) |

SOURCE: Reproduced from 2018 WGRA survey instrument provided in Breslin et al., 2019. Similar—and, in many cases, identical—questions were asked in the 2016 WGRA (Davis et al., 2017). Important differences between the two surveys are noted below. TDY/TAD = temporary duty/temporary additional duty.

[a] This item is included in the survey because touching an area of someone's body other than "private" areas can qualify as a sexual assault under the UCMJ if it was done for a sexual purpose. However, because the survey includes victims who can only speculate on the perpetrator(s)'s intentions (i.e., the WGRA is not a survey of perpetrators), it is unclear whether individuals who experienced only these acts actually experienced an incident that lines up with the definition of sexual assault under the UCMJ. For that reason, we exclude these items.

[b] In 2016, an additional survey measure asked whether at least one perpetrator was a member of the same service branch.

[c] The response option of "military peer(s) of about the same rank as you" was not included on the 2016 WGRA. This answer choice was the most common answer on the 2018 WGRA, and we noticed large differences in the response patterns (especially endorsement of "not sure") across years, which could be attributed to the difference in answer choices. For this reason, we report only responses to this question using 2018 data.

[d] The "delayed training program" portion of this response option was added in 2018.

[e] This response option was included only on the 2016 WGRA. It was not endorsed by a large number of respondents. The item is relatively difficult to interpret; it is not clear how respondents interpreted "being intimate with the person." However, we continue to include the item in our descriptions of experiences.

The text of three questions changed substantially from the 2016 to 2018 WGRA instruments. The first was the question on the professional relationship between the victim and the perpetrator, which added the option to indicate that the perpetrator was a military peer of the victim. This is by far the most endorsed option on the 2018 WGRA, and we believe (and will show in Chapter 3) that the addition of this option changed the probability of endorsing the other response options. Additionally, the bullying and hazing questions begin with the definitions of

9

bullying and hazing, which are substantially different between the two years. In both cases, respondents were provided with definitions of bullying and hazing, followed by a question about whether the respondent would describe their experience as bullying or hazing. Table 2.3 compares the definitions of bullying and hazing from the two survey years. We believe that the change in definition might have materially changed the way that respondents interpreted these questions, and that responses in 2016 and 2018 are therefore not comparable. We therefore present only data from the 2018 WGRA for these questions in the experience descriptions, except for in Chapter 3, where we discuss the changes to the text of the questions in more depth and demonstrate the changes in response patterns from year to year. Other changes in the survey instrument from 2016 to 2018 are minor and most likely did not affect respondents' interpretation of the questions. Most are small changes to wording. There was one question where the answer choices changed from 2016 to 2018: In 2016, the question on when the event took place included an answer option for "while being intimate with the person," which was removed from the 2018 instrument. This answer choice was rarely endorsed, so we believe that it did not change the pattern of responses. Throughout the text, when we present statistics about this answer choice, we use data from 2016 only.

**Table 2.3. Definitions of Hazing and Bullying in the 2016 versus 2018 WGRA**

| 2016 WGRA | 2018 WGRA |
|---|---|
| Hazing refers to things done to humiliate or "toughen up" people prior to accepting them into a group. | Hazing is any conduct through which members of the armed forces or DoD civilian employees, without a proper military or governmental purpose (but with a connection to military service or DoD civilian employment), <u>physical or psychologically injure</u>, or create a risk for such injuries, for the purpose of <u>initiation/admission into or affiliation with</u>, change in status or position with, or as a condition of continued membership in any military or DoD civilian organization. |
| Bullying refers to repeated verbally or physically abusive behaviors that are threatening, humiliating, or intimidating. | Bullying is an act of <u>aggression</u> by members of the armed forces or DoD civilian employees, with a connection to military service or DoD civilian employment, with the <u>intent of harming</u> a member of the armed forces or DoD civilian employee physical or psychologically, <u>without a proper military or governmental purpose</u>. Bullying may involve singling out of an individual from his or her co-workers or unit for ridicule because he or she is considered different or weak. It often involves an imbalance of power between the aggressor and the victim. |

SOURCE: Source for 2016 is Davis et al., 2017. Source for 2018 is Breslin et al., 2019.

## Administrative Data on Military Personnel

Text in this section is reproduced in part from the description of the construction of experience descriptions in Chapter 2 of Calkins et al., 2021, with modifications as necessary for differences between the two reports.

We used administrative personnel data from the DMDC Active Duty Master File to link active-component soldiers to the locations where they served during the one-year period prior to survey participation. We associated individuals with the installation to which they were assigned for the majority of their time in the 12 months prior to the survey date. If the individual spent equal months at multiple installations, we assigned the individual to their most recent installation prior to the survey date. We excluded personnel who were assigned to the Pentagon or military academies from all analyses because these personnel face very different types of sexual assault risk than personnel assigned to other installations. The Pentagon is the installation with the lowest prevalence of sexual assault in the Army (Matthews et al., 2021). The WGRA samples do not include cadets and midshipmen at the service academies, so estimates would provide information about only other personnel stationed there.[14]

## Construction of Sexual Assault Experience Descriptions

Text in this section is reproduced in part from the description of the construction of experience descriptions in Chapter 2 of Calkins et al., 2021, with modifications as necessary for differences between the two reports.

We developed descriptions of sexual assault for victims in the active-component Army using information from *both* the sexual assault screening questions and the follow-up questions about the soldiers' most serious experiences of sexual assault in the 2016 and 2018 WGRA. Our descriptions are meant to illuminate the context of sexual assaults experienced by active-component soldiers: specifically, what types of sexual assault behaviors are involved (both in all sexual assaults and during victims' worst experiences); respondents' beliefs about perpetrators' intentions; the types of coercion involved; who the typical perpetrators are; where and when sexual assaults occur; whether alcohol is involved; and whether the sexual assault co-occurred with hazing, bullying, sexual harassment, or stalking. We produced these descriptions for the entire active-component Army and aggregating the two survey years, separately by survey years, separately for high-risk and non–high-risk installations as groups, separately by gender, and separately by gender and sexual orientation. The descriptions are constructed using only the experiences of soldiers who were sexually assaulted during the year prior to the administration of the 2016 and 2018 WGRA.

We produced figures displaying the estimated percentages of sexual assault victims who indicated experiencing each characteristic of their sexual assault experience. Corresponding tabular results are provided in Appendix C of this report. For the sexual assault screener questions on behaviors, the percentages should be interpreted as the percentage of victims in a given group who indicated that they experienced a particular type of behavior during *any* sexual assault experience over the year prior to the survey. For the questions on perpetrator intent, the percentages should be interpreted as the percentage of victims in each group who did not qualify

---

[14] Cadets and midshipmen at the service academies are surveyed separately by OPA (Davis et al., 2019).

as having been sexually assaulted on the first type of behavior who indicated that they believed the perpetrator had a particular intent *during the sexual assault including the type of behavior on which they qualified as having been sexually assaulted.* For the sexual assault screener questions on type of coercion, the percentages should be interpreted as the percentage of victims in each group who indicated that they experienced a particular type of coercion *during the sexual assault including the type of behavior on which they qualified as having been sexually assaulted.* For the follow-up questions involving soldiers' most serious experience of sexual assault, including information on types of sexual assault behaviors involved in the most serious experience; perpetrator characteristics; time and place of the assault; alcohol and drug involvement; and co-occurrence with hazing, bullying, sexual harassment and stalking, the percentages should be interpreted as the percentage of victims in each group who indicated that *their most serious experience* involved each characteristic.

We first produce these percentages for all soldiers in the active-component Army who were sexually assaulted. We then compare the experiences of the following groups:

- sexual assault victims in the 2016 versus 2018 WGRA samples (Chapter 3)
- female sexual assault victims versus male sexual assault victims (Chapter 4)
- sexual assault victims who identify as heterosexual versus other sexual orientations (Chapter 5)
- sexual assault victims assigned to installations where they face a high risk of sexual assault versus soldiers who are assigned to installations where they do not face a high risk of sexual assault, where *high risk* is defined as above-average risk of sexual assault for either male or female soldiers (Chapter 6).

To protect respondents' privacy, we do not report results for any group of soldiers with fewer than 30 respondents who were sexually assaulted.

We report 95-percent confidence intervals (CIs) for each estimated percentage using Clopper-Pearson exact CIs (Clopper and Pearson, 1934; see Appendix B). The confidence intervals reflect the uncertainty in the estimates, and the results should be interpreted with this uncertainty in mind. We suppress any estimate for which the difference between the estimate and either boundary of the confidence interval (i.e., upper or lower) is greater than 15 percentage points because the level of uncertainty is too high to provide a useful interpretation of the estimate. We still report the confidence interval in these cases to communicate the range of estimates that are consistent with the data. These cases are displayed in figures as confidence intervals only. In tabular results, we also report only confidence intervals in these cases, with "S" (meaning suppressed) in place of the point estimate.

The results presented in this report are descriptive and are meant to describe the observed descriptions of sexual assault. Given the large set of results presented, we used *p*-values from Rao-Scott chi-squared tests to indicate potential sources of differences across survey years, between men's and women's experiences, between high-risk and non–high-risk installations, by sexual orientation, and across high-risk installations. No adjustments for multiple hypothesis testing were used because the goal of using the *p*-values was to highlight potential sources of differences, and we interpret the results with this in mind.[15]

We used a *p*-value cutoff of 0.05 as the criterion for flagging potential differences of interest. If the *p*-value for a given statistical test was less than or equal to 0.05, we interpreted that as a statistically significant difference in the frequency of a characteristic of the most serious sexual assault experience between the groups being compared. It is important to keep in mind that a *p*-value greater than 0.05 does not mean that no differences exist; it means that there is not enough evidence to verify the existence of differences. Similarly, although a *p*-value of less than or equal to 0.05 indicates that there are statistically significant differences in the most serious sexual assault experiences across survey years, gender, sexual orientation, or installation risk level, the differences might not be large enough to be of practical importance for policymaking.

It is important to keep in mind that a statistically significant difference and a substantive difference between groups are not the same. When sample sizes are large or variation is low, estimates may be precise enough to find very small statistically significant differences, but the difference between the two estimates may not be of practical importance for policymaking. For instance, if a characteristic applies to either a very large or very small percentage of sexual assault victims (i.e., more than 90 percent or less than 5 percent) and the difference is smaller than 5 percentage points, the difference likely is not especially important to the Army's approach to sexual assault prevention. We also highlight some cases where a statistically significant difference on a question with more than two answer choices is driven by a larger proportion of victims responding with "not sure" (for instance, a difference in alcohol involvement in assaults at high-risk versus non–high-risk installations; see Chapter 6) or where we believe that there are important contextual factors to keep in mind (for instance, a difference in the proportion of victims at high-risk versus non–high-risk installations indicating that their most serious assault occurred while deployed; see Chapter 6).

The descriptions of sexual assault described in this report are based on relatively small sample sizes because they are limited to individuals in the active-component Army who responded to the WGRA in 2016 or 2018 and were sexually assaulted during the 12 months prior to the survey date. These individuals are then divided into meaningful groups to compare characteristics of their sexual assault experiences. Because of the limited sample sizes, true differences between groups have a high probability of being detected as statistically significant only when that true difference between groups is large. When a difference between groups is not statistically significant, the reader should not interpret that failure to reject the null hypothesis as evidence that differences of a small or medium effect size do not exist in the population. The

---

[15] See Appendix B for a more detailed explanation of the methods used in this report, including hypothesis testing and power calculations.

limited data do not allow us to identify all of the true differences between groups with standard levels of statistical confidence. Appendix B provides detailed power analyses corresponding to the analyses in each chapter of this report. Ultimately, our goal was to identify parts of the sexual assault experience in the active-component Army that differ across survey years, genders, sexual orientations, and installation risk level in ways that are of practical importance for the Army's approach to sexual assault prevention and response. These analyses are likely to achieve that goal whenever the differences between these groups are descriptively large.

Other approaches for estimating and identifying differences across installations, such as small area estimation techniques, were considered. However, we chose our approach because it meets the goals of this report without unnecessary complexity and provides simple-to-interpret results. It is unlikely that alternative estimation strategies would substantively change our results.

# Chapter 3. Sexual Assaults in the Active-Component Army in 2016 and 2018

In this chapter, we present the most common characteristics of sexual assaults of active-component soldiers in the 2016 WGRA sample, the 2018 WGRA sample, and the combined 2016 and 2018 WGRA samples. We examine the types of sexual assault behaviors involved, perceived perpetrator intentions, and types of coercion involved in all sexual assaults across the active-component Army. We also examine types of sexual assault behaviors; perpetrator characteristics; time and place of the assault; alcohol involvement; and co-occurrence with bullying, hazing, sexual harassment, and stalking for soldiers' most serious sexual assault experience.

Appendix C includes tabular results for this chapter. Appendix D includes tabular results for differences by gender and year.

## Sexual Assault Prevalence in the Active-Component Army

We provide the prevalence of sexual assault in the active-component Army, here and in the remaining chapters, for context. Across the two WGRA samples of sexual assault victims in 2016 and 2018, 1.3 percent of active-component soldiers were sexually assaulted over the year prior to survey administration. The rate of sexual assault in the Army rose from 1.1 percent in 2016 to 1.5 percent in 2018. Information on the prevalence of sexual assault by gender in both years is provided in Chapter 4.

## Sexual Assault Screening Questions

Figure 3.1 displays the percentage of sexual assault victims in the active-component Army who indicated that they experienced each type of sexual assault behavior on the sexual assault screener questions (that is, during all sexual assault experiences of the prior year), with results pooled for both surveys and separately by survey year. Note that the responses for types of sexual assault behaviors could be from *any* sexual assault experienced over the year prior to the survey rather than solely the most serious sexual assault experience. Corresponding tabular results are available in Table C.1.

All figures in this chapter are produced in the same format. The labels on the x-axis represent responses to the survey questions. The three icons above each label represent the designated percentage from the graph, with the purple squares (leftmost icon) representing the percentage of all active-component soldiers across both survey years who were sexually assaulted (i.e., all sexual assault victims) who indicated each characteristic of their experience, the teal circles (center icon) representing the percentage of all active-component soldiers in the 2016 WGRA sample who were sexually assaulted (i.e., sexual assault victims in the 2016 sample) who indicated each characteristic of their experience, and the lime-green triangles (rightmost icon) representing the percentage of all active-component soldiers in the 2018 WGRA sample who were sexually assaulted (i.e., sexual assault victims in the 2018 sample) who indicated each characteristic of their experience. The lines surrounding these icons represent the 95-percent CI. If no icon is provided, that means that we have suppressed the icon because the confidence interval is too wide to provide a useful estimate. Bolded labels indicate a statistically significant difference across the two WGRA survey years.

**Figure 3.1. Types of Sexual Assault Behaviors from Screener Questions, All Sexual Assault Victims by WGRA Survey Year**

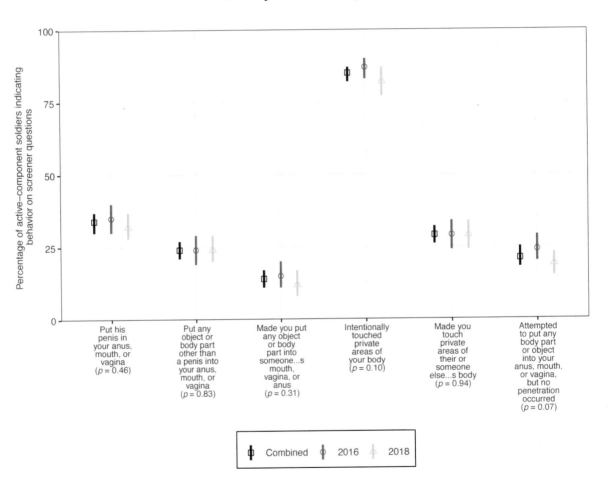

SOURCE: Authors' calculations using the 2016 and 2018 WGRA.
NOTE: Percentages are made up of only soldiers who were sexually assaulted during the year prior to WGRA administration. Percentages are available in Table C.1.

The most common type of behavior experienced by soldiers during any sexual assault experience over the year prior to the survey date (experienced by 85 percent of sexual assault victims) was having someone intentionally touch private areas of the respondent's body, either directly or through clothing. The second most common, at 34 percent of victims, was having someone put his penis into the victim's anus, mouth, or vagina. The other types of sexual assault behaviors indicated on the screener questions, from most to least common, were having someone make the victim touch private areas of the perpetrator's or someone else's body (29 percent); having someone put any object or body part other than a penis into the victim's anus, mouth, or vagina (24 percent); having someone make an unsuccessful attempt to put a penis, other body part, or object into the victim's anus, mouth, or vagina (21 percent); and having someone make the victim put any object or body part into someone's anus, mouth, or vagina (14 percent). There were no statistically significant changes across survey years in the types of sexual assault behaviors indicated on the screener questions.

Figure 3.2 displays the percentage of sexual assault victims indicating that they were assaulted more than once, each type of perpetrator intent, and each type of coercion, with results pooled for both surveys and separately by survey year. Note that the responses for types of sexual assault behaviors could be from *any* sexual assault experienced over the year prior to the survey rather than solely the most serious sexual assault experience. Corresponding tabular results are available in Table C.2 (perpetrator intentions and types of coercion).

**Figure 3.2. Perpetrator Intent and Type of Coercion from Screener Questions, All Sexual Assault Victims by WGRA Survey Year**

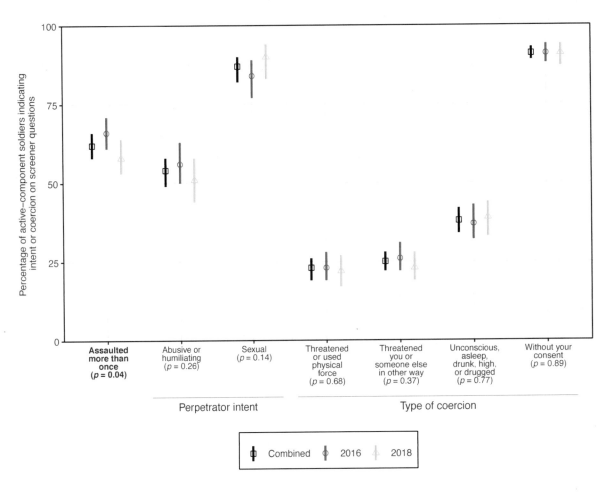

SOURCE: Authors' calculations using the 2016 and 2018 WGRA.
NOTE: Percentages are made up of only soldiers who were sexually assaulted during the year prior to WGRA administration. Perpetrator intent and type of coercion percentages are for the behavior on which the respondent qualified as having been sexually assaulted. Intent questions were not asked of respondents who qualified as having been sexually assaulted under the first sexual assault behavior (someone put his penis into the respondent's anus, mouth, or vagina), because the UCMJ does not require abusive, humiliating, or sexual intent for this behavior to qualify as rape or sexual assault. These percentages, therefore, have the denominator as individuals who qualified as having been sexually assaulted on one of the other behaviors. See Chapter 2 for further details. Percentages are available in Table C.2.

Across the two survey years, 62 percent of sexual assault victims indicated that they were assaulted more than once. This percentage differed across the two survey years (66 percent in 2016 versus 58 percent in 2018).

When it comes to perpetrator intentions, 54 percent of victims across survey years indicated that they believed that the perpetrator(s)'s intentions were to abuse or humiliate the victim, and 87 percent indicated that they believed that the perpetrator assaulted them for a sexual reason. There were no statistically significant changes in perpetrator intent across survey years. Note that, as described in Chapter 2, these results exclude individuals who qualified as having been sexually assaulted under the first sexual assault behavior (someone put his penis into the victim's anus, mouth, or vagina), because those individuals were not given these two questions.

When it comes to type of coercion, 23 percent of victims across survey years indicated that the perpetrator either used or threatened physical force as part of the behavior(s) experienced by the victim. Twenty-five percent of victims indicated that the perpetrator had threatened them or someone else in some way other than physical force, and 38 percent indicated that the behavior occurred while they were unconscious, asleep, or incapacitated by alcohol or drugs. Ninety-one percent of victims endorsed the item indicating that the behavior occurred without their consent; the other nine percent of victims must have endorsed one of the other three type of coercion items to qualify as having been sexually assaulted, and those three types of coercion are violations of the victim's consent regardless of whether the victim recognized it as such. There were no statistically significant changes in type of coercion across survey years.

## Soldiers' Most Serious Sexual Assault Experience

### Types of Sexual Assault Behaviors

Figure 3.3 displays the percentage of victims indicating that they experienced each type of unwanted behavior during their most serious experience of sexual assault over the year prior to the administration of either WGRA, with results pooled for both surveys and separately by survey year. Corresponding tabular results are available in Table C.3.

**Figure 3.3. Types of Sexual Assault Behaviors During Most Serious Experience, All Sexual Assault Victims by WGRA Survey Year**

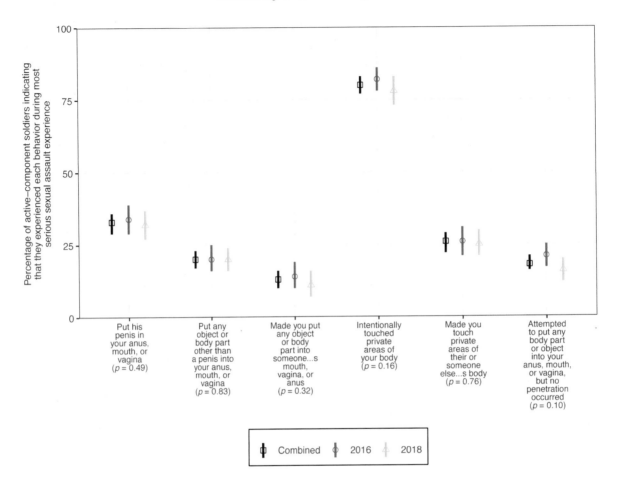

SOURCE: Authors' calculations using the 2016 and 2018 WGRA.
NOTE: Percentages are made up of only soldiers who were sexually assaulted during the year prior to WGRA administration. Respondents are instructed to select all that apply. Percentages are available in Table C.3.

The most common type of behavior experienced by soldiers during their most serious sexual assault experience (which was experienced by 80 percent of victims) was having someone intentionally touch private areas of the victim's body, either directly or through clothing. The second most common, experienced by 33 percent of victims, was having someone put his penis into the victim's anus, mouth, or vagina. The other types of sexual assault behaviors indicated on the screener questions, from most to least common, were having someone make the victim touch private areas of the perpetrator's or someone else's body (26 percent); having someone put any object or body part other than a penis into the victim's anus, mouth, or vagina (20 percent); having someone make an unsuccessful attempt to put a penis, other body part, or object into the victim's anus, mouth, or vagina (18 percent); and having someone make the victim put any object or body part into someone's anus, mouth, or vagina (13 percent). There were no statistically significant changes across survey years in the types of sexual assault behaviors included in victims' most serious experiences.

These behaviors are similar in magnitude to those presented in Figure 3.1, indicating that soldiers' most serious experiences of sexual assault are similar to all sexual assault experiences over the 12 months prior to the survey date in terms of the types of sexual assault behaviors involved. We therefore do not present other information on the types of sexual assault behaviors involved in soldiers' most serious experience in other chapters, although the tabular results are available in the appendix.

### Characteristics of Perpetrators

Tabular results for all figures in this section are available in Table C.4 in Appendix C.

Figure 3.4 displays the most common numbers, military statuses, and genders of perpetrators of active-component soldiers' most serious experiences of sexual assault, with results pooled for both surveys and separately by survey year. One-third (33 percent) of victims indicated that their most serious experience had more than one perpetrator, 63 percent indicated that their most serious experience had only one perpetrator, and 4 percent were not sure how many perpetrators were involved. The overwhelming majority of victims' most serious experiences had military perpetrators: Seventy-eight percent of victims indicated that all the perpetrators were in the military and 6 percent indicated that some, but not all, of the perpetrators were in the military (for a total of 84 percent indicating that at least one perpetrator was a member of the military). Twelve percent of victims indicated that none of the perpetrators were in the military, and 4 percent were not sure whether any of the perpetrators were in the military. The typical perpetrator of the most serious experience was male: Seventy-eight percent of victims indicated that all perpetrators were men, 8 percent indicated that the perpetrators were a mix of men and women, 11 percent indicated that all perpetrators were women, and 3 percent were not sure of the perpetrators' genders. Of victims who indicated at least one military perpetrator, 84 percent indicated that at least one perpetrator was enlisted or a warrant officer, 16 percent indicated that at least one perpetrator was an officer, and 8 percent were not sure of the perpetrator's pay grade.[16]

---

[16] Respondents were able to select more than one category of perpetrator, so these percentages will not sum to 100 percent.

**Figure 3.4. Number, Military Status, and Gender of Perpetrators of Most Serious Experience, All Sexual Assault Victims by WGRA Survey Year**

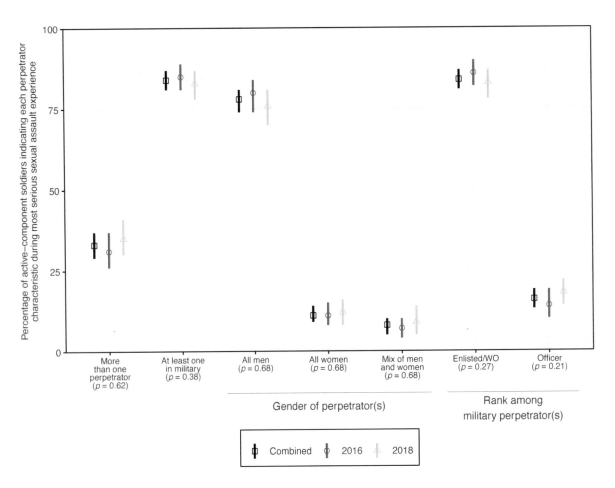

SOURCE: Authors' calculations using the 2016 and 2018 WGRA.
NOTE: Percentages are made up of only soldiers who were sexually assaulted during the year prior to WGRA administration. "At least one in military" is an aggregation of answer choices "yes, they all were" and "yes, some were, but not all" from the question on whether the perpetrator(s) was or were in the military. Rank is determined from a question asking the pay grade(s) of perpetrator(s), which was asked only of respondents who indicated that "all" or "some, but not all" of the perpetrators were members of the military. Respondents were instructed to select all pay grades that applied; the "not sure" response is not presented in this figure. Percentages are available in Table C.4. WO= warrant officer.

Figure 3.5 displays the most common professional relationship between the victim and the perpetrators of active-component soldiers' most serious experiences of sexual assault, with results pooled for both surveys and separately by survey year. As we noted in Chapter 2, there is a major change in the text of the question from 2016 to 2018. Specifically, the 2018 survey instrument introduced the option to indicate that the perpetrator was a military peer of similar rank to the victim. This is problematic because the military peer option was by far the most endorsed on the 2018 survey. There are large, statistically significant decreases in the proportion of victims choosing every other answer choice except for those indicating that at least one perpetrator was the victim's supervisor, for those indicating that at least one perpetrator was higher-ranked and outside the victim's chain of command, and for those indicating that at least one perpetrator was a government contractor or civilian. The decrease is especially large for the response "not sure" (37 percent versus 15 percent, $p < 0.0001$). We were concerned that the introduction of the new answer option changed respondents' understanding of the question in ways that shifted response patterns. We therefore use only responses from 2018 in the rest of the report for this characteristic of perpetrators, and we consider them to be our main results in this section.

**Figure 3.5. Professional Relationship Between Victim and Perpetrator of Most Serious Experience, All Sexual Assault Victims by WGRA Survey Year**

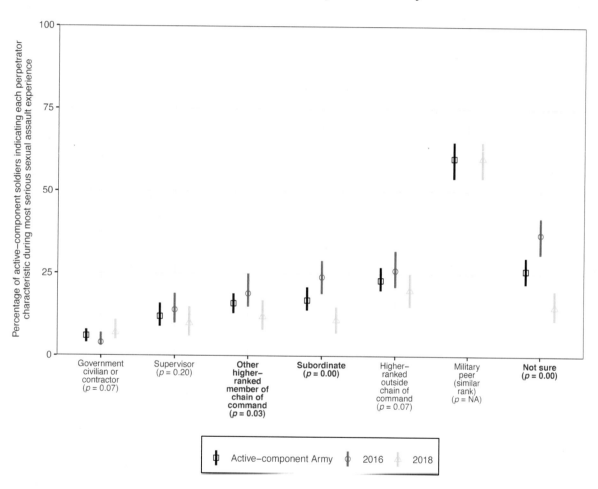

SOURCE: Authors' calculations using the 2016 and 2018 WGRA.
NOTE: Percentages are made up of only soldiers who were sexually assaulted during the year prior to WGRA administration. Respondents were instructed to select all that apply. "Military peer of similar rank" was not an available answer choice on the 2016 WGRA. "Government civilian or contractor" is a combination of the following two answer choices: "DoD/government civilian(s) working for the military" and "Contractor(s)." Percentages are available in Table C.4. NA = not applicable.

In the 2018 WGRA, the most common professional relationship between the victim and the perpetrators was that they were military peers of similar rank (60 percent). The second most common professional relationship was higher-ranked and outside the victim's chain of command (20 percent). The remaining professional relationship choices, from most to least common, were not sure (15 percent), a higher-ranked member of the victim's chain of command other than the victim's supervisor (12 percent), a subordinate or someone the victim managed (11 percent), the victim's supervisor (10 percent), and a DoD or government civilian or contractor (7 percent).

Figure 3.6 displays the most common personal relationship between the victim and the perpetrators of active-component soldiers' most serious experiences of sexual assault, with results pooled for both surveys and separately by survey year. The most common personal relationship between the victim and perpetrator is that they were friends or acquaintances, at 53 percent. The second most common answer choice was "none of the above," at 27 percent, which indicates an individual the victim knew but who did not fall into any of the other options. We believe that this answer choice likely includes military coworkers who the victim would not consider friends. The other responses, from most to least common, were that at least one perpetrator was a stranger (16 percent), the victim's significant other (6 percent), not sure (5 percent), the victim's current or former spouse or someone with whom they had a child (4 percent), and a family member of the victim (1 percent). The only statistically significant change between the two survey years was in the percentage of victims who indicated that at least one perpetrator was their current or former spouse or someone with whom they had a child, which decreased from 6 percent in 2016 to 2 percent in 2018 ($p = 0.001$).

**Figure 3.6. Personal Relationship Between Victim and Perpetrator of Most Serious Experience, All Sexual Assault Victims by WGRA Survey Year**

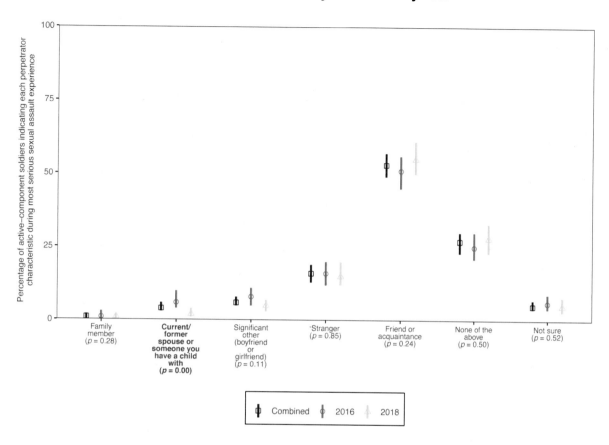

SOURCE: Authors' calculations using the 2016 and 2018 WGRA.
NOTE: Percentages are made up of only soldiers who were sexually assaulted during the year prior to WGRA administration. Respondents were instructed to select all that apply. "Current/former spouse or someone you have a child with" is an aggregation of the following response options: "your current or former spouse" and "someone you have a child with (your child's mother or father)." "Significant other (boyfriend or girlfriend)" is an aggregation of the following response options: "your significant other (boyfriend or girlfriend) who you <u>live</u> with" and "your significant other (boyfriend or girlfriend) who you <u>do/did not</u> live with." Percentages are available in Table C.4.

## Place and Time of Assault

Corresponding tabular results for this section are available in Table C.5.

Figure 3.7 displays the percentage of sexual assault victims who indicated that their most serious sexual assault experience occurred at each place, with results pooled for both surveys and separately by survey year. Across the two survey years, 69 percent of victims indicated that their most serious sexual assault occurred at a military installation, and 56 percent indicated that their most serious sexual assault occurred during a required military activity. Those required military activities include the following: while at work during duty hours (see Figure 3.8); while on temporary duty (TDY) or during field exercises or alerts (19 percent); during an official military function either on or off base (17 percent); while deployed to a combat zone or transitioning between operational theaters (13 percent); during basic, officer, or technical training (13 percent); and during any military combat training other than basic training (9 percent). Across the two survey years, 39 percent of victims indicated that their most serious experience occurred off base. There are two statistically significant differences across survey years in the place that soldiers' most serious sexual assault experience occurred. The percentage of victims who indicated that their most serious assault experience occurred at a military installation decreased from 73 percent to 64 percent ($p = 0.02$), and the percentage of victims who indicated that their most serious assault experience occurred during any military combat training other than basic training increased from 7 percent to 12 percent ($p = 0.04$).

**Figure 3.7. Place of Most Serious Experience, All Sexual Assault Victims by WGRA Survey Year**

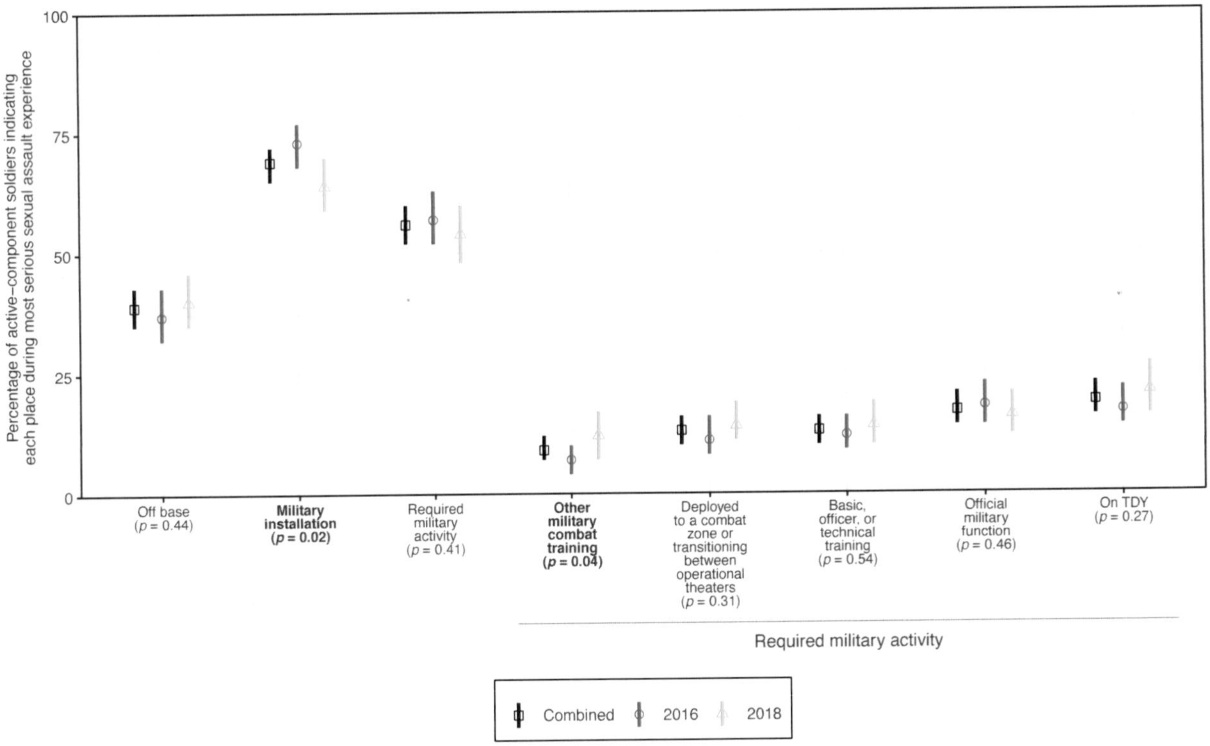

SOURCE: Authors' calculations using the 2016 and 2018 WGRA.
NOTE: Percentages are made up of only soldiers who were sexually assaulted during the year prior to WGRA administration. Respondents were instructed to select all places that applied. "Deployed to a combat zone or transitioning between operational theaters" is an aggregation of the following response options: "while you were deployed to a combat zone or to an area where you drew imminent danger pay or hostile fire pay," "during an overseas port visit while deployed," and "while transitioning between operational theaters (for example, going to or returning from forward deployment)." "Basic, officer, or technical training" is an aggregation of the following response options: "while you were in recruit training/basic training," "while you were in Officer Candidate or Training School/Basic or Advanced Officer Course," and "while you were attending military occupational specialty school/technical training/advanced individual training/professional military education." "Any required military activity" is an aggregation of the following response options: "deployed to a combat zone or transitioning between operational theaters," "basic, officer, or technical training," "while you were on TDY/TAD, at sea, or during field exercises/alerts," "while you were in any other type of military combat training," "while at an official military function (either on or off base)," and (from the "when" question displayed in Figure 3.8) "while you were at work during duty hours." The answer choice "while you were in a delayed entry program (DEP) or delayed training program (DTP)" is excluded from this figure but was indicated by 4 percent of victims; this choice includes only pre-accession assaults. Percentages are available in Table C.5.

Figure 3.8 displays the percentage of sexual assault victims who indicated that their most serious sexual assault experience occurred at each time, with results pooled for both surveys and separately by survey year. Across the two survey years, the three most common times for victims' most serious experiences of sexual assault were at work during duty hours (38 percent), in the victim's or someone else's home or quarters (37 percent), and while out with friends or at a party (36 percent). Less common times included while being intimate with the person (8 percent; available in 2016 only), while on approved leave (7 percent), and while on a date (4 percent). Additionally, 11 percent of victims indicated "none of the above," and 2 percent of victims indicated "do not recall." There were no statistically significant changes across survey years in the time of soldiers' most serious sexual assault experiences.

**Figure 3.8. Time of Most Serious Experience, All Sexual Assault Victims by WGRA Survey Year**

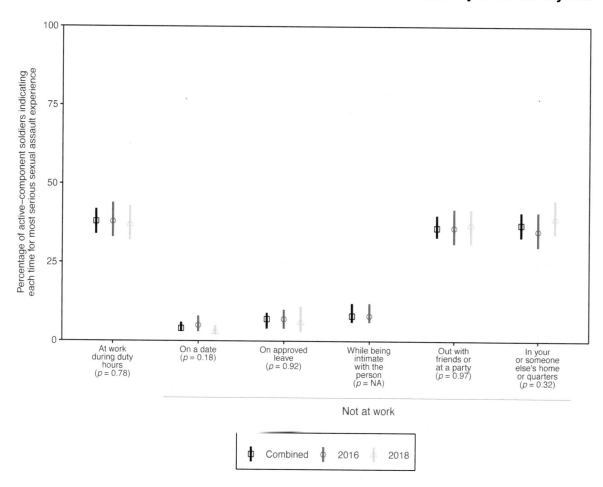

SOURCE: Authors' calculations using the 2016 and 2018 WGRA.
NOTE: Percentages are made up of only soldiers who were sexually assaulted during the year prior to WGRA administration. Respondents were instructed to select all times that apply. The response option "while being intimate with the person" was available in 2016 only. This figure does not present results for "none of the above" or "do not recall." Percentages are available in Table C.5.

*Alcohol and Drug Involvement*

Figure 3.9 displays the percentage of sexual assault victims who indicated that their most serious sexual assault experience involved alcohol or drugs, with results pooled for both surveys and separately by survey year. The figure presents only the percentage responding "yes;" respondents were also given the option to respond with "no" or either "don't know" or "not sure" for all questions, and the percentages of victims who chose those answers are reported in Table C.6.

**Figure 3.9. Alcohol and Drug Involvement in Most Serious Experience, All Sexual Assault Victims by WGRA Survey Year**

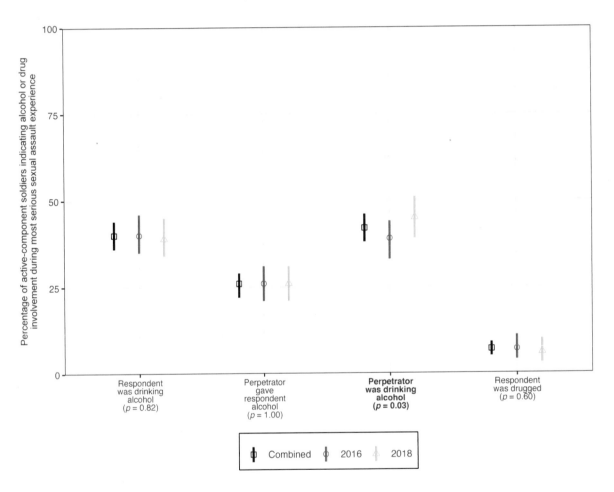

SOURCE: Authors' calculations using the 2016 and 2018 WGRA.
NOTES: Percentages are made up of only soldiers who were sexually assaulted during the year prior to WGRA administration. Percentages are for "Yes" responses to each question; respondents also had the choices of "no" and either "not sure" or "I don't know" (depending on the question). Percentages are available in Table C.6.

Across the two survey years, 40 percent of victims indicated that they were drinking alcohol during their most serious sexual assault experience, whereas 58 percent indicated they were not drinking alcohol, and 3 percent indicated "not sure" (results do not sum to 100 percent because

28

of rounding). Overall, 26 percent of victims indicated that the perpetrator either bought or gave them alcohol, 72 percent indicated that the perpetrator did not buy or give them alcohol, and 3 percent did not know. Forty-two percent of victims indicated that the perpetrator was drinking alcohol, 39 percent indicated that the perpetrator was not drinking alcohol, and 19 percent did not know. Seven percent of victims believed that they were drugged without their knowledge or consent, 80 percent did not believe that they were drugged, and 13 percent did not know. The only statistically significant difference across survey years is in the percentage of victims who indicated that the perpetrator of their most serious experience was drinking alcohol: The percentage of victims who indicated that the perpetrator was drinking alcohol rose from 39 percent to 45 percent, the percentage of victims who indicated that the perpetrator was not drinking fell from 44 percent to 34 percent, and the percentage of victims who did not know rose from 17 percent to 21 percent ($p = 0.03$).

## Hazing, Bullying, Sexual Harassment, and Stalking

Figure 3.10 displays the percentage of sexual assault victims who indicated that their most serious sexual assault experience co-occurred with bullying, hazing, sexual harassment, or stalking, with results pooled for both surveys and separately by survey year. Corresponding tabular results are available in Table C.7.

**Figure 3.10. Bullying, Hazing, Sexual Harassment, and Stalking During Most Serious Experience, All Sexual Assault Victims by WGRA Survey Year**

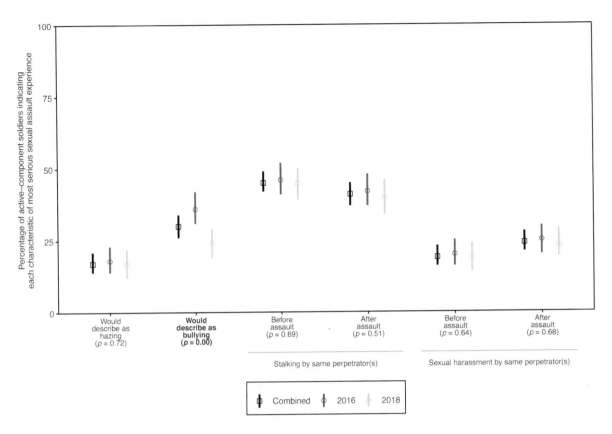

SOURCE: Authors' calculations using the 2016 and 2018 WGRA.
NOTES: Percentages are made up of only soldiers who were sexually assaulted during the year prior to WGRA administration. Definitions of bullying and hazing changed substantially between survey years; see Table 2.3. Percentages are available in Table C.7.

Across the two surveys, 17 percent of sexual assault victims indicated that they would describe their most serious sexual assault experience as hazing, and 30 percent would describe it as bullying. There was no statistically significant change from 2016 to 2018 in the percentage of victims who described their experience as hazing (18 percent versus 17 percent, $p = 0.72$), but there was a statistically significant decrease in the percentage who described their experience as bullying (36 percent versus 24 percent, $p = 0.001$). However, we believe that the reduction in bullying may not reflect an actual decrease in sexual assaults meant to bully the victim because the questions measuring bullying and hazing changed substantially between the 2016 and 2018 WGRA survey instruments (see Table 2.3). We therefore consider the percentages from 2018 to be our main results.

Consistent with earlier findings in Schell, Cefalu, et al., 2021, and Matthews et al., 2021, sexual harassment and sexual assault often co-occur. Forty-five percent of victims across both survey years indicated that they were sexually harassed before the assault by the same perpetrators, and 41 percent indicated that they were sexually harassed after the assault by the

30

same perpetrators.[17] There was no statistically significant change from 2016 to 2018 (before assault: 46 percent versus 45 percent, $p = 0.69$; after assault: 42 percent versus 40 percent, $p = 0.51$).

Stalking and sexual assault also often co-occur, though less often than sexual assault and sexual harassment. Across both survey years, 19 percent of victims indicated that they were stalked before the assault by the same perpetrators, and 24 percent of victims indicated that they were stalked after the assault by the same perpetrators. There was no statistically significant change from 2016 to 2018 (before assault: 20 percent versus 19 percent, $p = 0.64$; after assault: 25 percent versus 23 percent, $p = 0.68$).

## Summary

In this chapter, we presented the typical circumstances surrounding sexual assaults of soldiers in the active-component Army and described changes from 2016 to 2018.

By far the most common type of sexual assault, both for all sexual assault experiences over the 12 months prior to the survey date and for soldiers' most serious experiences, is a nonpenetrative one, where someone intentionally touched private areas of the victim's body. Penetrative sexual assaults with a penis were the second most common type of sexual assault but were substantially less likely than intentional touching of private parts. Nearly 90 percent of victims believed that the assault was committed for a sexual reason, and more than half indicated that the assault was meant to be abusive or humiliating (which can co-occur).

The typical perpetrator of soldiers' most serious sexual assault experience is a male member of the military acting alone, and most military perpetrators were enlisted or a warrant officer. Perpetrators were most often military peers of the victim, but slightly more than 40 percent of victims indicated that at least one perpetrator was the victim's supervisor, another higher-ranked member of the victim's chain of command, or higher-ranked and outside the victim's chain of command. Slightly more than half of victims indicated that the perpetrator was their friend or acquaintance, perpetrators who were strangers to the victim were uncommon, and assaults by spouses, significant others, or family members were comparatively rare.

Approximately two-thirds of soldiers' most serious experiences of sexual assault occurred at military installations. Slightly more than half of victims indicated that their most serious experience occurred during a required military activity, the most common of which was while at work during duty hours. Victims were approximately equally likely to be assaulted while at work, while in their or someone else's home or quarters, and while out with friends or at a party.

---

[17] Prior research on the best way to assess whether an individual was sexually harassed indicates that questions like this one, which simply ask whether the respondent was sexually harassed instead of asking several questions about specific behaviors the respondent experienced, tend to underestimate the rate of sexual harassment. See Morral, Gore, and Schell, 2014, for a review of the literature.

Forty percent of victims indicated that they were drinking alcohol during their most serious sexual assault experience, 42 percent indicated that the perpetrator was drinking alcohol during their most serious sexual assault experience, and 25 percent indicated that the perpetrator either bought or gave them alcohol.

Sexual assaults often co-occur with sexual harassment, and less often with stalking, either before or after, by the same perpetrators. Co-occurrence with hazing and bullying is not comparable across years, but in 2018, 17 percent of victims described their most serious experience as hazing, and 24 percent described their most serious experience as bullying.

There were few statistically significant changes in the circumstances surrounding sexual assault from 2016 to 2018, and fewer are of substantive importance for policymaking. Among soldiers who had been sexually assaulted at least once, the percentage of victims who were assaulted multiple times decreased across survey years. There was a small but statistically significant reduction in the percentage of victims who indicated that at least one of the perpetrators was their current or former spouse or the parent of their child, but such assaults are comparatively rare and therefore should not be a primary focus of sexual assault prevention. There was a statistically significant decrease in the percentage of most serious sexual assault experiences that occurred at military installations and a statistically significant increase in the percentage of most serious experiences that occurred during any military combat training other than basic training. Finally, there was a statistically significant increase in the percentage of victims who indicated that the perpetrator was drinking alcohol.

# Chapter 4. Differences in the Sexual Assault Experience by Gender

In this chapter, we compare male and female active-component soldiers' experiences of sexual assault. We examine gender differences in the types of sexual assault behaviors involved, perceived perpetrator intentions, and types of coercion involved in all sexual assaults during the year prior to survey administration. We also examine types of sexual assault behaviors; perpetrator characteristics; time and place; alcohol involvement; and co-occurrence with bullying, hazing, sexual harassment, and stalking for soldiers' most serious sexual assault experience.

Appendix C includes tabular results for this chapter.

## Sexual Assault by Gender in the Active-Component Army

Women face substantially higher risk of sexual assault than men in the active-component Army. In 2018, 5.7 percent of female active-component soldiers and 0.7 percent of male active-component soldiers were sexually assaulted (Breslin et al., 2019). In 2016, 4.4 percent of female active-component soldiers and 0.6 percent of male active-component soldiers were sexually assaulted (Davis et al., 2017).

## Sexual Assault Screening Questions

Figure 4.1 displays the percentage of sexual assault victims who indicated that they experienced each type of sexual assault behavior on the sexual assault screener questions, by gender. The responses for types of sexual assault behaviors could be from *any* sexual assault experienced over the year prior to the survey rather than solely the most serious sexual assault experience. Corresponding tabular results are available in Table C.8.

All figures in this chapter are produced in the same format. The labels on the x-axis represent responses to the survey questions. The three icons above each label represent the designated percentage from the graph. The purple squares (leftmost icon) represent the percentage of all active-component soldiers who were sexually assaulted who indicated each characteristic of their experience, which is reproduced from Chapter 3, except in cases where we use 2018 data only. The teal circles (center icon) represent the percentage of male active-component soldiers who were sexually assaulted (i.e., male victims) who indicated each characteristic of their experience, and the lime-green triangles (rightmost icon) represent the percentage of female active-component soldiers who were sexually assaulted (i.e., female victims) who indicated each characteristic of their experience. The lines surrounding these icons represent the 95-percent CIs.

If no icon is provided, that means that we have suppressed the icon because the confidence interval is too wide to provide a useful estimate. Bolded labels indicate a statistically significant difference between high-risk and non–high-risk installations.

**Figure 4.1. Types of Sexual Assault Behaviors from Screener Questions, All Sexual Assault Victims by Gender**

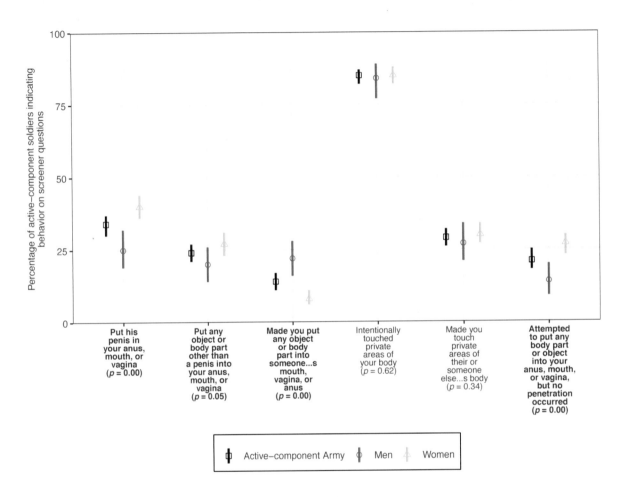

SOURCE: Authors' calculations using the 2016 and 2018 WGRA.
NOTE: Percentages are made up of only soldiers who were sexually assaulted during the year prior to WGRA administration. Percentages are available in Table C.8.

There are substantial differences by victim gender in the types of sexual assault behaviors indicated on the sexual assault screener questions. Among sexually assaulted active-component soldiers, male and female victims were approximately equally likely to indicate that they experienced the two nonpenetrative sexual assault behaviors (having someone touch private areas of the victim's body or having someone make the victim touch private areas of their or someone else's body) during any sexual assault of the prior year. Among soldiers who had been sexually assaulted, male and female victims were also equally likely to indicate that they had been assaulted multiple times. However, there were substantial differences in penetrative sexual

34

assaults and attempted penetrative sexual assaults. Female victims were statistically significantly more likely to experience a sexual assault or attempted sexual assault where they were penetrated by someone else: Forty percent of women and 25 percent of men indicated that they had been penetrated with a penis ($p = 0.0002$), 27 percent of women and 20 percent of men indicated that they had been penetrated with an object or body part other than a penis ($p = 0.047$), and 27 percent of women and 14 percent of men indicated that someone had unsuccessfully attempted to penetrate them with a penis, another body part, or an object ($p = 0.0003$). In contrast, male victims were statistically significantly more likely to indicate that they had been made to penetrate someone (either the perpetrator or someone else) with any object or body part (22 percent versus 8 percent, $p < 0.0001$).

Figure 4.2 displays the percentage of sexual assault victims who indicated that they were assaulted more than once, each type of perpetrator intent, and each type of coercion, by gender. Corresponding tabular results are available in Table C.9.

**Figure 4.2. Perpetrator Intent and Type of Coercion from Screener Questions, All Sexual Assault Victims by Gender**

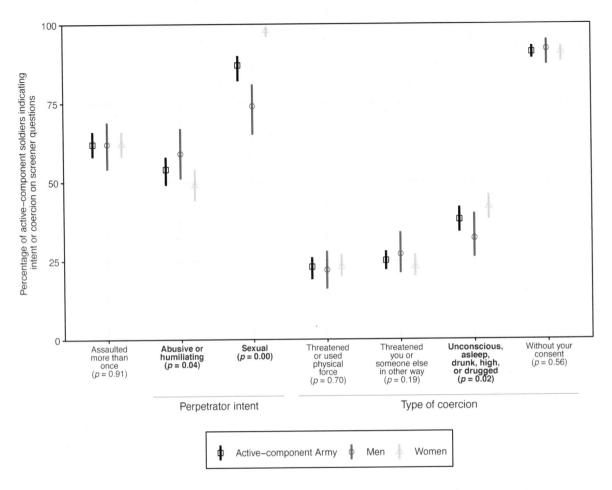

SOURCE: Authors' calculations using the 2016 and 2018 WGRA.
NOTE: Percentages are made up of only soldiers who were sexually assaulted during the year prior to WGRA administration. Perpetrator intent and type of coercion percentages are for the behavior on which the respondent qualified as having been sexually assaulted. Intent questions were not asked of respondents who qualified as having been sexually assaulted under the first sexual assault behavior (someone put his penis into the respondent's anus, mouth, or vagina) because the UCMJ does not require abusive, humiliating, or sexual intent for this behavior to qualify as rape or sexual assault. These percentages, therefore, have the denominator as individuals who qualified as having been sexually assaulted on one of the other behaviors. See Chapter 2 for further details. Percentages are available in Table C.9.

There are large and statistically significant differences in perpetrator intent by victim gender. Male victims were statistically significantly more likely to indicate that they believed that the perpetrator intended to abuse or humiliate them (59 percent versus 49 percent, $p = 0.04$). Female victims were statistically significantly more likely to indicate that they believed the perpetrator had a sexual purpose (98 percent versus 74 percent, $p < 0.0001$). There is also one statistically significant difference in types of coercion. Female victims were statistically significantly more likely to indicate that they were unconscious, asleep, or incapacitated by alcohol or drugs during the assault including the behavior on which they qualified as having been sexually assaulted (42 percent versus 32 percent, $p = 0.02$). We did not find statistically significant differences in the likelihood of being assaulted more than once (among all soldiers who were sexually assaulted).

## Soldiers' Most Serious Sexual Assault Experiences

### Types of Sexual Assault Behaviors

With one exception, gender differences in the types of sexual assault behaviors involved in soldiers' most serious sexual assault experiences are similar to gender differences in the answers to the screener questions we discussed in the previous section. Unlike in the screener questions, there was no statistically significant gender difference in the percentage of victims who indicated that their most serious sexual assault experience included being penetrated with an object or body part other than a penis. See Table C.10 in Appendix C.

### Characteristics of Perpetrators

Corresponding tabular results for all figures in this section are available in Table C.11.

Figure 4.3 displays the most common numbers, military statuses, and genders of perpetrators of active-component soldiers' most serious experiences of sexual assault, by gender of the victim. Although the typical perpetrator for both male and female victims was a male enlisted member of the military acting alone, there are substantial gender differences in the frequency of multiple perpetrators, nonmilitary or officer perpetrators, and female perpetrators. Female victims were less likely than male victims to indicate that their most serious experience had more than one perpetrator: Fifty-seven percent of men indicated a single perpetrator, 37 percent indicated multiple perpetrators, and 6 percent indicated that they were not sure how many perpetrators there were, whereas 68 percent of women indicated one perpetrator, 30 percent indicated multiple perpetrators, and 2 percent were not sure ($p = 0.01$). Female victims were more likely than male victims to indicate that at least one perpetrator was a member of the military: Eighty-six percent of women indicated that all perpetrators were in the military, 5 percent indicated that some but not all were in the military, 7 percent indicated that none of the perpetrators were in the military, and 2 percent were not sure, compared with 66 percent, 8 percent, 18 percent, and 8 percent of men, respectively ($p < 0.0001$). Men were statistically significantly more likely to indicate at least one female perpetrator: Fifty-four percent of men indicated that all perpetrators were male, 26 percent indicated that all perpetrators were female, 13 percent indicated that the perpetrators were a mix of men and women, and 6 percent indicated that they were not sure of the perpetrator's gender or perpetrators' genders, compared with 94 percent, 1 percent, 4 percent, and 1 percent of women ($p < 0.0001$). Among victims who indicated at least one military perpetrator, male victims were statistically significantly more likely than female victims to indicate that at least one perpetrator was a commissioned officer (21 percent versus 13 percent, $p = 0.01$).

37

**Figure 4.3. Number, Military Status, and Gender of Perpetrators of Most Serious Experience, All Sexual Assault Victims by Gender**

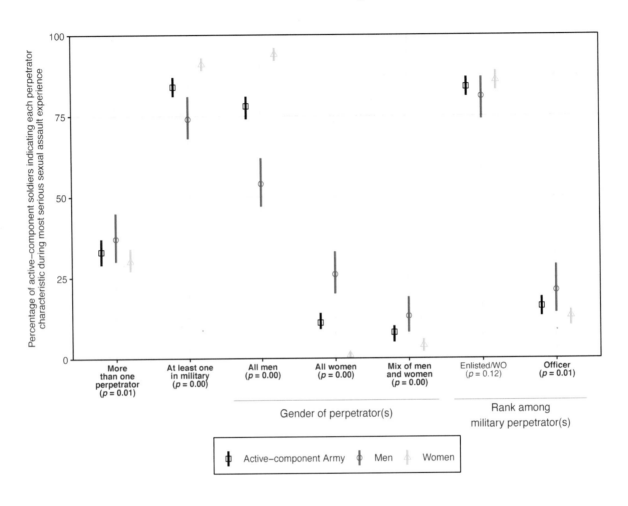

SOURCE: Authors' calculations using the 2016 and 2018 WGRA.
NOTE: Percentages are made up of only soldiers who were sexually assaulted during the year prior to WGRA administration. "At least one in the military" is an aggregation of answer choices "yes, they all were" and "yes, some were, but not all" from the question on whether the perpetrator(s) was or were in the military. Rank is determined from a question asking the pay grade(s) of perpetrator(s), which was asked of only respondents who indicated that "all" or "some, but not all" of the perpetrators were members of the military. Respondents were instructed to select all pay grades that apply; the "not sure" response is not presented in this figure. WO = warrant officer.

Figure 4.4 displays the most common professional relationship between the victim and the perpetrators of active-component soldiers' most serious experiences of sexual assault, by gender. There is only one statistically significant gender difference in the professional relationship between the victim and perpetrator: Male victims were statistically significantly more likely than female victims to indicate that at least one perpetrator was a subordinate or someone they managed (17 percent versus 7 percent, $p = 0.01$).

38

**Figure 4.4. Professional Relationship Between Victim and Perpetrator of Most Serious Experience, All Sexual Assault Victims by Gender**

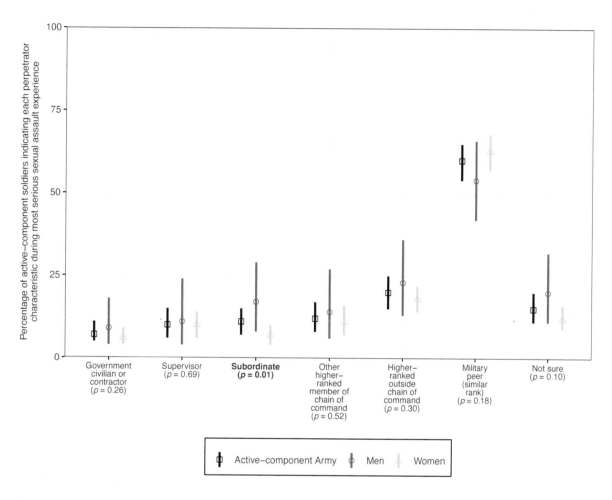

SOURCE: Authors' calculations using the 2018 WGRA.
NOTE: Percentages are made up of only soldiers who were sexually assaulted during the year prior to WGRA administration. Respondents were instructed to select all that apply. We include only responses from 2018 because "military peer of similar rank" was not an available answer choice in 2016. "Government civilian or contractor" is a combination of the following two answer choices: "DoD/government civilian(s) working for the military" and "Contractor(s)."

Figure 4.5 displays the most common personal relationship between the victim and the perpetrators of active-component soldiers' most serious experiences of sexual assault, by gender. There are three statistically significant gender differences in the personal relationship between the victim and perpetrator of victims' most serious sexual assault experience. Women were statistically significantly more likely to indicate that at least one perpetrator was a friend or acquaintance (57 percent versus 46 percent, $p = 0.01$). Men were statistically significantly more likely to indicate "none of the above," which, as noted in Chapter 3, we believe includes military coworkers who the victim would not describe as friends (32 percent versus 23 percent, $p = 0.01$). Men were also statistically significantly more likely to indicate "not sure" (9 percent versus 3 percent, $p = 0.0008$).

**Figure 4.5. Personal Relationship Between Victim and Perpetrator of Most Serious Experience, All Sexual Assault Victims by Gender**

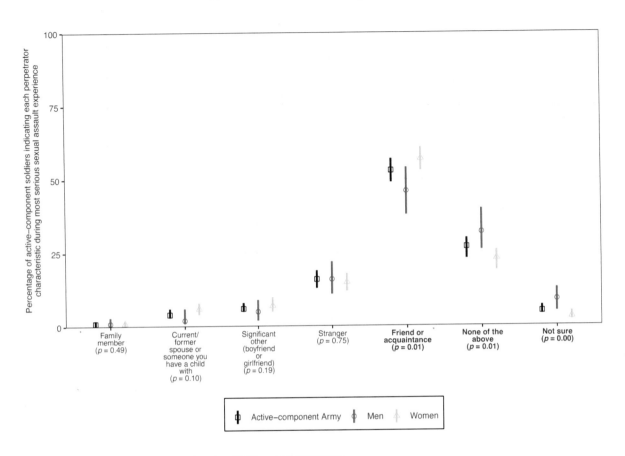

SOURCE: Authors' calculations using the 2016 and 2018 WGRA.
NOTE: Percentages are made up of only soldiers who were sexually assaulted during the year prior to WGRA administration. Respondents were instructed to select all that apply. "Current/former spouse or someone you have a child with" is an aggregation of the following response options: "your current or former spouse" and "someone you have a child with (your child's mother or father)." "Significant other (boyfriend or girlfriend)" is an aggregation of the following response options: "your significant other (boyfriend or girlfriend) who you <u>live</u> with" and "your significant other (boyfriend or girlfriend) who you <u>do/did not</u> live with."

## Place and Time of Assault

Corresponding tabular results for both figures in this section are available in Table C.12.

Figure 4.6 displays the percentage of sexual assault victims indicating that their most serious sexual assault experience occurred at each place, by gender. Overall, men are more likely than women to have been sexually assaulted in a work context. Male victims were statistically significantly more likely than female victims to indicate that their most serious experience occurred during a required military activity (which includes TDY, deployment, any type of training, official military functions, and, from Figure 4.7, while at work during duty hours; 65 percent versus 50 percent, $p = 0.0005$). In particular, men were statistically significantly more likely to indicate that their most serious experience occurred during TDY (28 percent versus 13 percent, $p < 0.0001$), during military combat training other than basic training (14 percent versus

40

5 percent, $p = 0.0003$), and during an official military function (23 percent versus 13 percent, $p = 0.0007$).

**Figure 4.6. Place of Most Serious Experience, All Sexual Assault Victims by Gender**

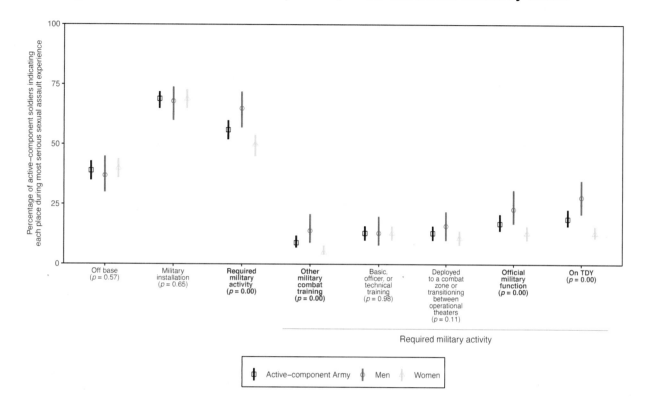

SOURCE: Authors' calculations using the 2016 and 2018 WGRA.
NOTE: Percentages are made up of only soldiers who were sexually assaulted during the year prior to WGRA administration. Respondents were instructed to select all places that apply. "Deployed to a combat zone or transitioning between operational theaters" is an aggregation of the following response options: "while you were deployed to a combat zone or to an area where you drew imminent danger pay or hostile fire pay," "during an overseas port visit while deployed," and "while transitioning between operational theaters (for example, going to or returning from forward deployment)." "Basic, officer, or technical training" is an aggregation of the following response options: "while you were in recruit training/basic training," "while you were in Officer Candidate or Training School/Basic or Advanced Officer Course," and "while you were attending military occupational specialty school/technical training/advanced individual training/professional military education." "Any required military activity" is an aggregation of the following response options: "deployed to a combat zone or transitioning between operational theaters," "basic, officer, or technical training," "while you were on TDY/TAD, at sea, or during field exercises/alerts," "while you were in any other type of military combat training," "while at an official military function (either on or off base)," and (from the "when" question displayed in Figure 4.7) while "at work during duty hours." The "while you were in a delayed entry program (DEP) or delayed training program (DTP)" answer choice is excluded from this figure but was indicated by 4 percent of victims; this choice includes only pre-accession assaults.

Figure 4.7 displays the percentage of sexual assault victims indicating that their most serious sexual assault experience occurred at each time, by gender. Male victims were statistically significantly more likely than female victims to indicate that their most serious sexual assault experience occurred while at work during duty hours (50 percent versus 29 percent, $p < 0.0001$). Female victims were statistically significantly more likely than male victims to indicate that their most serious experience occurred in their own or someone else's home or quarters (44 percent versus 27 percent, $p < 0.0001$).

**Figure 4.7. Time of Most Serious Experience, All Sexual Assault Victims by Gender**

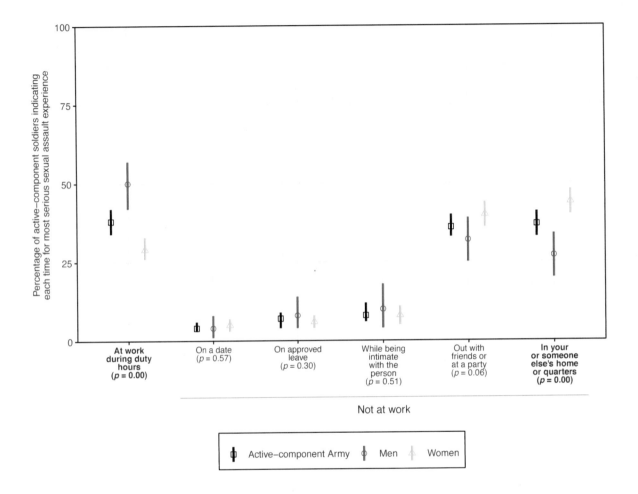

SOURCE: Authors' calculations using the 2016 and 2018 WGRA.
NOTE: Percentages are made up of only soldiers who were sexually assaulted during the year prior to WGRA administration. Respondents were instructed to select all times that apply. The "while being intimate with the person" option was available only in 2016. The figure does not present results for "none of the above" or "do not recall."

*Alcohol and Drug Involvement*

Figure 4.8 displays the percentage of sexual assault victims indicating that their most serious sexual assault experience involved alcohol or drugs, by gender. The figure presents only the percentage responding "yes;" respondents were also given the option to respond with "no" or "don't know" for all questions, and the percentages of respondents who chose those answers are reported in Table C.13.

**Figure 4.8. Alcohol and Drug Involvement in Most Serious Experience, All Sexual Assault Victims by Gender**

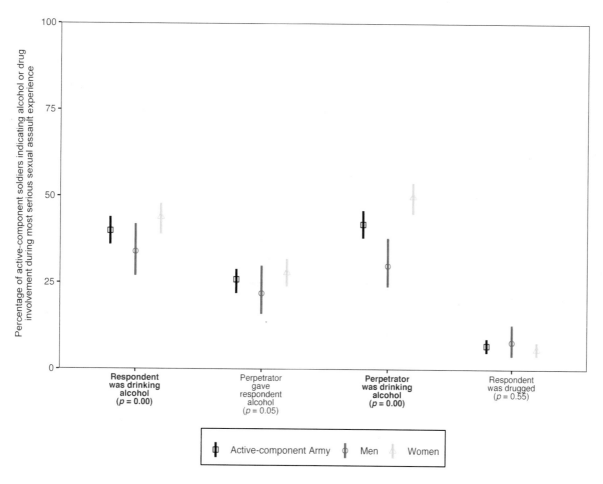

SOURCE: Authors' calculations using the 2016 and 2018 WGRA.
NOTE: Percentages are made up of only soldiers who were sexually assaulted during the year prior to WGRA administration. Percentages are for "yes" responses to each question; respondents also had the choices of "no" and (depending on the question) "not sure" or "I don't know."

In general, women's most serious sexual assault experiences were more likely than men's to involve alcohol. Women were statistically significantly more likely to indicate that they were drinking alcohol at the time of their most serious sexual assault experience: Forty-four percent of women indicated "yes," 56 percent indicated "no," and 1 percent indicated "not sure," compared with 34 percent, 61 percent, and 5 percent of men, respectively ($p = 0.0006$). Women were also statistically significantly more likely to indicate that the perpetrator was drinking alcohol at the time of their most serious sexual assault experience: Fifty percent of women indicated "yes," 36 percent indicated "no," and 15 percent indicated "I don't know," compared with 30 percent, 44 percent, and 26 percent of men, respectively ($p < 0.0001$).

*Hazing, Bullying, Sexual Harassment, and Stalking*

Figure 4.9 displays the percentage of sexual assault victims indicating that their most serious sexual assault experience co-occurred with bullying, hazing, sexual harassment, or stalking, by gender. Corresponding tabular results are available in Table C.14. Male victims were substantially more likely than female victims to describe their most serious sexual assault experience as hazing (29 percent versus 9 percent, $p < 0.0001$).

**Figure 4.9. Bullying, Hazing, Sexual Harassment, and Stalking During Most Serious Experience, All Sexual Assault Victims by Gender**

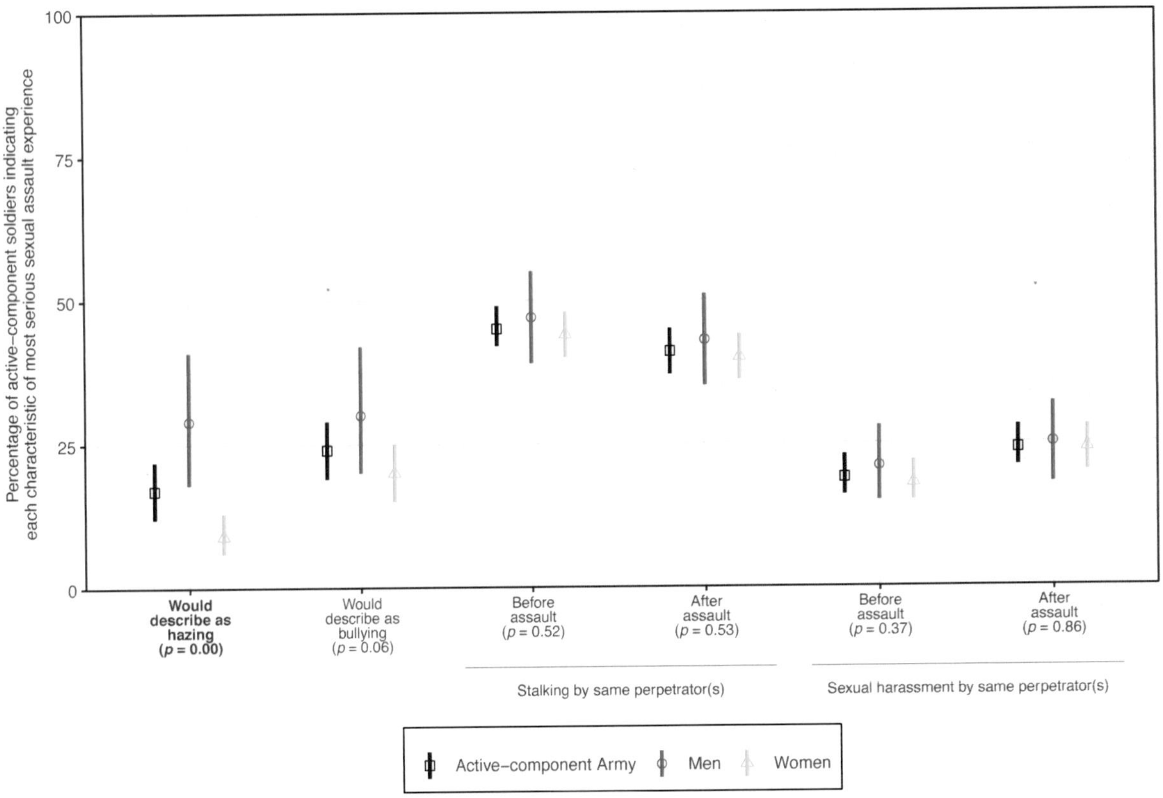

SOURCE: Authors' calculations using the 2016 and 2018 WGRA.
NOTE: Percentages are made up of only soldiers who were sexually assaulted during the year prior to WGRA administration. Bullying and hazing use only 2018 data because of changes in definitions across the two survey years; see Table 2.3 in Chapter 2.

## Summary

Male and female victims tend to experience different types of sexual assault behaviors, and there are differences in perpetrator intent and methods of coercion as well. Among soldiers who were sexually assaulted during the year prior to survey administration, and among all sexual assault experiences over the 12 months prior to the survey date, female sexual assault victims were more likely than male victims to experience completed or attempted sexual assaults where they were penetrated by someone else, whereas male victims were more likely than female victims to experience sexual assaults where they were made to penetrate someone else. Nonpenetrative sexual assaults were equally common for male and female victims. Male victims were more likely than female victims to indicate that they believed that the perpetrator intended to abuse or humiliate them, whereas female victims were more likely than male victims to indicate that they believed that the perpetrator had a sexual reason for their actions. Female victims were also more likely than male victims to indicate that they were sexually assaulted while asleep, unconscious, or incapacitated by drugs or alcohol.

The typical perpetrator of soldiers' most serious sexual assault experience was similar for male and female victims: a male enlisted member of the military acting alone. However, the frequency of an atypical perpetrator was higher for men: Men were more likely to indicate multiple perpetrators; at least one female perpetrator; nonmilitary perpetrators; and, among military perpetrators, perpetrators who were commissioned officers. There were also gender differences in the relationships between victims and perpetrators. In terms of professional relationships, perpetrators were most often military peers for both male and female victims, but male victims were more likely than female victims to indicate that at least one perpetrator was their subordinate or someone they managed. In terms of personal relationships, female victims were more likely than male victims to describe the perpetrator as a friend or acquaintance, whereas male victims were more likely than female victims to describe the perpetrator as someone they knew, but who was not a family member, current or former spouse or intimate partner, or friend or acquaintance—a category that might include some military coworkers. Men were also more likely than women to indicate that they were not sure on the personal relationship item.

In terms of time and place, male victims were more likely than female victims to indicate that their most serious sexual assault experience occurred during required military activities, particularly while on TDY, during official military functions, during military combat training other than basic training, and while at work during duty hours. Female victims were more likely than male victims to indicate that their most serious sexual assault experience occurred in a private, nonwork setting, particularly while in their or someone else's home or quarters. Relatedly, female victims were more likely than male victims to indicate that they and/or the perpetrator were drinking alcohol during their most serious sexual assault experience, and male victims were more likely than female victims to describe their most serious experience as hazing.

# Chapter 5. Differences in the Sexual Assault Experience by Sexual Orientation

In this chapter, we describe differences in sexual assault experiences by sexual orientation. We examine the types of sexual assault behaviors involved, perceived perpetrator intentions, and types of coercion involved in all sexual assaults over the year prior to survey administration. We also examine types of sexual assault behaviors; perpetrator characteristics; time and place; alcohol involvement; and co-occurrence with bullying, hazing, sexual harassment, and stalking for soldiers' most serious sexual assault experience. Because of small sample sizes, we must aggregate active-component soldiers who did not identify as heterosexual (i.e., *sexual minorities*) into relatively large groups. Sexual minorities in the Army are disproportionately female, so an examination of experiences by sexual orientation only likely would be biased because of the different gender balance of individuals in the two groups. We therefore present results separately by victim gender and sexual orientation.

Appendix C includes tabular results for this chapter.

## Sexual Assault of Sexual Minorities in the Active-Component Army

There is currently no published reference on rates of sexual assault by gender and sexual orientation in the Army. We therefore present that information here. Table 5.1 shows the prevalence of soldiers who self-identified with different sexual orientations among both the total active-component Army and among only those soldiers who reported a sexual assault. Survey item response options included "heterosexual," "lesbian or gay," "bisexual," "other," and "prefer not to answer" (PNA).[18] We also constructed a no response (NR) group of respondents who skipped the survey question about sexual orientation.

The majority of active-component soldiers identify as heterosexual, although the size of that majority shrinks among soldiers who experienced a sexual assault (78 percent versus 51 percent).

---

[18] There are several reasons why a respondent would select PNA when asked about their sexual orientation. This list is not exhaustive. First, for some, the selection is essentially a "don't know" response. That is, these individuals may be asexual or questioning their sexual orientation and do not know how to answer the question. This may be less likely in the WGRA, however, because the "other" response option does include these as examples. It may also be the case that some respondents simply do not understand the question stem or the response options. Second, some military respondents may be especially concerned about the confidentially surrounding their response. A service member who has not disclosed their status to friends and family, other unit members, or leadership may not want to respond to a question about sexual orientation. Third, some portion of respondents might have found the question offensive or not relevant, believing that it should not be part of the WGRA, and thus chose not to provide a response. The WGRA does not ask respondents why they selected PNA.

Whereas 4 percent of all active-component soldiers identify as lesbian, gay, bisexual, or other (LGBO), more than four times as many sexually assaulted soldiers (17 percent) fall into this combined group. The LGBO group is overrepresented among both male and female sexual assault victims in the active-component Army (12 versus 15 percent for women and 3 versus 21 percent for men).

We also have a substantial group of soldiers for whom we are missing information on sexual orientation. The PNA group is represented at roughly equal (or perhaps slightly smaller) levels in the group of soldiers who were sexually assaulted and in the active-component Army as a whole, but the NR group is overrepresented in the group of soldiers who were sexually assaulted (28 percent in the sexually assaulted group compared with 12 percent across the active-component Army). These two groups combined make up 18 percent of all active-component soldiers (23 percent of women and 17 percent of men) but 32 percent of active-component soldiers who were sexually assaulted (32 percent of women and 31 percent of men). According to the pattern of responses, we believe that the bulk of the NR group exited the survey prior to the sexual orientation question, which is one of the last questions on the survey.

**Table 5.1. Self-Identified Sexual Orientation by Gender and Sexual Assault Experience, 2016 and 2018 WGRA**

| | Total Active Component | | | Active-Component Soldiers Who Were Sexually Assaulted | | |
|---|---|---|---|---|---|---|
| | All Soldiers (%) | Women (%) | Men (%) | All Soldiers (%) | Women (%) | Men (%) |
| Heterosexual | 78 | 65 | 80 | 51 | 53 | 49 |
| Gay/lesbian | 2 | 5 | 1 | 5 | 3 | 8 |
| Bisexual | 2 | 5 | 1 | 9 | 9 | 8 |
| Other[a] | 1 | 2 | 1 | 3 | 2 | 5 |
| PNA | 5 | 7 | 5 | 4 | 4 | 4 |
| NR (skipped question) | 12 | 16 | 12 | 28 | 28 | 26 |
| LGBO (combined) | 4 | 12 | 3 | 17 | 15 | 21 |
| PNA and NR (combined) | 18 | 23 | 17 | 32 | 32 | 31 |
| LGBO, PNA, and NR (combined) | 22 | 35 | 20 | 49 | 47 | 51 |

SOURCE: Authors' calculations using the 2016 and 2018 WGRA.
NOTES: In 2016, the sexual orientation question was used only on the paper survey form, so a small proportion of respondents were not given the question. These individuals are dropped from the remainder of this chapter's analyses. Percentages may not sum exactly because of rounding.
[a] Other includes "questioning, asexual, undecided, self-identified."

Although we had intended to report sexual assault descriptions for each of the groups in Table 5.1, we were unable to do so because of the small sample size in some cells, especially among men. Therefore, for men, we grouped all categories other than heterosexual (i.e., LGBO,[19] PNA, and NR). By grouping in this way, we are able to present more point estimates for men. For women, who have higher rates of sexual assault, we are able to compare across three groups: heterosexual, LGBO, and PNA and NR.

## Results for Women by Sexual Orientation

### *Sexual Assault Screening Questions*

Figure 5.1 displays the percentage of female victims who indicated that they experienced each type of sexual assault behavior on the sexual assault screener questions, by sexual orientation. The responses for types of sexual assault behaviors could be from *any* sexual assault experienced over the year prior to the survey rather than solely the most serious sexual assault experience. Corresponding tabular results are available in Table C.15.

Figures 5.1 through 5.9 are all in the same format. The labels on the x-axis represent responses to the survey questions. The three icons above each label represent the designated percentage from the graph. The purple squares (leftmost icon) represent the percentage of all female active-component soldiers who were sexually assaulted who indicated each characteristic of their experience, which is reproduced from Chapter 4. The dark blue circles (second icon from the left) represent the percentage of heterosexual female active-component soldiers who were sexually assaulted (i.e., heterosexual female victims) who indicated each characteristic of their experience. The teal triangles (second icon from the right) represent the percentage of female lesbian, gay, bisexual, or other active-component soldiers who were sexually assaulted (i.e., LGBO female victims) who indicated each characteristic of their experience. The lime-green bars (rightmost icon) represent the percentage of female active-component soldiers who did not respond or preferred not to answer the sexual orientation question who were sexually assaulted (i.e., NR/PNA female victims) who indicated each characteristic of their experience. The lines surrounding these icons represent the 95-percent CIs. If no icon is provided, that means that we have suppressed the icon because the confidence interval is too wide to provide a useful estimate. Bolded labels indicate a statistically significant difference between high-risk and non–high-risk installations.

---

[19] See the appendix in Morral and Schell, 2021, for a discussion of the treatment of the "other" sexual orientation group in the 2018 WGRA.

**Figure 5.1. Types of Sexual Assault Behaviors from Screener Questions, Female Sexual Assault Victims by Sexual Orientation**

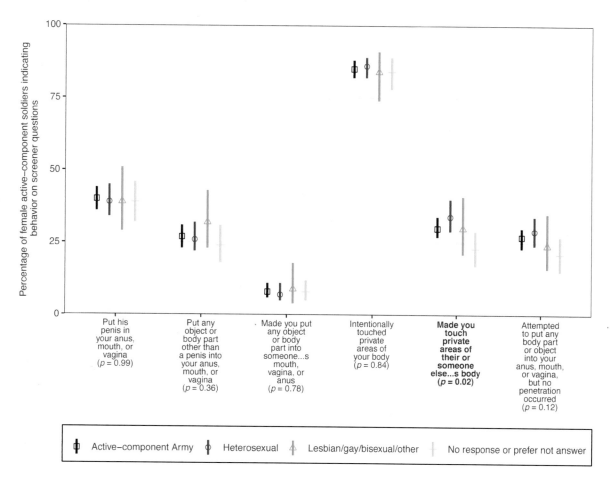

SOURCE: Authors' calculations using the 2016 and 2018 WGRA.
NOTE: Percentages are made up of only soldiers who were sexually assaulted during the year prior to WGRA administration. Percentages are available in Table C.15.

There is only one statistically significant difference by sexual orientation in the types of behaviors indicated on the screener questions. Heterosexual female victims were more likely than LGBO female victims to indicate that any sexual assault over the prior year included having someone make them touch private areas of someone else's body, and LGBO female victims were more likely to indicate the same behavior than NR/PNA female victims (34 percent versus 30 percent versus 23 percent, respectively, $p = 0.02$).

Figure 5.2 displays the percentage of female victims indicating that they were assaulted more than once, each type of perpetrator intent, and each type of coercion, by sexual orientation. Corresponding tabular results are available in Table C.16. There is one statistically significant difference in perpetrator intent: Forty-eight percent of heterosexual female victims, 37 percent of LGBO female victims, and 57 percent of NR/PNA female victims indicated that they believed that the perpetrator's intent was to abuse or humiliate them ($p = 0.04$).

**Figure 5.2. Perpetrator Intent and Type of Coercion from Screener Questions, Female Sexual Assault Victims by Sexual Orientation**

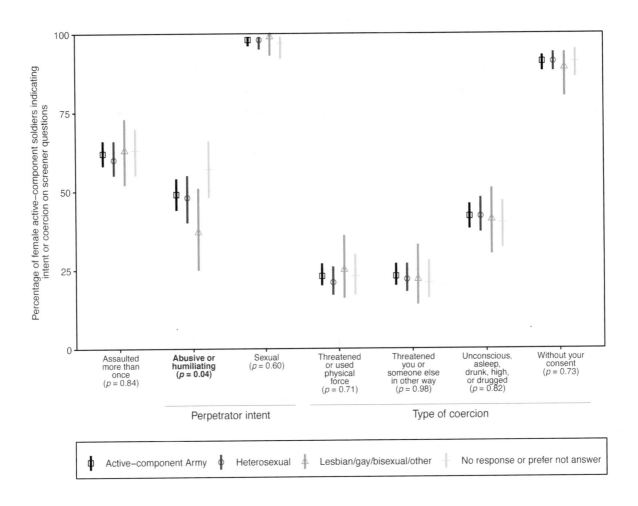

SOURCE: Authors' calculations using the 2016 and 2018 WGRA.
NOTE: Percentages are made up of only soldiers who were sexually assaulted during the year prior to WGRA administration. Perpetrator intent and type of coercion percentages are for the behavior on which the respondent qualified as having been sexually assaulted. Intent questions were not asked of respondents who qualified as having been sexually assaulted under the first sexual assault behavior (someone put his penis into the respondent's anus, mouth, or vagina), because the UCMJ does not require abusive, humiliating, or sexual intent for this behavior to qualify as rape or sexual assault. These percentages, therefore, have the denominator as individuals who qualified as having been sexually assaulted on one of the other behaviors. See Chapter 2 for further details. Percentages are available in Table C.16.

## Most Serious Sexual Assault Experience

### Types of Sexual Assault Behaviors

Similar to the results presented in Figure 5.1 for types of behaviors involved in all sexual assault experiences over the 12 months prior to the survey date, there are no differences by sexual orientation in the types of sexual assault behaviors indicated by female soldiers during their most serious sexual assault experience. See Table C.17.

## Characteristics of Perpetrators

Corresponding tabular results for all figures in this section are available in Table C.18.

Figure 5.3 displays the typical number, military status, and gender of perpetrators of female victims' most serious experiences of sexual assault, by sexual orientation. We found one statistically significant difference, which is that heterosexual women were less likely to indicate at least one female perpetrator ($p = 0.01$). Among heterosexual female victims, 97 percent indicated that all perpetrators were men, zero percent indicated that all perpetrators were female, 2 percent indicated that the perpetrators were a mix of men and women, and zero percent indicated that they were not sure. Among LGBO female victims, 93 percent indicated that all perpetrators were men, 1 percent indicated that all perpetrators were female, 4 percent indicated that the perpetrators were a mix of men and women, and 2 percent indicated that they were not sure. Among NR/PNA female victims, 90 percent indicated that all perpetrators were men, 2 percent indicated that all perpetrators were female, 6 percent indicated that the perpetrators were a mix of men and women, and 2 percent indicated that they were not sure. However, despite the statistically significant difference, perpetrators of women's most serious sexual assault experiences were overwhelmingly male. We do not believe that this difference is of substantive importance.

**Figure 5.3. Number, Military Status, and Gender of Perpetrators of Most Serious Experience, Female Sexual Assault Victims by Sexual Orientation**

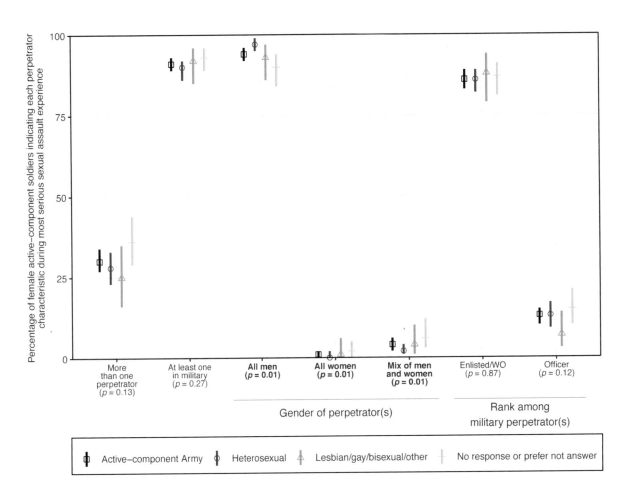

SOURCE: Authors' calculations using the 2016 and 2018 WGRA.
NOTE: Percentages are made up of only soldiers who were sexually assaulted during the year prior to WGRA administration. "At least one in the military" is an aggregation of the "yes, they all were" and "yes, some were, but not all" answer choices from the question on whether the perpetrator(s) was or were in the military. Rank is determined from a question asking the pay grade(s) of perpetrator(s), which was asked of only respondents who indicated that "all" or "some, but not all" of the perpetrators were members of the military. Respondents were instructed to select all pay grades that apply; the "not sure" response is not presented in the figure. WO = warrant officer.

Figure 5.4 displays the most common professional relationship between the victims and the perpetrators of female victims' most serious experiences of sexual assault, by sexual orientation. We found no statistically significant differences by sexual orientation.

**Figure 5.4. Professional Relationship Between Victim and Perpetrator of Most Serious Experience, Female Sexual Assault Victims by Sexual Orientation**

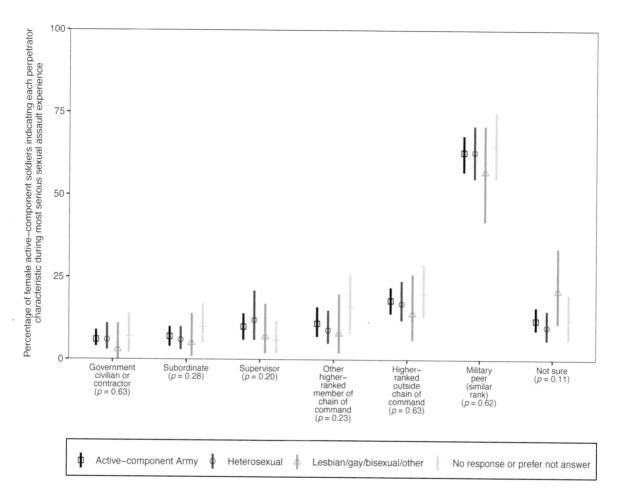

SOURCE: Authors' calculations using the 2018 WGRA.
NOTE: Percentages are made up of only soldiers who were sexually assaulted during the year prior to WGRA administration. Respondents were instructed to select all that apply. We include only responses from 2018 because "military peer of similar rank" was not an available answer choice in 2016. "Government civilian or contractor" is a combination of two answer choices: "DoD/government civilian(s) working for the military" and "Contractor(s)."

Figure 5.5 displays the most common personal relationship between the victims and the perpetrators of female victims' most serious experiences of sexual assault, by sexual orientation. We found one statistically significant difference in the percentage indicating "none of the above," which we believe includes military coworkers who the victim would not describe as a friend: Twenty-two percent of heterosexual female victims, 15 percent of LGBO female victims, and 30 percent of NR/PNA female victims indicated "none of the above" ($p = 0.01$).

53

**Figure 5.5. Personal Relationship Between Victim and Perpetrator of Most Serious Experience, Female Sexual Assault Victims by Sexual Orientation**

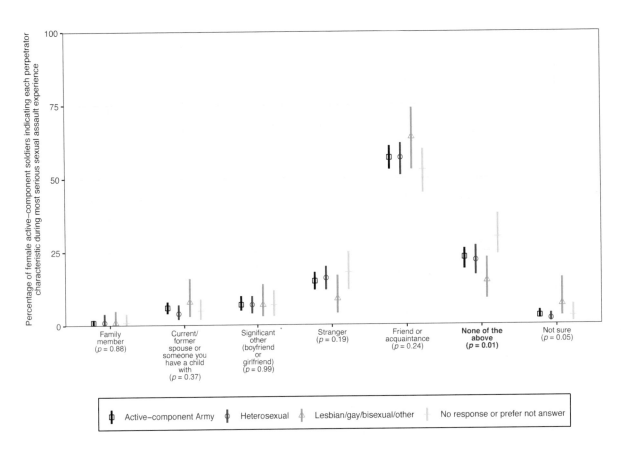

SOURCE: Authors' calculations using the 2016 and 2018 WGRA.
NOTE: Percentages are made up of only soldiers who were sexually assaulted during the year prior to WGRA administration. Respondents were instructed to select all that apply. "Current/former spouse or someone you have a child with" is an aggregation of the following two responses: "your current or former spouse" and "someone you have a child with (your child's mother or father)." "Significant other (boyfriend or girlfriend)" is an aggregation of the following two response options: "your significant other (boyfriend or girlfriend) who you <u>live</u> with" and "your significant other (boyfriend or girlfriend) who you <u>do/did not</u> live with."

Place and Time of Assault

Corresponding tabular results for both figures in this section are available in Table C.19.

Figure 5.6 displays the percentage of female victims indicating that their most serious sexual assault experience occurred at each place, by sexual orientation. We found a statistically significant difference by sexual orientation in the percentage who indicated that their most serious experience occurred at a military installation, at 64 percent of heterosexual female victims, 78 percent of LGBO female victims, and 76 percent of NR/PNA female victims ($p = 0.004$).

**Figure 5.6. Place of Most Serious Experience, Female Sexual Assault Victims by Sexual Orientation**

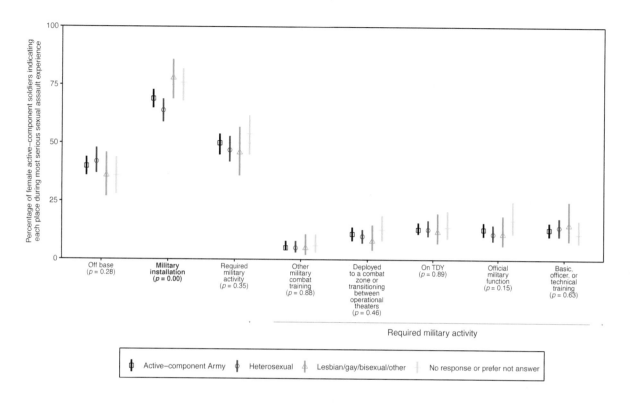

SOURCE: Authors' calculations using the 2016 and 2018 WGRA.
NOTE: Percentages are made up of only soldiers who were sexually assaulted during the year prior to WGRA administration. Respondents were instructed to select all places that apply. "Deployed to a combat zone or transitioning between operational theaters" is an aggregation of the following response options: "while you were deployed to a combat zone or to an area where you drew imminent danger pay or hostile fire pay," "during an overseas port visit while deployed," and "while transitioning between operational theaters (for example, going to or returning from forward deployment)." "Basic, officer, or technical training" is an aggregation of the following response options: "while you were in recruit training/basic training," "while you were in Officer Candidate or Training School/Basic or Advanced Officer Course," and "while you were attending military occupational specialty school/technical training/advanced individual training/professional military education." "Any required military activity" is an aggregation of the following response options: "deployed to a combat zone or transitioning between operational theaters," "basic, officer, or technical training," "while you were on TDY/TAD, at sea, or during field exercises/alerts," "while you were in any other type of military combat training," "while at an official military function (either on or off base)," and (from the "when" question displayed in Figure 5.7) while you were "at work during duty hours." The "while you were in a delayed entry program (DEP) or delayed training program (DTP)" answer choice is excluded from the figure but was indicated by 4 percent of respondents; this choice includes only pre-accession assaults.

Figure 5.7 displays the percentage of female victims who indicated that their most serious sexual assault experience occurred at each time, by sexual orientation. We found only one statistically significant difference by sexual orientation, which is in the percentage of female victims indicating that their most serious sexual assault experience occurred while being intimate with the person: Although we are unable to present a point estimate for LGBO women because of the wide confidence intervals, the range of possible estimates is substantially higher for LGBO women than the point estimates for NR/PNA or heterosexual women (5 percent each, $p = 0.02$).

55

**Figure 5.7. Time of Most Serious Experience, Female Sexual Assault Victims by Sexual Orientation**

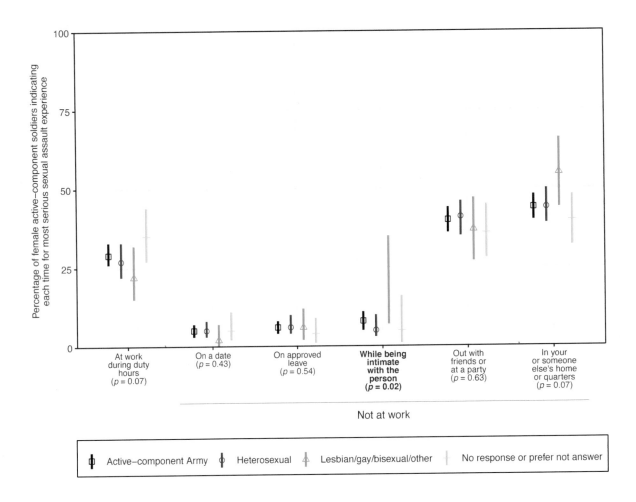

SOURCE: Authors' calculations using the 2016 and 2018 WGRA.
NOTE: Percentages are made up of only soldiers who were sexually assaulted during the year prior to WGRA administration. Respondents were instructed to select all times that apply. The "While being intimate with the person" response options was available only in 2016. The figure does not present results for "none of the above" or "do not recall."

Alcohol and Drug Involvement

Figure 5.8 displays the percentage of female victims who indicated that their most serious sexual assault experience involved alcohol or drugs, by sexual orientation. The figure presents only the percentage responding "yes;" respondents were also given the option to respond with "no" or either "don't know" or "not sure" for all questions, and the percentages choosing those answers are reported in Table C.20. We found no statistically significant differences by sexual orientation.

56

**Figure 5.8. Alcohol and Drug Involvement in Most Serious Experience, Female Sexual Assault Victims by Sexual Orientation**

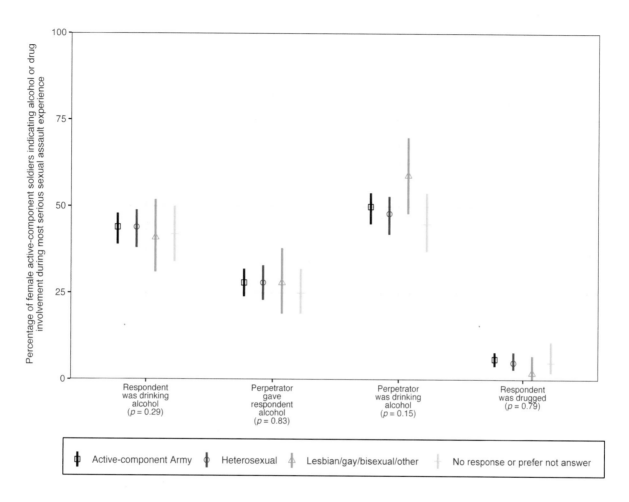

SOURCE: Authors' calculations using the 2016 and 2018 WGRA.
NOTE: Percentages are made up of only soldiers who were sexually assaulted during the year prior to WGRA administration. Percentages are for "Yes" responses to each question; respondents also had the choices of "no" and either "not sure" or "I don't know" (depending on the question).

## Hazing, Bullying, Sexual Harassment, and Stalking

Figure 5.9 displays the percentage of female victims who indicated that their most serious sexual assault experience co-occurred with bullying, hazing, sexual harassment, or stalking, by sexual orientation. Corresponding tabular results are available in Table C.21. We found a statistically significant difference by sexual orientation in the percentage of victims who indicated that they would describe their most serious sexual assault experience as bullying, at 17 percent of heterosexual female victims, 13 percent of LGBO female victims, and 29 percent of NR/PNA female victims.

**Figure 5.9. Bullying, Hazing, Sexual Harassment, and Stalking During Most Serious Experience, Female Sexual Assault Victims by Sexual Orientation**

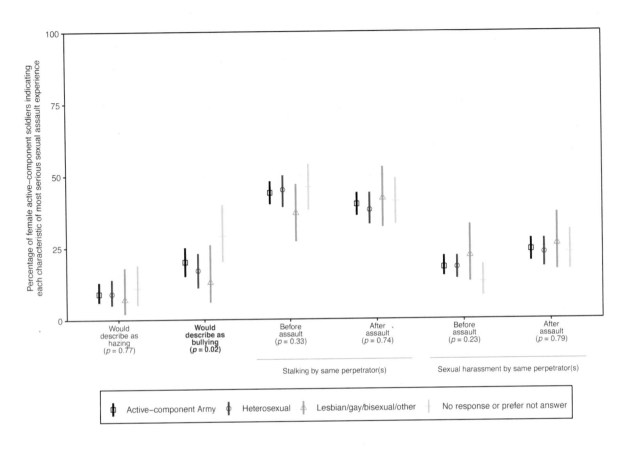

SOURCE: Authors' calculations using the 2016 and 2018 WGRA.
NOTE: Percentages are made up of only soldiers who were sexually assaulted during the year prior to WGRA administration. Bullying and hazing use only 2018 data because of changes in definitions across the two survey years; see Table 2.3 in Chapter 2.

*Summary of Results for Women by Sexual Orientation*

We examined differences in female victims' sexual assault experiences by sexual orientation. Because of small sample sizes, we aggregated sexual orientation into three categories for women: heterosexual or straight, LGBO, and NR/PNA. We found few differences between the sexual assault experiences of heterosexual and LGBO female victims but several differences between the sexual assault experiences of NR/PNA female victims and those of heterosexual and LBGO female victims.

We found two statistically significant differences from the screener questions on sexual assault. First, heterosexual female victims were more likely than LGBO female victims—and LGBO female victims were more likely than NR/PNA female victims—to indicate that they experienced a nonpenetrative sexual assault where they were made to touch private areas of someone else's body during any of their experiences during the year prior to the survey. Second, heterosexual female victims were more likely than LGBO female victims and less likely than

NR/PNA female victims to indicate that they believed that the perpetrator intended to abuse or humiliate them.

We found one difference in the characteristics of perpetrators that we believe is of substantive importance. NR/PNA female victims were more likely than heterosexual or LGBO female victims to indicate that (at least one of) the perpetrator(s) of their most serious sexual assault experience fell into the personal relationship category of "none of the above," meaning someone the victim knew but who was not a family member, current or former spouse or significant other, or friend or acquaintance. We believe that this category includes military coworkers who the victim did not consider friends. A similar pattern exists for whether the victim would describe their most serious experience as bullying. We also found that LGBO and NR/PNA female victims were statistically significantly more likely than heterosexual female victims to indicate that their most serious sexual assault experience occurred at a military installation and that LGBO women were statistically significantly more likely than heterosexual and NR/PNA women to indicate that their most serious experience occurred while being intimate with the other person.

Taken together, NR/PNA female victims indicated the highest levels of abusive or humiliating intent, perpetrators they knew but who they chose not to describe as friends (and who may well have been military coworkers, given that the majority of perpetrators were members of the military), and bullying. Heterosexual and LGBO female victims either indicated roughly equal levels or had lower levels for LBGO female victims. The lack of differences in experiences between heterosexual and LGBO victims is consistent with the findings of Trump-Steele et al., 2021, who used combined data for all DoD service branches from the 2018 WGRA. In only one case were LGBO female victims similar to NR/PNA female victims but different from heterosexual female victims in a substantively important way: LGBO and NR/PNA female victims were more likely than heterosexual female victims to indicate that their most serious experience occurred at a military installation. These findings indicate that the female sexual assault victims who most often experienced sexual assaults meant to abuse, humiliate, or bully were not the LGBO female victims; they were the NR/PNA female victims. Although this seems important, we cannot say definitively who these victims are, which makes it difficult to determine the actual policy implications because it is not clear how these victims identify themselves in terms of sexual orientation. It is possible, given that the majority of the NR/PNA group falls into the NR category and the bulk of the NR category appears to have exited the survey prior to the sexual orientation question, that the reason for the difference is that female soldiers who experienced assaults meant to abuse, humiliate, or bully dropped out of the survey earlier rather than the break-off being related to sexual minority status. In supplemental analyses in which we examined the NR and PNA groups separately, we found suggestive evidence that the NR group experienced somewhat more-violent sexual assaults (e.g., sexual assaults of women in this group more often involved the use of physical force or threats thereof, although the difference was not statistically significant because of small sample size), but the small sample size for the PNA group prevents us from drawing definitive conclusions. Further study is needed to better understand who the PNA soldiers are and whether their sexual assault experiences differed from those of other groups of soldiers.

## Results for Men by Sexual Orientation

### *Sexual Assault Screening Questions*

Figure 5.10 displays the percentage of male victims who indicated that they experienced each type of sexual assault behavior on the sexual assault screener questions, by sexual orientation. The responses for types of sexual assault behaviors could be from *any* sexual assault experienced over the year prior to the survey rather than solely the most serious sexual assault experience. Corresponding tabular results are available in Table C.22.

Figures 5.10 through 5.18 are all in the same format. The labels on the x-axis represent responses to the survey question. The three icons above each label represent the designated percentage who indicated each behavior. The purple squares (leftmost icon) represent the percentage of all male active-component soldiers who were sexually assaulted who indicated each characteristic of their experience, which is reproduced from Chapter 4. The teal circles (center icon) represent the percentage of heterosexual male active-component soldiers who were sexually assaulted (i.e., heterosexual male victims) who indicated each characteristic of their experience, and the lime-green triangles (rightmost icon) represent the percentage of male active-component soldiers who either did not respond to the sexual orientation question (either by skipping it or responding with "prefer not to answer") or who identified with any orientation other than heterosexual who were sexually assaulted (i.e., LGBO, NR, and PNA male victims) who indicated each characteristic of their experience. The lines surrounding these icons represent the 95-percent CI. If no icon is provided, that means that we have suppressed the icon because the confidence interval is too wide to provide a useful estimate. Bolded labels indicate a statistically significant difference between high-risk and non–high-risk installations.

**Figure 5.10. Types of Sexual Assault Behaviors from Screener Questions, Male Sexual Assault Victims by Sexual Orientation**

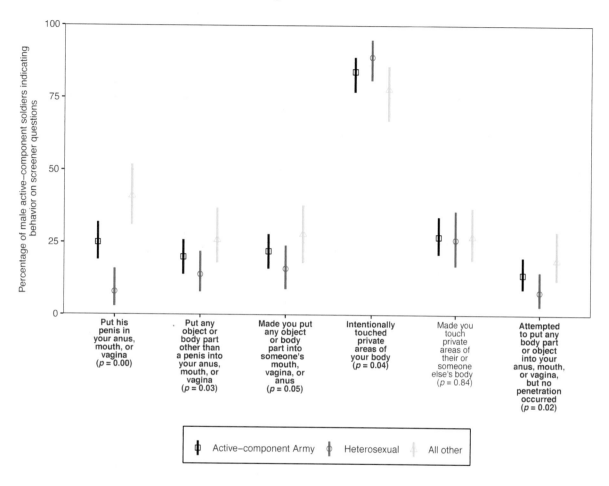

SOURCE: Authors' calculations using the 2016 and 2018 WGRA
NOTE: Percentages are made up of only soldiers who were sexually assaulted during the year prior to WGRA administration. All other = LGBO, PNA, and NR. Corresponding tabular results are available in Table C.22.

We found several large, statistically significant differences by sexual orientation in the types of behaviors that men indicated on the sexual assault screener questions. LGBO, NR, and PNA male victims were more likely than heterosexual male victims to indicate that, during any sexual assault over the year prior to the survey, they had been penetrated with a penis (41 percent versus 8 percent, $p < 0.0001$), had been penetrated with another body part or an object (26 percent versus 14 percent, $p = 0.03$), were made to penetrate another person with any body part or object (28 percent versus 16 percent, $p = 0.049$), and/or had someone unsuccessfully attempt to penetrate them with any body part or object (19 percent versus 8 percent, $p = 0.02$). LGBO, NR, and PNA male victims were less likely than heterosexual male victims to indicate that someone intentionally touched private areas of their body (78 percent versus 89 percent, $p = 0.02$).

Figure 5.11 displays the percentage of male victims who indicated that they were assaulted more than once, each type of perpetrator intent, and each type of coercion, by sexual orientation. Corresponding tabular results are available in Table C.23.

61

**Figure 5.11. Perpetrator Intent and Type of Coercion from Screener Questions, Male Sexual Assault Victims by Gender**

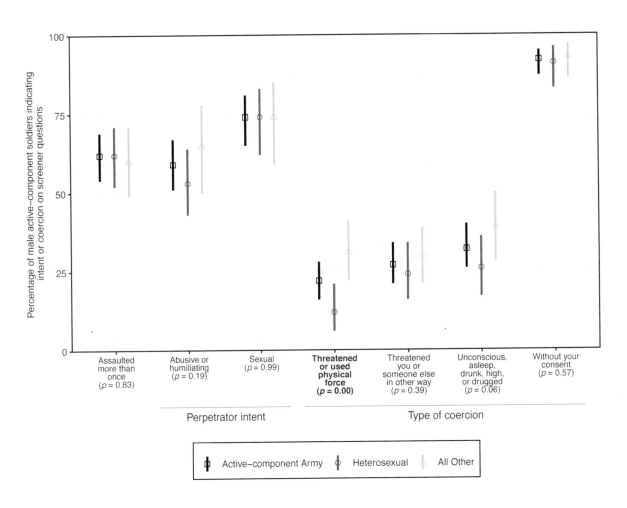

SOURCE: Authors' calculations using the 2016 and 2018 WGRA.
NOTE: Percentages are made up of only soldiers who were sexually assaulted during the year prior to WGRA administration. Perpetrator intent and type of coercion percentages are for the behavior on which the respondent qualified as having been sexually assaulted. Intent questions were not asked of respondents who qualified as having been sexually assaulted under the first sexual assault behavior (someone put his penis into the respondent's anus, mouth, or vagina), because the UCMJ does not require abusive, humiliating, or sexual intent for this behavior to qualify as rape or sexual assault. These percentages, therefore, have the denominator as individuals who qualified as having been sexually assaulted on one of the other behaviors. See Chapter 2 for further details. Percentages are available in Table C.23.

We also found one statistically significant difference in types of coercion. LGBO, NR, and PNA male victims were statistically significantly more likely to indicate that the perpetrator threatened or used physical force to make them comply (31 percent versus 12 percent, $p = 0.003$). We also found one marginally significant difference in methods of coercion that might account for some uncertainty in the identity of the perpetrators, which we discuss later in this chapter: LGBO, NR, and PNA male victims were more likely than heterosexual male victims to indicate that they were assaulted while asleep, unconscious, or incapacitated by alcohol or drugs ($p = 0.06$).

We did not find statistically significant differences in the percentage of men indicating that they were assaulted multiple times or in perpetrator intent.

### Most Serious Sexual Assault Experience

#### Types of Sexual Assault Behaviors

The pattern of differences in the types of behaviors involved in men's most serious sexual assault experience by sexual orientation is similar to the patterns for the screener questions: LGBO, NR, and PNA male victims were more likely than heterosexual male victims to experience all types of penetrative and attempted penetrative sexual assault behaviors and less likely to experience nonpenetrative sexual assaults. See Table C.24.

#### Characteristics of Perpetrators

Corresponding tabular results for all figures in this section are available in Table C.25.

Figure 5.12 displays the most common numbers, military statuses, and genders of perpetrators of male victims' most serious experiences of sexual assault, by sexual orientation. We found three statistically significant differences by sexual orientation. First, LGBO, NR, and PNA male victims were less likely to indicate that at least one perpetrator was in the military (82 percent versus 66 percent, $p = 0.01$). This difference is driven both by a larger proportion of nonmilitary perpetrators and by a larger proportion of experiences in which the victim was not sure of the perpetrator's military status: Fifty-two percent of LGBO, NR, and PNA male victims indicated that all perpetrators were in the military, 14 percent indicated that some but not all were in the military, 23 percent indicated that none were in the military, and 11 percent were not sure, compared with 80 percent, 2 percent, 14 percent, and 4 percent of heterosexual male victims, respectively.

Second, LGBO, NR, and PNA male victims were less likely to indicate that all perpetrators of their most serious sexual assault experience were women (14 percent versus 40 percent), more likely to indicate that the perpetrators were a mixed-gender group (23 percent versus 4 percent), and more likely to indicate that they were unsure of the gender of the perpetrator(s) (11 percent versus 2 percent), but approximately equally likely to indicate that all perpetrators were men (52 percent versus 54 percent) ($p < 0.0001$).

Third, among those who indicated that at least one perpetrator was in the military, LGBO, NR, and PNA male victims were more likely than heterosexual male victims to indicate that they were not sure of the perpetrator(s)'s pay grade (12 percent versus 4 percent, $p = 0.04$). There is also one marginally significant difference that could account for some of the statistically significant differences we see here: A larger proportion of LGBO, NR, and PNA male victims indicated more than one perpetrator of their most serious experience ($p = 0.052$), which is necessary for the perpetrators to be a mix of military and nonmilitary members or a mix of men and women. The "not sure" responses for military status may be driven by a higher percentage of

LGBO, NR, and PNA male victims who indicated that at least one perpetrator was a stranger (see Figure 5.14); the higher percentage of LGBO, NR, and PNA male victims who believed that they were drugged (see Figure 5.17); or by the previously discussed marginally significant difference in the percentage of sexual minority men who indicated that they were assaulted while unconscious, asleep, or incapacitated by alcohol or drugs.

**Figure 5.12. Number, Military Status, and Gender of Perpetrators of Most Serious Experience, Male Sexual Assault Victims by Sexual Orientation**

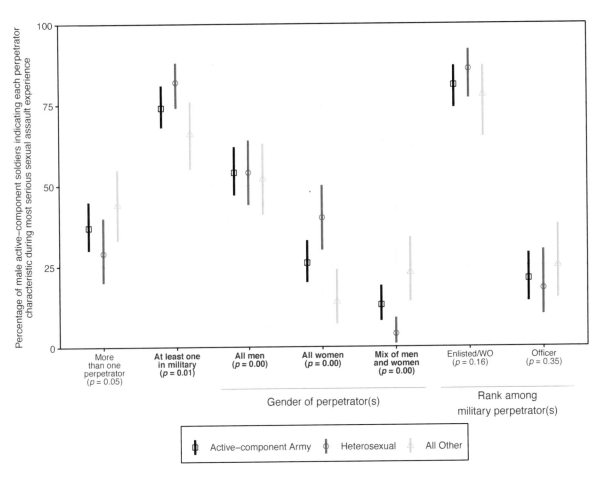

SOURCE: Authors' calculations using the 2016 and 2018 WGRA.
NOTE: Percentages are made up of only soldiers who were sexually assaulted during the year prior to WGRA administration. "At least one in the military" is an aggregation of the answer choices "yes, they all were" and "yes, some were, but not all" from the question on whether the perpetrator(s) was or were in the military. Rank is determined from a question asking the pay grade(s) of perpetrator(s), which was asked of only respondents who indicated that "all" or "some, but not all" of the perpetrators were members of the military. Respondents were instructed to select all pay grades that apply; the "not sure" response is not presented. All other = LGBO, PNA, and NR.

Figure 5.13 displays the most common professional relationship between the victims and the perpetrators of male victims' most serious experiences of sexual assault, by sexual orientation. Because of the small sample size, the confidence intervals for LGBO, NR, and PNA male victims are too large to provide exact estimates. However, LGBO, NR, and PNA male victims were statistically significantly more likely than heterosexual male victims to indicate that the perpetrator of their most serious sexual assault experience was their supervisor ($p = 0.01$) or another higher-ranked member of their chain of command ($p = 0.01$). LGBO, NR, and PNA male victims were also more likely to indicate "not sure" ($p = 0.01$).

**Figure 5.13. Professional Relationship Between Victim and Perpetrator of Most Serious Experience, Male Sexual Assault Victims by Sexual Orientation**

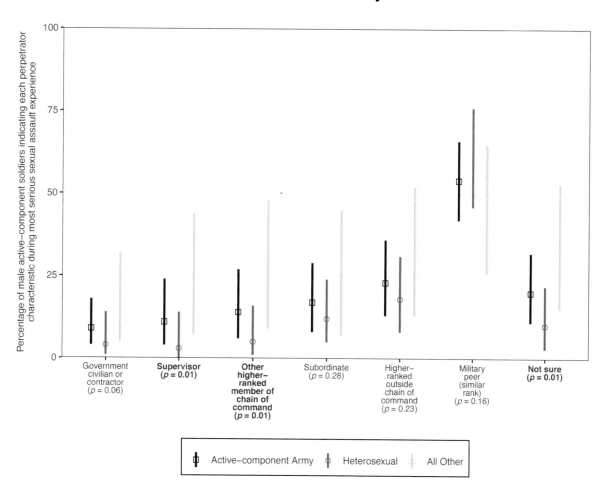

SOURCE: Authors' calculations using the 2018 WGRA.
NOTE: Percentages are made up of only soldiers who were sexually assaulted during the year prior to WGRA administration. Respondents were instructed to select all that apply. We include only responses from 2018 because "military peer of similar rank" was not an available answer choice in 2016. "Government civilian or contractor" is a combination of two answer choices: "DoD/government civilian(s) working for the military" and "Contractor(s)."

Figure 5.14 displays the most common personal relationship between the victim and the perpetrators of male victims' most serious experiences of sexual assault, by sexual orientation. We found two statistically significant differences. First, LGBO, NR, and PNA male victims were statistically significantly more likely to indicate that at least one perpetrator was a stranger (23 percent versus 10 percent, $p = 0.01$). Second, LGBO, NR, and PNA male victims were statistically significantly more likely to indicate that they were not sure (13 percent versus 5 percent, $p$ = 0.03), which (as with gender or military status) could be related to the evidence on drug involvement discussed later in this chapter.

**Figure 5.14. Personal Relationship Between Victim and Perpetrator of Most Serious Experience, Male Sexual Assault Victims by Sexual Orientation**

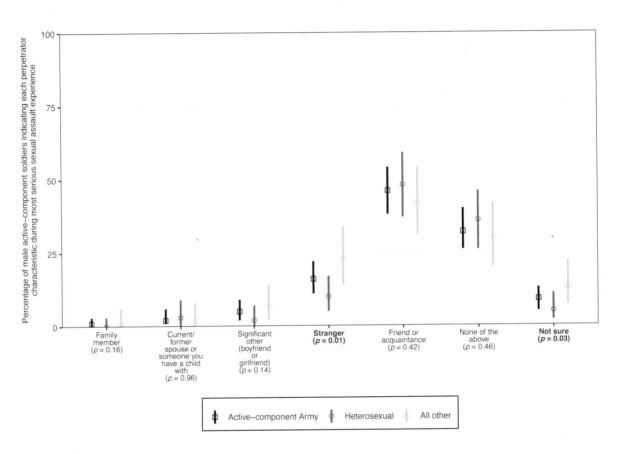

SOURCE: Authors' calculations using the 2016 and 2018 WGRA.
NOTE: Percentages are made up of only soldiers who were sexually assaulted during the year prior to WGRA administration. Respondents were instructed to select all that apply. "Current/former spouse or someone you have a child with" is an aggregation of the following two response options: "your current or former spouse" and "someone you have a child with (your child's mother or father)." "Significant other (boyfriend or girlfriend)" is an aggregation of the following two response options: "your significant other (boyfriend or girlfriend) who you <u>live</u> with" and "your significant other (boyfriend or girlfriend) who you <u>do/did not</u> live with." All other = LGBO, PNA, and NR.

Place and Time of Assault

Corresponding tabular results for both figures in this section are available in Table C.26.

Figure 5.15 displays the percentage of male victims who indicated that their most serious sexual assault experience occurred at each place, by sexual orientation. We found three statistically significant differences by sexual orientation. LGBO, NR, and PNA male victims are statistically significantly more likely than heterosexual male victims to indicate that their most serious sexual assault experience occurred while on TDY (35 percent versus 21 percent,

66

$p = 0.048$); during an official military function (30 percent versus 17 percent, $p = 0.04$); and during basic, officer, or technical training ($p = 0.01$).

**Figure 5.15. Place of Most Serious Experience, Male Sexual Assault Victims by Sexual Orientation**

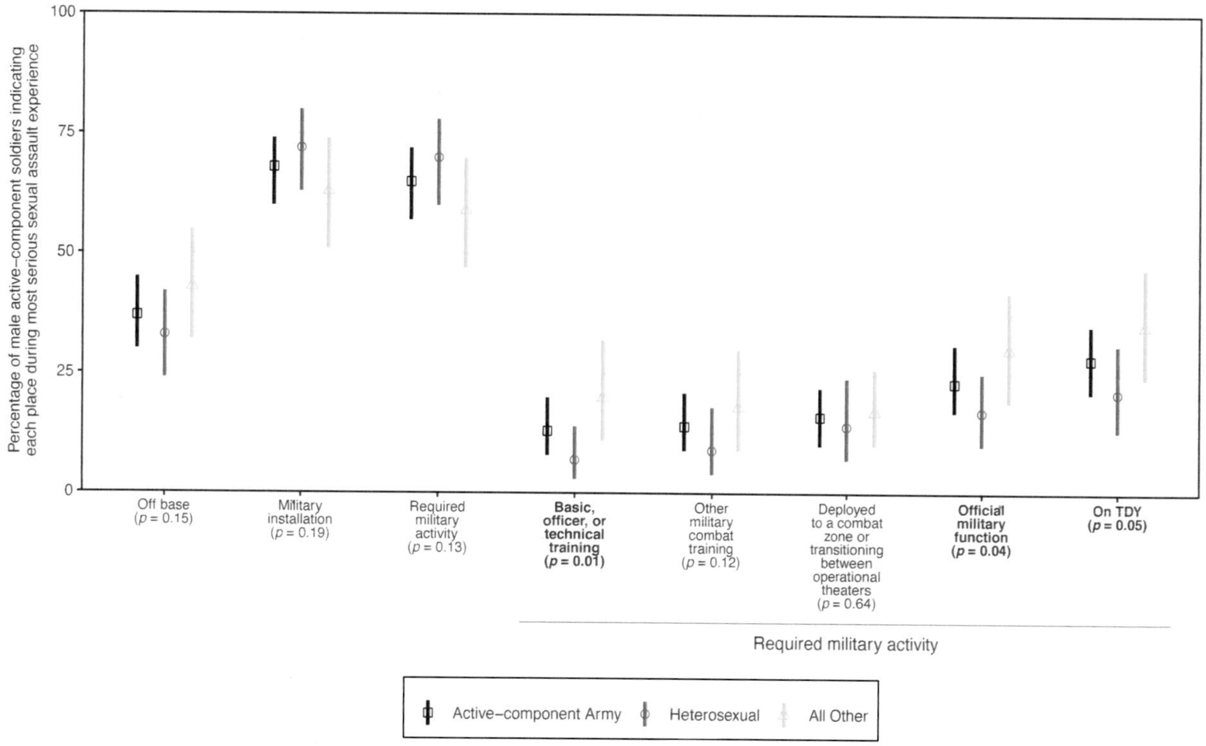

SOURCE: Authors' calculations using the 2016 and 2018 WGRA.
NOTE: Percentages are made up of only soldiers who were sexually assaulted during the year prior to WGRA administration. Respondents were instructed to select all places that apply. "Deployed to a combat zone or transitioning between operational theaters" is an aggregation of the following response options: "while you were deployed to a combat zone or to an area where you drew imminent danger pay or hostile fire pay," "during an overseas port visit while deployed," and "while transitioning between operational theaters (for example, going to or returning from forward deployment)." "Basic, officer, or technical training" is an aggregation of the following response options: "while you were in recruit training/basic training," "while you were in Officer Candidate or Training School/Basic or Advanced Officer Course," and "while you were attending military occupational specialty school/technical training/advanced individual training/professional military education." "Any required military activity" is an aggregation of the following response options: "deployed to a combat zone or transitioning between operational theaters," "basic, officer, or technical training," "while you were on TDY/TAD, at sea, or during field exercises/alerts," "while you were in any other type of military combat training," "while at an official military function (either on or off base)," and (from the "when" question displayed in Figure 5.16) while "at work during duty hours." The "while you were in a delayed entry program (DEP) or delayed training program (DTP)" answer choice is excluded from the figure but was indicated by 4 percent of respondents. This choice includes only pre-accession assaults. All other = LGBO, PNA, and NR.

Figure 5.16 displays the percentage of male victims who indicated that their most serious sexual assault experience occurred at each time, by sexual orientation. We found no statistically significant differences in the time of male soldiers' most serious sexual assault experience by sexual orientation.

**Figure 5.16. Time of Most Serious Experience, Male Sexual Assault Victims by Sexual Orientation**

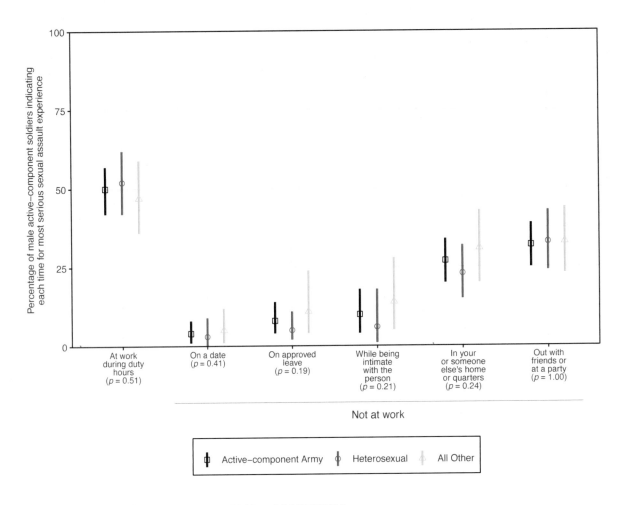

SOURCE: Authors' calculations using the 2016 and 2018 WGRA.
NOTE: Percentages are made up of only soldiers who were sexually assaulted during the year prior to WGRA administration. Respondents were instructed to select all times that apply. The "while being intimate with the person" response option was available only in 2016. This figure does not present results for "none of the above" or "do not recall." All other = LGBO, PNA, and NR.

Alcohol and Drug Involvement

Figure 5.17 displays the percentage of male victims who indicated that their most serious sexual assault experience involved alcohol or drugs, by sexual orientation. The figure presents only the percentage responding "yes;" respondents were also given the option to respond with "no" or "don't know" for all questions, and the percentages of respondents who chose those answers are reported in Table C.27. We found two statistically significant differences. First, LGBO, NR, and PNA male victims were more likely to indicate that they were drinking alcohol at the time of their sexual assault: Thirty-seven percent of LGBO, NR, and PNA male victims indicated that they were drinking alcohol, 53 percent indicated that they were not drinking alcohol, and 10 percent indicated that they were not sure, compared with 33 percent, 66 percent, and 1 percent of heterosexual male victims, respectively ($p = 0.02$, calculated across all response options). Second, LGBO, NR, and PNA male victims were more likely to believe or not know whether they were drugged without their knowledge or consent during their most serious experience. In total, 12 percent of LGBO, NR, and PNA male victims indicated that they believed they had been drugged, 69 percent indicated that they did not believe they had been drugged, and 20 percent indicated that they did not know, compared with 5 percent, 90 percent, and 6 percent of heterosexual male victims, respectively ($p = 0.01$, calculated across all response options).

**Figure 5.17. Alcohol and Drug Involvement in Most Serious Experience, Male Sexual Assault Victims by Sexual Orientation**

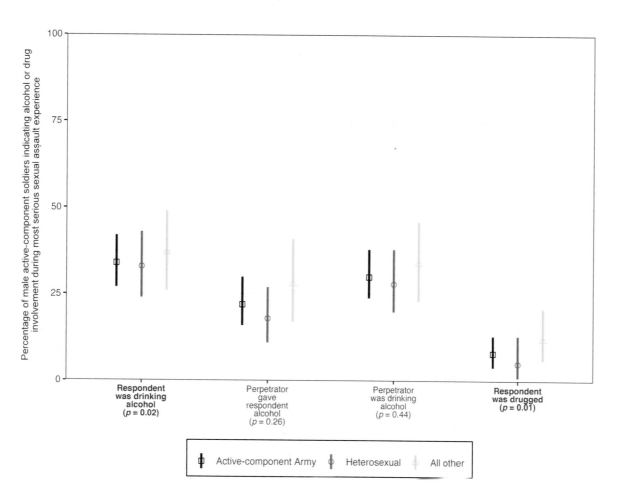

SOURCE: Authors' calculations using the 2016 and 2018 WGRA.
NOTE: Percentages are made up of only soldiers who were sexually assaulted during the year prior to WGRA administration. Percentages are for "yes" responses to each question; respondents also had the choices of "no" and either "not sure" or "I don't know" (depending on the question), and $p$-values are calculated across all response options. All other = LGBO, PNA, and NR.

## Hazing, Bullying, Sexual Harassment, and Stalking

Figure 5.18 displays the percentage of male victims who indicated that their most serious sexual assault experience co-occurred with bullying, hazing, sexual harassment, or stalking, by sexual orientation. Corresponding tabular results are available in Table C.28. LGBO, NR, and PNA male victims were statistically significantly more likely than heterosexual male victims to indicate that they were stalked before (30 percent versus 14 percent, $p = 0.01$) and/or after (34 percent versus 15 percent, $p = 0.002$) their most serious sexual assault experience. Additionally, while we suppress the point estimates for bullying and hazing because of imprecision, LGBO, NR, and PNA male victims were statistically significantly more likely than heterosexual male victims to indicate that they would describe their most serious sexual assault experience as hazing ($p = 0.05$) and bullying ($p = 0.01$).

**Figure 5.18. Bullying, Hazing, Sexual Harassment, and Stalking During Most Serious Experience, Male Sexual Assault Victims by Sexual Orientation**

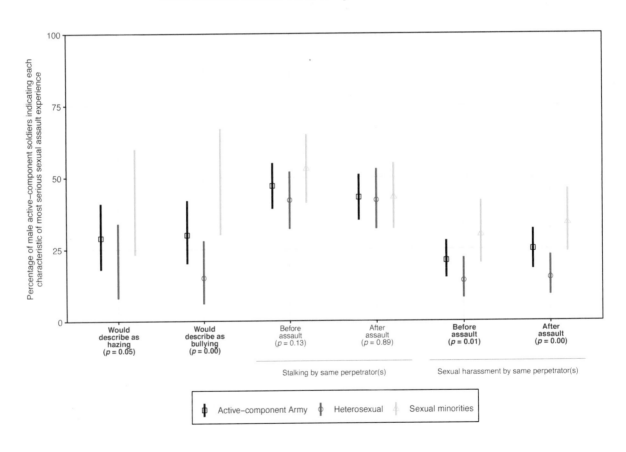

SOURCE: Authors' calculations using the 2016 and 2018 WGRA.
NOTE: Percentages are made up of only soldiers who were sexually assaulted during the year prior to WGRA administration. The bullying and hazing items reflect only 2018 data because of changes in definitions across the two survey years; see Table 2.3. Sexual minorities = LGBO, PNA, and NR.

## Summary of Results for Men by Sexual Orientation

Because of small sample size, we examined only differences between male sexual assault victims who did and did not identify as heterosexual, where we include men who did not respond to the sexual orientation survey question and who responded with "prefer not to answer." We found substantial evidence that LGBO, NR, and PNA male victims experienced more penetrative sexual assaults; experienced more-violent sexual assaults (i.e., those that involve physical force or threats thereof) than heterosexual male victims; were more likely to be sexually assaulted during work; and more often indicated co-occurrence with hazing, bullying, and stalking. The differences we found are qualitatively similar to those of Trump-Steele et al., 2021, p. 46, whose analysis includes members of all the military services combined.[20] However, the relatively small sample of LGBO, NR, and PNA male victims makes understanding their experiences in detail difficult, as does our lack of ability to study differences between gay men, bisexual men, men of other sexual orientations, and men who responded with "prefer not to answer." Supplemental analyses in which we split the LGBO, NR, and PNA group into (1) LGBO and (2) NR or PNA suggest that the differences are not driven solely by the NR and PNA group—that is, there are differences between the sexual assault experiences of LGBO men and those of heterosexual male victims. However, the sample sizes for the active-component Army are too small to draw definitive conclusions. Further study is needed to create a full picture of the sexual assault experiences of LGBO, NR, and PNA male victims in the active-component Army, which is crucial to the sexual assault prevention effort.

LGBO, NR, and PNA male victims are more likely than heterosexual male victims to indicate that they experienced all penetrative or attempted penetrative sexual assault behaviors during any sexual assault over the year prior to survey administration, and they were less likely to indicate that they experienced having someone touch private areas of their body. LGBO, NR, and PNA male victims were also statistically significantly more likely to indicate that the perpetrator used or threatened them with violence to make them comply.

LGBO, NR, and PNA male victims were less likely than heterosexual male victims to indicate that at least one perpetrator of their most serious sexual assault experience was a military member. They were also more likely to indicate that the perpetrators of their most serious experience were a mixed-gender group and less likely to indicate that all perpetrators were women (but equally likely to indicate that all perpetrators were men). In terms of professional relationship, LGBO, NR, and PNA male victims were more likely than heterosexual

---

[20] The executive summary provided by Trump-Steele et al., 2021, notes that the authors did not find statistically significant differences in sexual assault experiences by sexual orientation, but they did find substantive differences between heterosexual and sexual minority male victims that are similar in direction and magnitude to our results (Trump-Steele et al., 2021, p. 46). We believe that the difference in statistical significance is attributable to a difference in methods: First, their cutoff for statistical significance is a $p$-value of 0.01, which is more conservative than ours, and second, they exclude the NR/PNA group.

male victims to describe at least one of the perpetrators as their supervisor, another higher-ranked member of their chain of command, or "not sure." In terms of the personal relationship, LGBO, NR, and PNA male victims were also more likely than heterosexual male victims to describe at least one of the perpetrators of their most serious experience as a stranger. LGBO, NR, and PNA male victims were more likely than heterosexual male victims to indicate that they were not sure of the number, gender, military status, pay grade, and/or their personal relationship with the perpetrator(s) of their most serious experience, which may be related to the fact that they were more likely to be assaulted by strangers or to the involvement of drugs and/or alcohol.

LGBO, NR, and PNA male victims were more likely than heterosexual male victims to indicate that their most serious experience occurred during three types of required military activities: basic, officer, or technical training; official military functions; and while on TDY.

LGBO, NR, and PNA male victims also indicated different levels of alcohol and drug involvement than heterosexual male victims. LGBO, NR, and PNA male victims were more likely than heterosexual male victims to indicate that they were drinking alcohol or did not know whether they were drinking alcohol at the time of their most serious sexual assault experience. LGBO, NR, and PNA male victims were also more than twice as likely as heterosexual male victims to indicate that they believed they had been drugged, and they were more than three times as likely to indicate that they did not know whether they had been drugged. Although the difference is only marginally statistically significant, we found in the screener questions that LGBO, NR, and PNA male victims were more likely to indicate on the type of coercion questions that they were assaulted while asleep, unconscious, or incapacitated by alcohol or drugs, which is consistent with the evidence from the drug and alcohol involvement questions.

Finally, LGBO, NR, and PNA male victims were twice as likely to indicate that they were stalked both before and after their most serious sexual assault experience by the same perpetrator(s). LGBO, NR, and PNA male victims were also more likely than heterosexual male victims to describe their most serious experience as hazing and/or bullying.

# Chapter 6. Differences in the Sexual Assault Experience by Installation Risk Level

In this chapter, we examine differences in sexual assault experiences among soldiers assigned to high-risk versus non–high-risk installations. We examine the types of sexual assault behaviors involved, perceived perpetrator intentions, and types of coercion involved in all sexual assaults over the year prior to survey administration. We also examine types of sexual assault behaviors; perpetrator characteristics; time and place; alcohol involvement; and co-occurrence with bullying, hazing, sexual harassment, and stalking for soldiers' most serious sexual assault experience.

Appendix C includes tabular results for this chapter. Appendix E provides tabular results by gender and installation risk level; the results by gender and installation risk level do not differ substantially from the results presented in this chapter.

## High-Risk Installations in the Active-Component Army

Text in this section is reproduced in part from the description of the definition of high-risk installations in Chapter 2 of Calkins et al., 2021, with modifications as necessary for differences between the two reports.

We define a *high-risk installation* as one at which the rate of sexual assault indicated in the 2018 WGRA is higher than the overall rates in the active-component Army.[21] We chose 2018 because it reflects more-recent risk levels, but installation-level sexual assault risk tends to be stable over time (Matthews et al., 2021). We define *high risk* separately for men and women. During the year prior to the 2018 WGRA, 5.9 percent of female victims and 0.7 percent of male victims (excluding those assigned to the Pentagon and military academies) were sexually assaulted. *Non–high-risk installations* are those at which the rates of sexual assault indicated in the 2018 WGRA are at or below these average rates. We apply this definition of risk to both the 2016 and 2018 data. In total, we identified 13 high-risk installations for women and 21 high-risk installations for men. Overall, 7.4 percent of women at high-risk installations (versus 5.0 percent of women at non–high-risk installations) were sexually assaulted in the year prior to the survey period, and 0.8 percent of men at high-risk installations (versus 0.5 percent of men at non–high-risk installations) were sexually assaulted in the year prior to the survey period. In Table 6.1, we list the installations that we identified as high-risk and non–high-risk for men and women.

---

[21] Prior RAND work developed multiple definitions of the risk of sexual harassment and sexual assault at Army installations (Matthews et al., 2021). This definition corresponds to "total risk" from that work.

**Table 6.1. Installations with Above-Average Rates of Sexual Assault for Men and Women, 2018 WGRA**

| High-Risk Installations for Women | High-Risk Installations for Men |
|---|---|
| 20th ASG, Taegu, Korea | 20th ASG, Taegu, Korea |
| 23rd ASG, Camp Humphreys | Baumholder H.G. Smith Barracks |
| Fort Bliss | Camp Casey Dongducheon |
| Fort Campbell | Fort Bliss |
| Fort Carson | Fort Bragg |
| Fort Drum | Fort Campbell |
| Fort Hood | Fort Drum |
| Fort Huachuca | Fort Hood |
| Fort Polk | Fort Jonathan Wainwright |
| Fort Riley | Fort Lewis |
| Fort Sill | Fort Polk |
| Fort Stewart | Fort Richardson |
| Small foreign installations | Fort Riley |
| | Fort Stewart |
| | Grafenwohr, Germany |
| | Landstuhl Medical Center |
| | Osan, Korea |
| | Schofield Barracks |
| | Vicenza, Italy |
| | Vilseck |
| | Wiesbaden, Germany |

NOTE: ASG = area support group.

Soldiers assigned to high-risk installations were disproportionately male: Sixty-one percent of male soldiers who were sexually assaulted were assigned to high-risk installations, whereas 44 percent of female soldiers who were sexually assaulted were assigned to high-risk installations. We therefore present results by gender in Appendix E to be sure that any differences between high-risk and non–high-risk installations do not simply reflect the gender differences in sexual assault experiences.

It is important to keep in mind that there are substantial differences between high-risk and non–high-risk installations other than the prevalence of sexual assault. For one thing, installations with high prevalence of sexual assault often have a high proportion of personnel who are at high risk for sexual assault based on their individual characteristics—for instance, younger, unmarried personnel. However, even after taking into consideration the individual characteristics of personnel, there are other differences between high-risk and non–high-risk installations; for instance, high-risk installations tend to have higher operational tempo (i.e., days deployed on a mission for the Global War on Terrorism), and female soldiers at installations with more civilians face lower risk of sexual assault (Matthews et al., 2021).

## Sexual Assault Screening Questions

Figure 6.1 displays the percentage of sexual assault victims who indicated that they experienced each type of sexual assault behavior on the sexual assault screener questions, by installation risk level. Note that the responses for types of sexual assault behaviors could be from *any* sexual assault experienced over the year prior to the survey rather than solely the most serious sexual assault experience. Corresponding tabular results are available in Table C.29.

All figures in this chapter are in the same format. The labels on the x-axis represent responses to the survey question. The three icons above each label represent the designated percentage from the graph. The purple squares (leftmost icon) represent the percentage of all active-component soldiers who were sexually assaulted who indicated each characteristic of their experience, which is reproduced from Chapter 3 except in cases where we use 2018 data only. The teal circles (center icon) represent the percentage of all active-component soldiers assigned to high-risk installations who were sexually assaulted (i.e., sexual assault victims at high-risk installations) who indicated each characteristic of their experience, and the lime-green triangles (rightmost icon) represent the percentage of all active-component soldiers assigned to non–high-risk installations who were sexually assaulted (i.e., sexual assault victims at non–high-risk installations) who indicated each characteristic of their experience. The lines surrounding these icons represent the 95-percent CIs. If no icon is provided, that means that we have suppressed the icon because the confidence interval is too wide to provide a useful estimate. Bolded labels indicate a statistically significant difference between high-risk and non–high-risk installations.

**Figure 6.1. Types of Sexual Assault Behaviors from Screener Questions, All Sexual Assault Victims by Installation Risk Level**

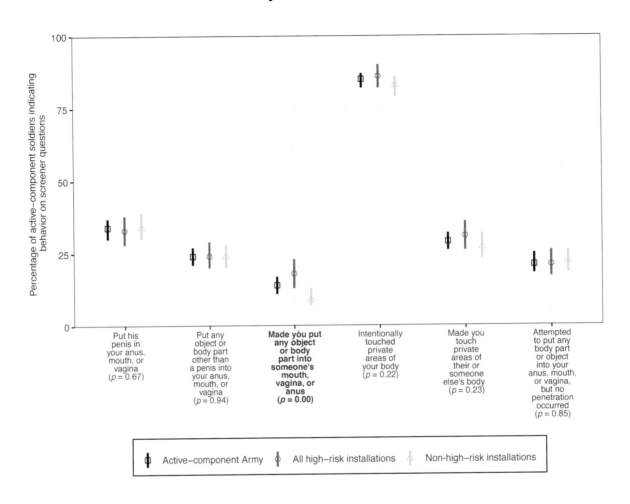

SOURCE: Authors' calculations using the 2016 and 2018 WGRA.
NOTE: Percentages are made up of only soldiers who were sexually assaulted during the year prior to WGRA administration. Tabular results are available in Table C.29.

Among the types of behaviors on the sexual assault screener questions, we found one statistically significant difference by installation risk level. A statistically significantly higher percentage of victims at high-risk installations indicated that any of their sexual assault experiences involved having someone make the victim put any object or body part into someone else's anus, mouth, or vagina (18 percent versus 9 percent, $p = 0.002$). The difference is present for both male and female victims, but is only statistically significant (and is larger) for men (see Table E.1 in Appendix E). Given that the difference is still present when looking only at male victims, it likely does not reflect only the fact that soldiers assigned to high-risk installations are disproportionately male. We also found one statistically significant difference that exists for female victims only: Female victims at high-risk installations were statistically significantly more likely than female victims at non–high-risk installations to indicate that someone made them touch private areas of the perpetrator's or someone else's body (35 percent versus 27 percent, $p = 0.048$, see Table E.1).

Figure 6.2 displays the percentage of sexual assault victims who indicated that they were assaulted more than once, each type of perpetrator intent, and each type of coercion, by installation risk level. Corresponding tabular results are available in Table C.30. Sexual assault victims who were assigned to high-risk installations were statistically significantly more likely to have been sexually assaulted more than once over the year prior to survey administration (68 percent versus 56 percent, $p = 0.002$). There are no statistically significant differences in the perpetrator intent or types of coercion indicated in the sexual assault screener questions by installation risk level.

**Figure 6.2. Perpetrator Intent and Type of Coercion from Screener Questions, All Sexual Assault Victims by Installation Risk Level**

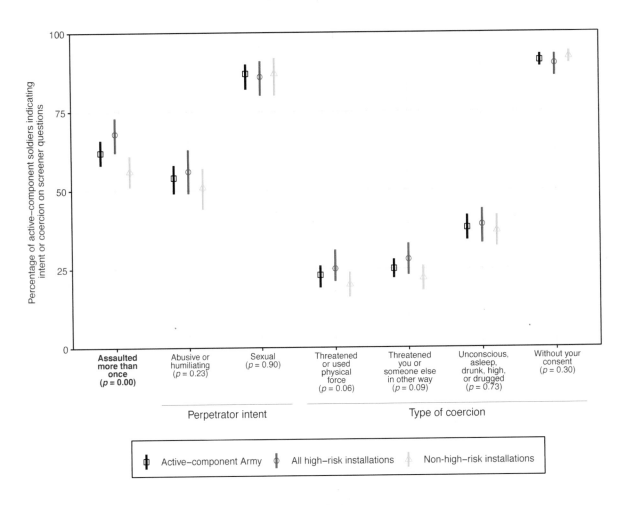

SOURCE: Authors' calculations using the 2016 and 2018 WGRA.
NOTE: Percentages are made up of only soldiers who were sexually assaulted during the year prior to WGRA administration. Perpetrator intent and type of coercion percentages are for the behavior on which the respondent qualified as having been sexually assaulted. Intent questions were not asked of respondents who qualified as having been sexually assaulted under the first sexual assault behavior (someone put his penis into the respondent's anus, mouth, or vagina), because the UCMJ does not require abusive, humiliating, or sexual intent for this behavior to qualify as rape or sexual assault. These percentages, therefore, have the denominator as individuals who qualified as having been sexually assaulted on one of the other behaviors. See Chapter 2 for further details. Percentages are available in Table C.30.

## Soldiers' Most Serious Sexual Assault Experience

### Types of Sexual Assault Behaviors

As we did for the screener questions, we found that a statistically significantly higher percentage of victims at high-risk installations indicated that their most serious sexual assault experience involved someone making the victim put any object or body part into someone else's anus, mouth, or vagina (16 percent versus 8 percent, $p = 0.003$). However, we did not find that the difference in behaviors for women only in the screener questions extends to the most serious experience. See Tables C.31 and Table E.3.

## Characteristics of Perpetrators

Corresponding tabular results for all figures in this section are available in Table C.32.

Figure 6.3 displays the percentage of victims who indicated each number, military status, and gender of the perpetrator(s) of their most serious sexual assault experience, by installation risk level. The only statistically significant difference in this set of results is in the number of perpetrators: Victims at high-risk installations were statistically significantly more likely to indicate that there was more than one perpetrator in their most serious sexual assault experience (37 percent indicating more than one, 58 percent indicating one, and 5 percent indicating not sure at high-risk installations versus 29 percent indicating more than one, 69 percent indicating one, and 2 percent indicating not sure at non–high-risk installations, $p = 0.01$). This difference is also statistically significant only for men. We also found a statistically significant difference for women only in the proportion of victims who indicated that at least one perpetrator was a member of the military (94 percent versus 89 percent, $p = 0.02$), but this difference is not large enough to be of practical importance for policymaking.

**Figure 6.3. Number, Military Status, and Gender of Perpetrators of Most Serious Experience, All Sexual Assault Victims by Installation Risk Level**

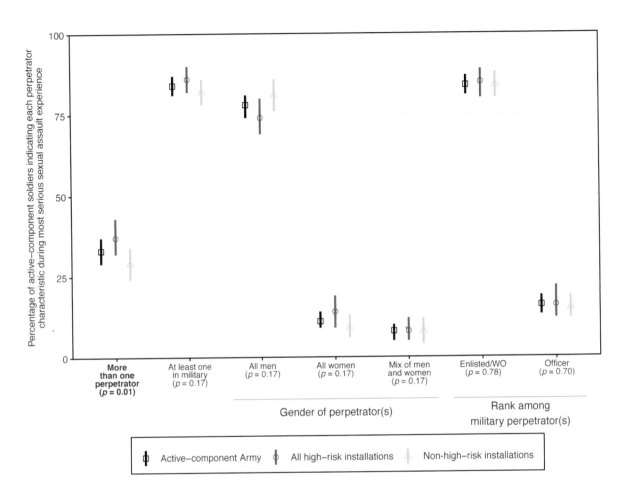

SOURCE: Authors' calculations using the 2016 and 2018 WGRA.
NOTE: Percentages are made up of only soldiers who were sexually assaulted during the year prior to WGRA administration. "At least one in the military" is an aggregation of the answer choices "yes, they all were" and "yes, some were, but not all" from the question on whether the perpetrator(s) was or were in the military. Rank is determined from a question asking the pay grade(s) of perpetrator(s), which is asked of only respondents who indicated that "all" or "some, but not all" of the perpetrators were members of the military. Respondents were instructed to select all pay grades that apply; the "not sure" response is not presented. WO = warrant officer.

Figure 6.4 displays the percentage of victims indicating each type of professional relationship with the perpetrator(s) of their most serious sexual assault experience, by installation risk level. We found no statistically significant differences by installation risk level in the professional relationship between the victim and perpetrator.

**Figure 6.4. Professional Relationship Between Victim and Perpetrator of Most Serious Experience, All Sexual Assault Victims by Installation Risk Level**

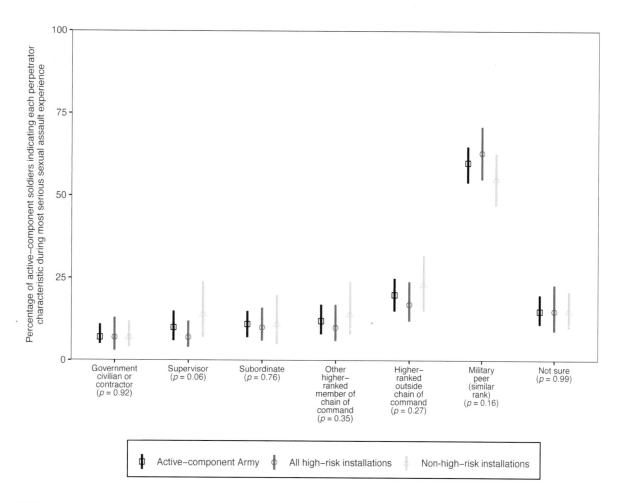

SOURCE: Authors' calculations using the 2018 WGRA.
NOTE: Percentages are made up of only soldiers who were sexually assaulted during the year prior to WGRA administration. Respondents were instructed to select all that apply. We include only responses from 2018 because "military peer of similar rank" was not an available answer choice in 2016. "Government civilian or contractor" is a combination of the following two answer choices: "DoD/government civilian(s) working for the military" and "Contractor(s)."

Figure 6.5 displays the percentage of victims who indicated each type of personal relationship with the perpetrator(s) of their most serious sexual assault experiences, by installation risk level. We found no statistically significant differences by installation risk level in the professional relationship between the victim and perpetrator.

**Figure 6.5. Personal Relationship Between Victim and Perpetrator of Most Serious Experience, All Sexual Assault Victims by Installation Risk Level**

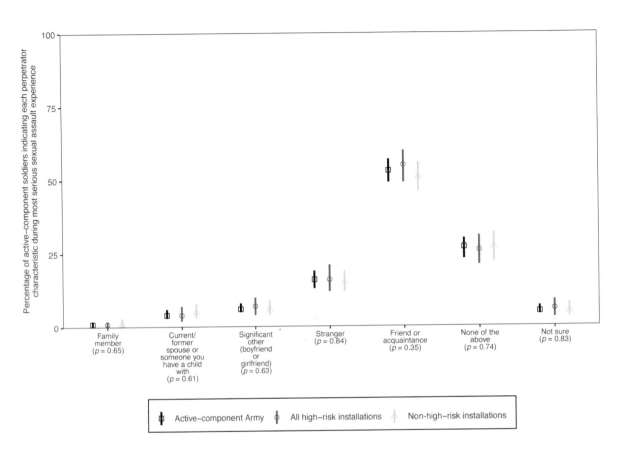

SOURCE: Authors' calculations using the 2016 and 2018 WGRA.
NOTE: Percentages are made up of only soldiers who were sexually assaulted during the year prior to WGRA administration. Respondents were instructed to select all that apply. "Current/former spouse or someone you have a child with" is an aggregation of the following response options: "your current or former spouse" and "someone you have a child with (your child's mother or father)." "Significant other (boyfriend or girlfriend)" is an aggregation of the following response options: "your significant other (boyfriend or girlfriend) who you <u>live</u> with" and "your significant other (boyfriend or girlfriend) who you <u>do/did not</u> live with."

*Place and Time of Assault*

Corresponding tabular results for both figures in this section are available in Table C.33.

Figure 6.6 displays the percentage of sexual assault victims who indicated that their most serious sexual assault experience occurred at each place, by installation risk level. We found only one statistically significant difference by installation risk level: Victims assigned to high-risk installations were statistically significantly more likely than victims assigned to non–high-risk installations to indicate that their most serious sexual assault experience occurred while deployed to a combat zone or transitioning between operational theaters (16 percent versus 9 percent, $p = 0.01$). We believe that this difference occurs because the installations we have classified as high-risk are more likely to deploy soldiers rather than because soldiers assigned to high-risk installations are more likely to be sexually assaulted conditional on deployment. This difference is therefore unlikely to be of practical importance for policymaking.

**Figure 6.6. Place of Most Serious Experience, All Sexual Assault Victims by Installation Risk Level**

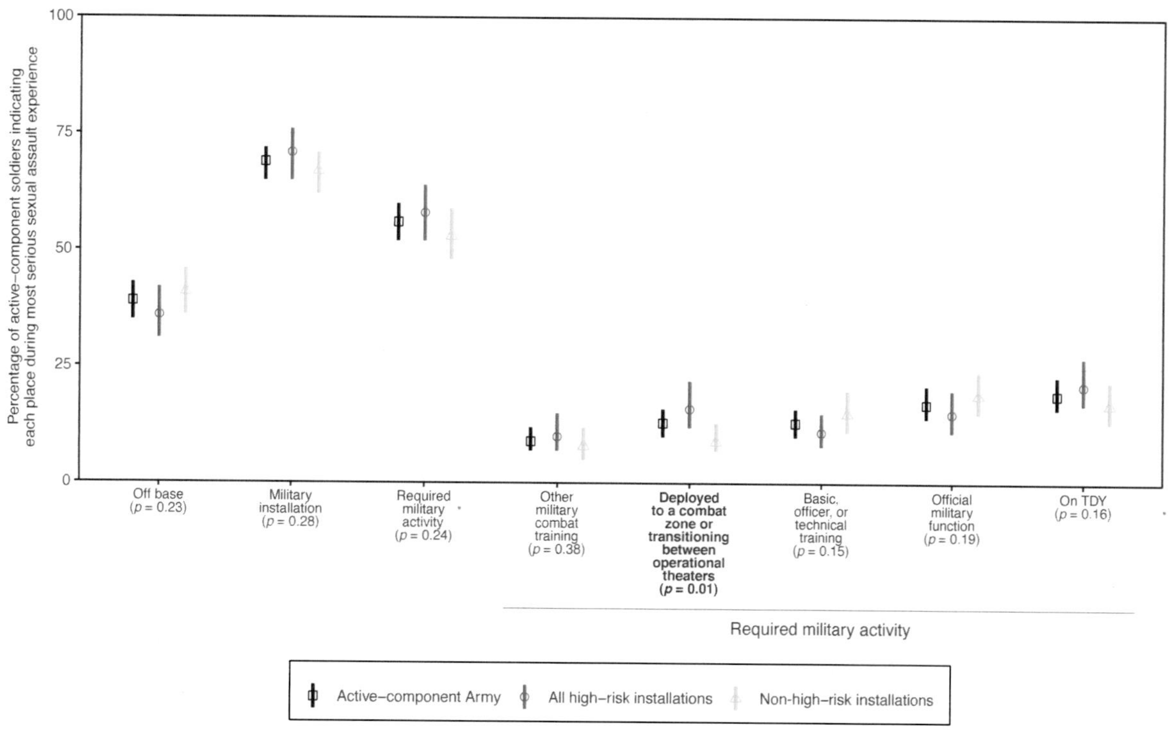

SOURCE: Authors' calculations using the 2016 and 2018 WGRA.
NOTE: Percentages are made up of only soldiers who were sexually assaulted during the year prior to WGRA administration. Respondents were instructed to select all places that apply. "Deployed to a combat zone or transitioning between operational theaters" is an aggregation of the following response options: "while you were deployed to a combat zone or to an area where you drew imminent danger pay or hostile fire pay," "during an overseas port visit while deployed," and "while transitioning between operational theaters (for example, going to or returning from forward deployment)." "Basic, officer, or technical training" is an aggregation of the following response options: "while you were in recruit training/basic training," "while you were in Officer Candidate or Training School/Basic or Advanced Officer Course," and "while you were attending military occupational specialty school/technical training/advanced individual training/professional military education." "Any required military activity" is an aggregation of the following response options: "deployed to a combat zone or transitioning between operational theaters," "basic, officer, or technical training," "while you were on TDY/TAD, at sea, or during field exercises/alerts," "while you were in any other type of military combat training," "while at an official military function (either on or off base)," and (from the "when" question displayed in Figure 6.7) while "at work during duty hours." The "while you were in a delayed entry program (DEP) or delayed training program (DTP)" answer choice is excluded from the figure but was indicated by 4 percent of victims; this choice includes only pre-accession assaults.

Figure 6.7 displays the percentage of sexual assault victims who indicated that their most serious sexual assault experience occurred at each time, by installation risk level. We found no statistically significant differences by installation risk level in the time that soldiers' most serious sexual assault experience took place.

83

**Figure 6.7. Time of Most Serious Experience, All Sexual Assault Victims by Installation Risk Level**

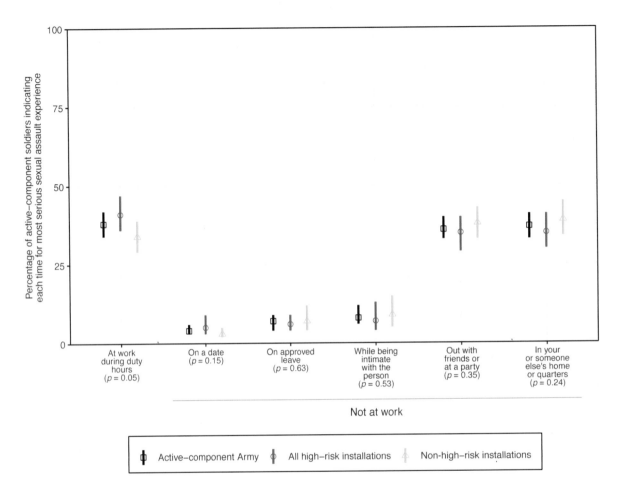

SOURCE: Authors' calculations using the 2016 and 2018 WGRA.
NOTE: Percentages are made up of only soldiers who were sexually assaulted during the year prior to WGRA administration. Respondents were instructed to select all times that apply. The "while being intimate with the person" response option is available only in 2016. The figure does not present results for "none of the above" or "do not recall."

## Alcohol and Drug Involvement

Figure 6.8 displays the percentage of sexual assault victims who indicated that their most serious sexual assault experience involved alcohol or drugs, by installation risk level. The figure presents only the percentage responding "yes;" respondents were also given the option to respond with "no" and either "don't know" or "not sure" for all questions, and the percentages choosing those answers are reported in Table C.34.

**Figure 6.8. Alcohol and Drug Involvement in Most Serious Experience, All Sexual Assault Victims by Installation Risk Level**

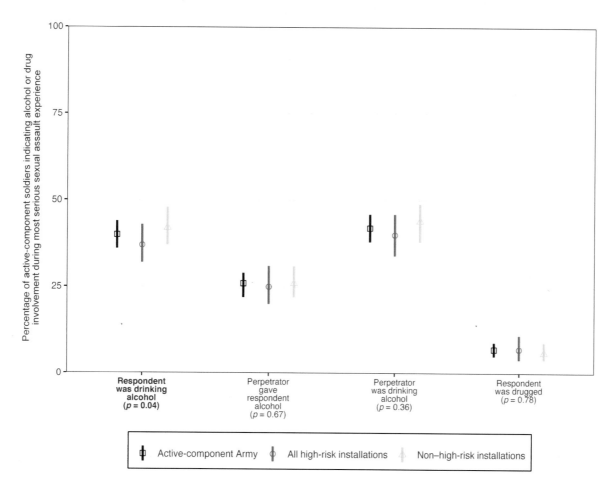

SOURCE: Authors' calculations using the 2016 and 2018 WGRA.
NOTE: Percentages are made up of only soldiers who were sexually assaulted during the year prior to WGRA administration. Percentages are for "Yes" responses to each question; respondents also had the choices of "no" and either "not sure" or "I don't know" (depending on the question).

We found one statistically significant difference by installation risk level, which is in the percentage of victims who indicated that they were drinking alcohol at the time of their most serious sexual assault experience. At high-risk installations, 37 percent of soldiers who were sexually assaulted indicated that they were drinking alcohol during their most serious sexual assault experience, 59 percent indicated that they were not drinking alcohol, and 4 percent indicated that they were not sure whether they were drinking alcohol. At non–high-risk installations, 42 percent of soldiers who were sexually assaulted indicated that they were drinking alcohol during their most serious sexual assault experience, 56 percent indicated that they were not drinking alcohol, and 1 percent indicated that they were not sure whether they were drinking alcohol ($p = 0.04$). The difference by installation risk level appears to be driven by men (see Table E.6), although the difference for men is not statistically significant (likely because of lack of power). Because these differences are relatively small and driven in part by less certainty at high-risk installations, they are unlikely to be of substantive importance.

*Hazing, Bullying, Sexual Harassment, and Stalking*

Figure 6.9 displays the percentage of sexual assault victims who indicated that their most serious sexual assault experience co-occurred with bullying, hazing, sexual harassment, or stalking, by installation risk level. Corresponding tabular results are available in Table C.35. We found no statistically significant differences in hazing, bullying, sexual harassment, and stalking during soldiers' most serious sexual assault experience by installation risk level.

**Figure 6.9. Bullying, Hazing, Sexual Harassment, and Stalking During Most Serious Experience, All Sexual Assault Victims by Installation Risk Level**

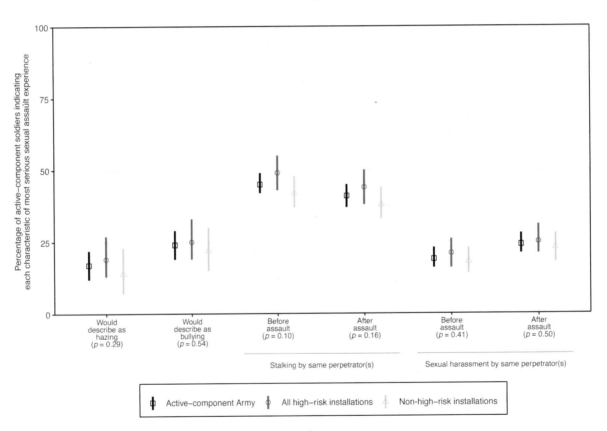

SOURCE: Authors' calculations using the 2016 and 2018 WGRA.
NOTE: Percentages are made up of only soldiers who were sexually assaulted during the year prior to WGRA administration. Bullying and hazing use only 2018 data because of changes in definition across the two survey years; see Table 2.3.

86

## Summary

We found a small number of differences between soldiers' sexual assault experiences by installation risk level, only some of which are large enough to be of practical importance for prevention policy.

Most of the differences occur on the sexual assault screening questions. In particular, sexual assault victims at high-risk installations were more likely to indicate that any of their sexual assault experiences involved someone making them penetrate another person with any object or body part, with the difference driven by male victims. Additionally, female victims at high-risk installations were statistically significantly more likely than female victims at non–high-risk installations to indicate that someone made them touch private areas of the perpetrator's or someone else's body. Victims at high-risk installations were also more likely than victims at non–high-risk installations to indicate that, conditional on being sexually assaulted at least once, they were assaulted multiple times over the year prior to the survey administration.

There are also two differences in the characteristics of perpetrators. A higher proportion of victims at high-risk installations indicated either multiple perpetrators or that they were unsure of the number of perpetrators in their most serious sexual assault experience. This difference is driven by male victims. Additionally, female victims at high–risk installations were statistically significantly more likely than female victims at non–high-risk installations to indicate military perpetrators in their most serious sexual assault experience, but the difference is not large enough to be of practical importance.

Victims at high-risk installations were more likely than victims at non–high-risk installations to indicate that their most serious sexual assault experience occurred while deployed to a combat zone or transitioning between operational theaters. However, like in Calkins et al., 2021, we believe that this is because the installations we have classified as high-risk are more likely to deploy victims rather than because victims assigned to high-risk installations face a higher risk of sexual assault conditional on deployment.

Finally, victims at high-risk installations were more likely than victims at non–high-risk installations to indicate either that they were not drinking alcohol or that they did not know whether they were drinking alcohol at the time of their most serious experience. However, this difference is too small to be of substantive importance.

# Chapter 7. Conclusion

Sexual assault prevention in the active-component Army depends critically on having information about the circumstances surrounding sexual assaults experienced by soldiers: what types of sexual assaults are most common; who perpetrators are and what their intentions were; when and where assaults most often occur; and other context, such as methods of coercion, alcohol involvement, and co-occurrence with bullying, hazing, sexual harassment, and stalking. In this report, we used data from the 2016 and 2018 WGRA to describe the circumstances surrounding sexual assaults of active-component soldiers. We also describe differences for important subgroups of victims: the 2016 versus 2018 samples, men versus women, victims who do and do not identify as heterosexual, and victims assigned to high-risk versus non–high-risk installations. Such information is helpful for understanding what types of behaviors and contexts the Army's sexual assault prevention effort should target.

By far the most common type of sexual assault, both for all assaults and for soldiers' most serious experiences, is a nonpenetrative one, where someone intentionally touched private areas of the victim's body. Penetrative sexual assaults with a penis were the second most common type of sexual assault but were substantially less likely than intentional touching of private parts. The typical perpetrator of soldiers' most serious sexual assault experience was a male member of the military acting alone, and most military perpetrators were enlisted or warrant officers. Perpetrators were most often military peers or friends or acquaintances of the victim. Perpetrators who were strangers to the victim were uncommon. Soldiers' most serious experience of sexual assault typically occurred at a military installation, and slightly more than half of victims indicated that their most serious experience occurred during a required military activity. Victims were approximately equally likely to be assaulted while at work, while in their or someone else's home or quarters, and while out with friends or at a party. Roughly 40 percent of victims indicated that they and/or the perpetrator were drinking alcohol during their most serious sexual assault experience. Nearly half of sexual assaults co-occur with sexual harassment either before or after (which is consistent with prior RAND research), and roughly 20 percent of assaults co-occur with stalking, bullying, or hazing.

We found no differences by survey year and few differences by installation risk level that are of substantive importance for prevention. However, we found substantial differences by gender, especially in terms of the types of sexual assault behaviors victims experienced and in terms of the setting in which victims were sexually assaulted. We also found some evidence suggesting that sexual minorities—that is, individuals who identify with a sexual orientation other than heterosexual—may experience more-violent sexual assaults and more assaults that are meant to abuse, humiliate, haze, or bully, especially among men. However, in many cases, our analyses by sexual orientation were hampered by our relatively small sample of sexual minority sexual assault victims. Although sexual minority soldiers face substantially higher risk of sexual assault than heterosexual soldiers (Morral and Schell, 2021; Trump-Steele et al., 2021), only 4 percent of active-component soldiers in our sample identified as lesbian, gay, bisexual, or another sexual orientation other than heterosexual.

## Limitations

Text in this section draws heavily from Calkins et al., 2021, which has similar limitations to the analysis used in this report.

Our analytic sample is limited to individuals who responded to the 2016 and 2018 WGRA who were sexually assaulted during the year prior to survey administration. As described in greater detail in Chapter 2, sexual assault is defined in the 2018 WGRA according to respondents' answers to a series of questions about their experiences with events that are likely to align with the definition of sexual assault or other sex crimes under the UCMJ. Responses can be subjective, especially for such follow-up questions as those asking about what victims believe perpetrators' intentions to have been. Therefore, there may be individuals who are coded in the data as having been sexually assaulted over the year prior to survey administration whose allegations would not have been classified as sex crime under the UCMJ by an official investigation. Likewise, an official investigation of the experiences of some individuals who are coded as not having been sexually assaulted over the year prior to survey administration could have classified those experiences as sex crime under the UCMJ. However, the WGRA data have the benefit of providing information about sexual assault experiences for all active-component soldiers who responded to the survey rather than just the group who chose to make an official report.

Furthermore, our descriptions of sexual assault—aside from questions about types of sexual assault behaviors involved, perceived perpetrator intentions, and types of coercion—are based on a series of questions in the 2016 and 2018 WGRA that ask respondents about their self-identified *most serious* sexual assault experience over the year prior to survey administration. Our results, therefore, are not a description of *all* sexual assaults experienced by active-component soldiers but instead a description of a subset of experiences that are more serious.

Finally, it is important to keep the scope of this report in mind. We do not provide additional information on risk of sexual assault in the Army. Furthermore, there is a need for more-specific information (e.g., detailed characteristics of perpetrators) that this report is unable to provide. We do not examine associations (or correlations) between different characteristics of victims' experiences, and it may not be the case that all of the most common characteristics of victims' experiences necessarily co-occur. Additionally, there are likely important differences between different groups of victims (e.g., male versus female victims, victims assigned to high and non–high risk installations) that are not captured by the data used in our analysis.

## Policy Implications

### *Sexual Assault Prevention Training Should Be Aligned with Soldiers' Experiences*

The first major policy implication of this report is that the approach to sexual assault response and prevention in the Army should be informed by soldiers' experiences. In particular, **sexual assault prevention training materials should emphasize the most common behaviors and scenarios outlined in this report, as we recommended for sexual harassment and gender discrimination in our companion report** (Calkins et al., 2021).

The approach to sexual assault prevention in the Army is, in many ways, geared toward addressing the sexual assault of heterosexual women. A 2015 report by the U.S. Government Accountability Office noted that DoD was not taking steps to address sexual assaults of men (Farrell, 2015), and our findings show that there are large gender differences in the circumstances surrounding sexual assault in the Army. Additionally, sexual assault prevention training materials typically do not include the unique experiences of sexual minorities, which, as we found in this report, may differ substantially (especially for men). **Sexual assault prevention training materials should be expanded to incorporate the experiences of men, sexual minorities, and others whose sexual assault experiences differ from those of heterosexual women.**

Previous RAND research identified several differences between installations where soldiers do and do not face higher-than-average sexual assault risk (Matthews et al., 2021). However, we found that the sexual assault experiences of soldiers at high-risk and non–high-risk installations are broadly similar. Among the large number of variables examined, we found differences only in the types of sexual assault behaviors some victims experienced, the likelihood of multiple perpetrators, and the likelihood of being sexually assaulted multiple times. In short, sexual assault looks broadly the same across installations; high-risk installations simply have higher prevalence. We therefore conclude that **there is no need to tailor the *content* of training materials to individual installations.** For example, a program that uses vignettes as discussion prompts does not need to generate different vignettes for low- and high-risk installations. Our conclusion is not meant to imply that high-risk installations should be treated exactly like non–high-risk installations, but that this particular portion of the prevention approach (i.e., training content) can be uniform across the Army. High-risk installations differ from non–high-risk installations in other ways, and may require additional prevention resources, additional funding, or other differences in the prevention approach (Matthews et al., 2021). For example, a high-risk installation might decide to invest proportionately more in prevention resources than a lower-risk installation.

## DoD-Level Policy Changes Are Needed to Allow Data Collection on the Experiences of Sexual Minorities in the Army

The second major policy implication of this report is that **there is a crucial lack of data on the sexual assault experiences of sexual minorities in the Army.** Because of small sample size, we were able to examine differences only between male sexual assault victims who do and do not identify as heterosexual, where we include men who did not respond to the sexual orientation question or responded with "prefer not to answer" in the sexual minorities category. Because we have a larger sample of women who were sexually assaulted, we were able to break them into three groups: heterosexual women, LGBO women, and women who did not respond to the sexual orientation question or who responded with "prefer not to answer." We found suggestive evidence that sexual minority male victims experienced more-violent sexual assaults and more assaults that were meant to haze or bully than heterosexual male victims, and we found some evidence that women who did not answer the sexual orientation question or who responded with "prefer not to answer" experienced more assaults that were meant to abuse, humiliate, or bully than heterosexual women or LGBO women. However, given the relatively small number of soldiers who identified with a sexual orientation other than heterosexual in the combined 2016 and 2018 WGRA and our resulting need to aggregate soldiers of differing sexual orientations, it is difficult for us to truly examine these soldiers' experiences in depth.

The effort to prevent and respond to sexual assault in the Army requires a detailed understanding of sexual assault experiences. One of the cross-cutting recommendations of the Independent Review Commission on Sexual Assault in the Military was that "DoD needs to improve data collection . . . to better reflect the experiences of Service members whose intersecting identities, such as race, ethnicity, sexual orientation, gender and gender identity, may place them at higher risk for sexual harassment and sexual assault" (Independent Review Commission on Sexual Assault in the Military, 2021, p. 32). We echo this recommendation: The lack of detailed information on the unique sexual assault experiences of sexual minorities hampers the effort to prevent and respond to sexual assault in the Army. A significant portion of service members who are sexually assaulted (especially male service members) are sexual minorities (Morral and Schell, 2021). If the prevention effort does not include specific efforts to prevent the sexual assault of sexual minorities, then there is a limit on the Army's ability to reduce the risk of sexual assault.

Currently, the lack of information on the sexual assault experiences of sexual minorities comes down to a data limitation, which is a fixable problem. **The Army should further investigate the sexual assault and other potentially discriminatory experiences of sexual minority soldiers by including sexual orientation as a sociodemographic variable in existing administrative data and in survey data collected in the future.** The WGRA is one of only a small number of data sources on service members that includes information on sexual orientation, which makes it nearly impossible to determine whether sexual minorities are at higher risk of mistreatment, discrimination, suicide, or other adverse workplace or behavioral health outcomes. If sexual orientation were treated as other sociodemographic characteristics (e.g., gender, race/ethnicity) are in administrative data, it would be possible to use sexual orientation data as part of analyses of administrative and other linked data and as a sampling and weighting variable in future data-collection efforts. The inclusion of sexual orientation items in other survey data might then allow the Army to provide a more comprehensive understanding of the unique experiences of sexual minority soldiers. We recognize that **such treatment of sexual orientation data will require a change in DoD-level policy, and the Army alone might not be able to implement the recommendation** (Under Secretary of Defense for Personnel and Readiness Clifford L. Stanley, 2011). Such a change also would require a thoughtful examination of how to protect sexual orientation data and the confidentiality of service members' identities. Sexual minorities are not a monolithic group. If the current restrictions on collecting sexual orientation data remain in place, both DoD and the Army will continue to be limited in their ability to determine whether there are differences between the experiences of sexual minority soldiers and their majority peers.

# Appendix A. Data Cleaning

## Types of Sexual Assault Behaviors Involved in Most Serious Experience

When asked about the type of most serious sexual assault they experienced, respondents were presented only with the options that they had endorsed when completing the screener questions (see Table 2.1). The data, therefore, include logical skips for individuals who were sexually assaulted but who did not experience a particular act. We imputed "No" responses to the questions on whether a particular act was involved in the respondent's most serious experience if that respondent did not experience that act at all during the year prior to the survey administration.

Additionally, respondents who endorsed only one act on the screener questions were not presented with the question on which act occurred during their most serious experience. For these individuals, we assumed that the single act they endorsed on the screener also occurred during their most serious experience.

Finally, a few individuals who indicated that they had been sexually assaulted did not answer the question about which type of act occurred during their most serious experience. Our analyses treated these individuals' most serious experience as including all types of sexual assault behaviors they endorsed on the screener questions.

## "Mark-All-That-Apply" Questions

We recoded responses to the following questions that instruct respondents to mark all that apply to capture whether the respondent skipped the question:

- **Rank of perpetrator.** This question presents several options of pay grades of the perpetrator(s). If none of the options were selected (i.e., all variables beginning with "SA1RNK" in SAS, a statistical software suite, are equal to "Not marked"), then we set all the variables for this question to missing. This question was asked only of individuals who indicated that either all or some of the perpetrator(s) were members of the military. Therefore, there will be individuals who did not respond to this question because they were not shown the question rather than because they were shown the question and did not answer. This changes the interpretation of responses.
- **Professional relationship between respondent and perpetrator(s).** This question presents several options of professional relationships between the respondent and the perpetrator(s), including "Not sure," but does not include a "None of the above" option. Therefore, there are likely respondents to whom none of the answer choices applied and who may have skipped the question for that reason rather than because they left the survey or intended to skip the question. We wanted to ensure that individuals for whom every answer choice was an implied "no" were left in the denominator when calculating percentages. We therefore recoded individuals to

missing if (1) all the variables related to the professional relationship between the respondent and perpetrator (i.e., SAS variables beginning with "SAOFFND") were "Not marked" and (2) the next question (personal relationship between respondent and perpetrator) appeared to have been skipped.

- **Personal relationship between respondent and perpetrator(s).** This question presents several options of personal relationships between the respondent and the perpetrator(s), including "Not sure" and "None of the above." The response options, therefore, should include the entire universe of possible responses. If the data indicated that every option for the personal relationship questions was not marked (i.e., all SAS variables beginning with "SAREL" were equal to "NOT MARKED"), we recoded all the "personal relationship" variables to missing. Additionally, for logical consistency, if either "Not Sure" or "None of the above" was selected along with another option, "Not Sure" and/or "None of the above" was set to "Not marked."

- **When the assault occurred.** This question presents several options of times that the assault occurred, including "Do not recall" and "None of the above." The response options, therefore, should include the entire universe of possible responses, meaning that at least one answer choice should apply to every respondent's most serious experience. Therefore, if the data indicated that every option for the "when" questions was not marked (i.e., all SAS variables beginning with "SAWHEN" were equal to "NOT MARKED"), we recoded all the "when" variables to missing. Additionally, for logical consistency, if either "Do not recall" or "None of the above" was selected along with another option, "Do not recall" and/or "None of the above" was set to "Not marked."

## Alcohol Questions

The WGRA survey instruments include three questions about the respondent's alcohol use during their most serious experience of sexual assault, as follows:

> 130. [123 in 2016] **At the time of this unwanted event, had you been drinking alcohol?** Even if you had been drinking, it does not mean that you are to blame for what happened.
>
> 131. [124 in 2016] **Just prior to this unwanted event . . .** *Mark one answer for each time.* [Answer choices are yes, no, don't know]
>
> - Did the person(s) who did this to you buy or give you alcohol to drink?
> - Do you think you might have been given a drug without your knowledge or consent? (Breslin et al., 2019; Davis et al., 2017)

The second and third questions in the survey instruments should be asked only of respondents who answered "yes" to the first question. According to the data, this appears to have been true for the second question (regarding whether the perpetrator had bought the victim alcohol). We therefore code individuals who said that they had *not* been drinking alcohol at the time of their most serious experience as a "No" on the second question. However, there are individuals in the data who answered to the third question (regarding believing that they had been drugged) despite having answered "No" on the first question. We therefore did *not* do any imputation on this question.

# Appendix B. Technical Details of Constructing Sexual Assault Experience Descriptions

This section is largely reproduced from Appendix A of Calkins et al., 2021, with modifications as necessary for differences between the two reports.

## Confidence Intervals

The 95-percent CIs for all percentages presented in the sexual assault descriptions were calculated using the Clopper-Pearson method (Clopper and Pearson, 1934). Confidence intervals for counts are computed using the standard normal approximation. Variance estimation is done with the Taylor series linearization method except in cases with a zero numerator. In those cases, confidence intervals were computed using the Hanley and Lippman-Hand, 1983, method with the sample size defined using the Kish, 1965, estimate for effective sample size.

## Hypothesis Testing

The analysis presented in this report is an exploratory descriptive analysis that is meant to shed light on potential differences in the sexual assault experience by gender, sexual orientation, and installation risk level in the active-component Army. Group differences in sexual assault experiences should not be interpreted as the results of formal hypothesis testing based on a causal analysis or random assignment; instead, the $p$-values produced by tests provide an indication of the ways in which the experience of sexual assault varies across groups of soldiers. Because of the nature of the analysis we are performing, we also did not correct for multiple tests. However, we explain here to provide context for the exploratory analysis we did perform.

Tests for statistically significant differences between high- and low-risk installations and between different high-risk installations were conducted using a Rao-Scott chi-squared test. The Rao-Scott chi-squared test shows whether any cell of a categorical table has a higher- or lower-than-expected share of respondents. For instance, when testing whether there were differences between the two survey years in the percentage of women who indicated that someone had put a penis in their anus, mouth, or vagina over the course of the prior year, we produced a table of responses to the question of whether this behavior was part of the self-identified most serious experience. This table is similar to Table B.1. The Rao-Scott test compares the observed weighted proportion of responses in each cell of the table with the proportion reporting each answer in the entire active-component Army, which is the value that would be expected if women were equally likely to experience this behavior during their self-identified most serious sexual assault experience in 2016 and 2018.

**Table B.1. Sample Categorical Table**

| Response to "Someone put a penis in your anus, mouth, or vagina" by Women | 2016 | 2018 | All Women in Active-Component Army, 2016 and 2018 |
|---|---|---|---|
| Yes (%) | 41 | 39 | 40 |
| No (%) | 59 | 69 | 60 |

When computing confidence intervals, we dropped installations where the estimated percentage is equal to zero from the numerator of the Clopper-Pearson exact confidence interval calculation, following the methodology of Hanley and Lippman-Hand, 1983. Because exact zeros cannot be used to calculate Rao-Scott $p$-values, in cases where no one in a given group indicated a particular characteristic of their most serious sexual assault experience, we calculated the $p$-value as if the individual in that group with the smallest survey weight *had* indicated that characteristic. This change was made only for the calculation of the $p$-value, not for the reported percentages, and results in a conservative $p$-value.

We interpret a $p$-value less than or equal to 0.05 as a statistically significant difference between the group of high-risk installations and the group of non–high-risk installations, or across high-risk installations. In cases where we are testing differences between two groups, a statistically significant difference means that we found sufficient evidence to say that a particular facet of the circumstances surrounding sexual assault is different among groups of active-component soldiers who were sexually assaulted. A $p$-value greater than 0.05, on the other hand, suggests that differences between our estimates for a given installation and the "expected" value are small enough that they could arise from natural variation. It is important to keep in mind that a failure to reject the null hypothesis does not mean that no differences exist, but that there is not enough evidence to verify the existence of differences. In cases where we are testing differences between two groups, a failure to reject the null hypothesis means that we have *not* found sufficient evidence to conclude that a particular facet of the circumstances surrounding sexual assault is different across groups of active-component soldiers who were sexually assaulted.

It is also important to keep in mind that a statistically significant difference and a substantive difference between groups are not the same. When sample sizes are sufficiently large or variation is sufficiently low, estimates may be precise enough to find even very small statistically significant differences, but the difference between the two estimates may not be of practical importance for policymaking. We note cases where this occurs in the main text.

## Weighting for Nonresponse

As is standard, we weight the data to correct for bias from nonresponse. We rescaled the standard weights provided in the WGRA data so that respondents who were sexually assaulted in

2016 had the same weight, on average, as respondents who were sexually assaulted in 2018 when combined across years.

## Power Calculations

In the following sections, we describe the statistical power associated with the analyses by chapter. We provide the effective sample size of the relevant groups using Kish's, 1965, approximation. The effective sample size is a measure of information available in the data that can be interpreted as the sample size from a simple random sample without nonresponse that yields the same statistical precision as our data. Given these effective sample sizes, we then calculated the minimum detectable difference in proportions between the groups. These calculations depend on the proportion of the variable of interest in one of the two groups being compared, so the calculations are repeated for a range of proportions.

### *Statistical Power for Detection of Differences by Survey Year*

The effective sample sizes for analyses in Chapter 3 were 354 and 334 for 2016 and 2018, respectively. Figure B.1 displays the minimal detectable difference comparing 2016 with 2018 for different values of the proportion in 2018 (assuming 80-percent power and a Type I error rate of 5 percent). For an item with 50-percent endorsement in 2018, we have 80-percent power to detect a difference as small as 10.6 percent. For an item with 5-percent endorsement in 2018, we have 80-percent power to detect a difference as small as 3.7 percent.

**Figure B.1. Minimum Detectable Difference in Proportions Between 2016 and 2018**

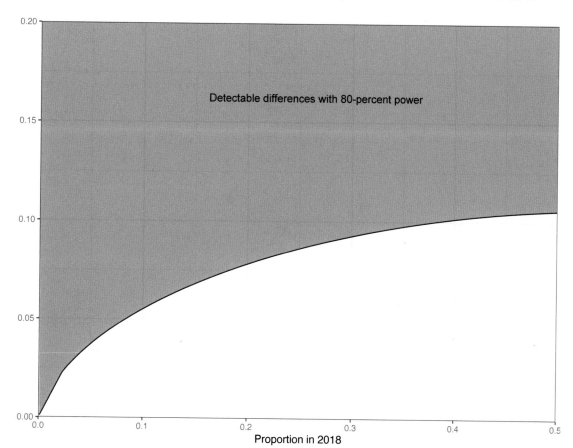

*Statistical Power for Detection of Differences by Gender*

The effective sample sizes for analyses in Chapter 4 were 190 and 618 for male and female victims, respectively. Figure B.2 displays the minimal detectable difference comparing men with women for different values of the proportion among men (assuming 80-percent power and a Type I error rate of 5 percent). For an item with 50-percent endorsement among men, we have 80-percent power to detect a difference as small as 11.5 percent. For an item with 5-percent endorsement among men, we have 80-percent power to detect a difference as small as 4.1 percent.

**Figure B.2. Minimum Detectable Difference in Proportions Between Male and Female Victims**

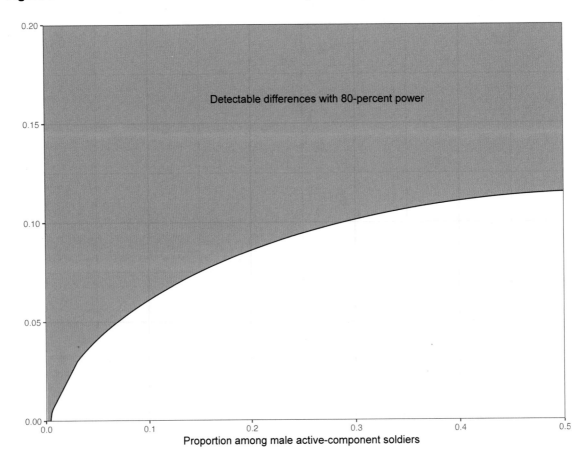

*Statistical Power for Detection of Differences by Sexual Orientation*

The effective sample sizes for analyses in Chapter 5 were 96 and 90 for heterosexual males and LGBO, NR, and PNA males, respectively. Figure B.3 displays the minimal detectable difference comparing heterosexual male victims with LGBO, NR, and PNA male victims for different values of the proportion among heterosexual male victims (assuming 80-percent power and a Type I error rate of 5 percent). For an item with 50-percent endorsement among heterosexual male victims, we have 80-percent power to detect a difference as small as 19.9 percent. For an item with 5-percent endorsement among heterosexual male victims, we have 80-percent power to detect a difference as small as 5.0 percent.

The effective sample sizes for analyses in Chapter 5 were 327, 89, and 187 for heterosexual women, LGBO women, and NR/PNA women, respectively. Figure B.4 displays the minimal detectable difference comparing heterosexual women with LGBO women for different values of the proportion among heterosexual women (assuming 80-percent power and a Type I error rate of 5 percent). For an item with 50-percent endorsement among heterosexual women, we have 80-percent power to detect a difference as small as 16.4 percent. For an item with 5-percent

100

endorsement among heterosexual women, we have 80-percent power to detect a difference as small as 4.9 percent.

Figure B.5 displays the minimal detectable difference comparing heterosexual women with NR and PNA women for different values of the proportion among heterosexual women (assuming 80-percent power and a Type I error rate of 5 percent). For an item with 50-percent endorsement among heterosexual women, we have 80-percent power to detect a difference as small as 12.7 percent. For an item with 5-percent endorsement among heterosexual women, we have 80-percent power to detect a difference as small as 4.4 percent.

Figure B.6 displays the minimal detectable difference comparing LGBO women with NR and PNA women for different values of the proportion among LGBO women (assuming 80-percent power and a Type I error rate of 5 percent). For an item with 50-percent endorsement among LGBO women, we have 80-percent power to detect a difference as small as 17.6 percent. For an item with 5-percent endorsement among LGBO women, we have 80-percent power to detect a difference as small as 5.0 percent.

**Figure B.3. Minimum Detectable Difference in Proportions Between Heterosexual and LGBO/NR/PNA Male Victims**

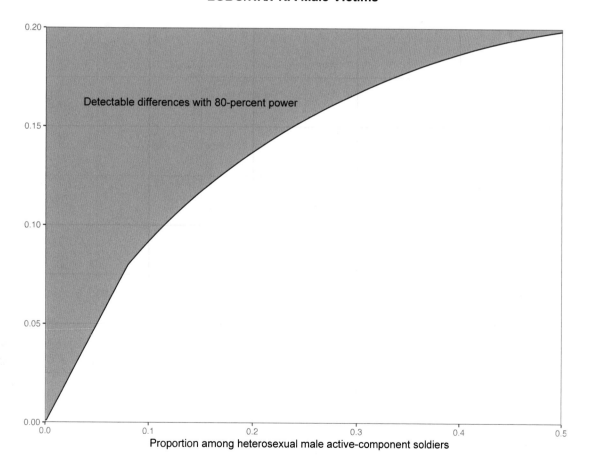

**Figure B.4. Minimum Detectable Difference in Proportions Between Heterosexual and LGBO Female Victims**

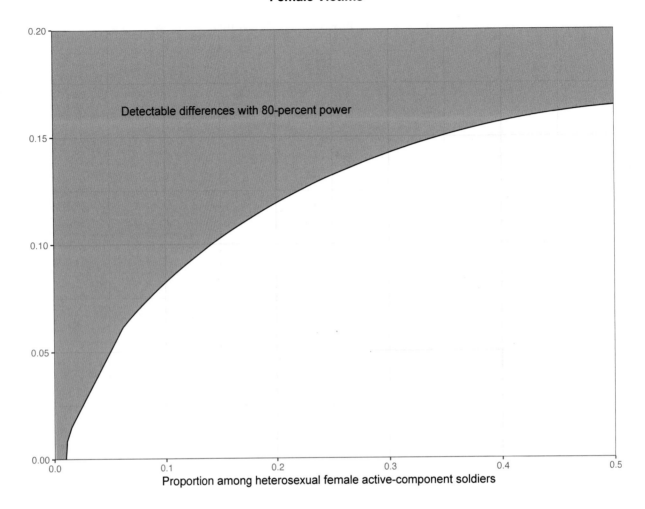

**Figure B.5. Minimum Detectable Difference in Proportions Between Heterosexual and NR/PNA Female Victims**

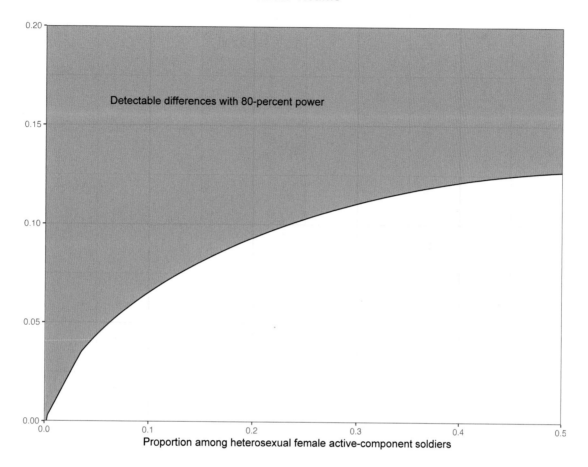

**Figure B.6. Minimum Detectable Difference in Proportions Between LGBO and NR/PNA Female Victims**

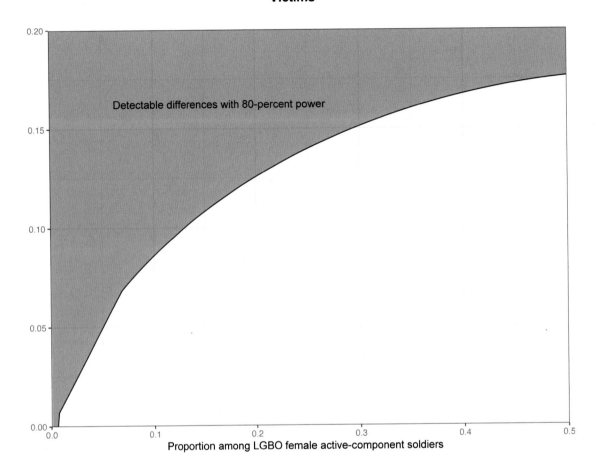

*Statistical Power for Detection of Differences by Installation Risk Level*

The effective sample sizes for analyses in Chapter 6 were 317 and 380 for high-risk installations and non–high-risk installations, respectively. Figure B.7 displays the minimal detectable difference comparing high-risk with non–high-risk installations for different values of the proportion among high-risk installations (assuming 80-percent power and a Type I error rate of 5 percent). For an item with 50-percent endorsement at high-risk-installations, we have 80-percent power to detect a difference as small as 10.5 percent. For an item with 5-percent endorsement at high-risk installations, we have 80-percent power to detect a difference as small as 3.7 percent.

**Figure B.7. Minimum Detectable Difference in Proportions Between High-Risk and Non–High-Risk Installations**

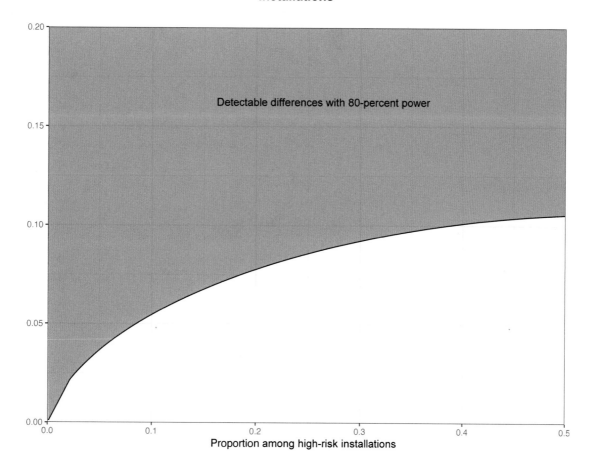

# Appendix C. Tabular Results for Chapters 3 Through 7

In Tables C.1–C.35, we provide results for Chapters 3 through 7. Corresponding figures are noted under each table.

## Tabular Results for Chapter 3

**Table C.1. Types of Sexual Assault Behaviors from Screener Questions, All Sexual Assault Victims by WGRA Survey Year**

| | Total Active-Component Army, 2016 and 2018 Combined | By Year | | |
| --- | --- | --- | --- | --- |
| | | 2016 | 2018 | p-Value for Difference |
| Put their penis in your anus, mouth, or vagina | 34% (30%–37%) | 35% (30%–40%) | 32% (28%–37%) | 0.46 |
| Put any object or any body part other than a penis into your anus, mouth, or vagina | 24% (21%–27%) | 24% (19%–29%) | 24% (20%–29%) | 0.83 |
| Made you put any part of your body or any object into someone's mouth, vagina, or anus | 14% (11%–17%) | 15% (11%–20%) | 12% (8%–17%) | 0.31 |
| Intentionally touched private areas of your body | 85% (82%–87%) | 87% (83%–90%) | 82% (77%–87%) | 0.10 |
| Made you touch private areas of their body or someone else's body | 29% (26%–32%) | 29% (24%–34%) | 29% (24%–34%) | 0.94 |
| Attempted to put a penis, an object, or any body part into your anus, mouth, or vagina, but no penetration actually occurred | 21% (18%–25%) | 24% (20%–29%) | 19% (15%–23%) | 0.07 |

SOURCE: Authors' calculations using the 2016 and 2018 WGRA.
NOTE: Percentages are made up of only soldiers who were sexually assaulted during the year prior to WGRA administration; 95-percent CIs are shown in parentheses. This table corresponds to Figure 3.1.

**Table C.2. Perpetrator Intent and Type of Coercion from Screener Questions, All Sexual Assault Victims by WGRA Survey Year**

| | Total Active-Component Army, 2016 and 2018 Combined | By Year | | |
| --- | --- | --- | --- | --- |
| | | 2016 | 2018 | p-Value for Difference |
| Assaulted more than once | 62% (58%–66%) | 66% (61%–71%) | 58% (53%–64%) | 0.04 |
| Perpetrator intent[a] | | | | |
| Abusive or humiliating | 54% (49%–58%) | 56% (50%–63%) | 51% (44%–58%) | 0.26 |

106

| | Total Active-Component Army, 2016 and 2018 Combined | By Year | | |
| --- | --- | --- | --- | --- |
| | | 2016 | 2018 | p-Value for Difference |
| Sexual purpose | 87% (82%–90%) | 84% (77%–89%) | 90% (83%–94%) | 0.14 |
| Type of coercion | | | | |
| Threatened or used physical force | 23% (19%–26%) | 23% (19%–28%) | 22% (17%–27%) | 0.68 |
| Threatened you or someone else in another way | 25% (22%–28%) | 26% (22%–31%) | 23% (19%–28%) | 0.37 |
| You were unconscious, asleep, or drunk, high, or drugged | 38% (34%–42%) | 37% (32%–43%) | 39% (33%–44%) | 0.77 |
| It happened without your consent | 91% (89%–93%) | 91% (88%–94%) | 91% (87%–94%) | 0.89 |

SOURCE: Authors' calculations using the 2016 and 2018 WGRA.
NOTES: Percentages are made up of only soldiers who were sexually assaulted during the year prior to WGRA administration and are for the behavior on which the respondent qualified as having been sexually assaulted; 95-percent CIs are shown in parentheses. This table corresponds to Figure 3.1.
[a] Perpetrator intent questions were not asked of respondents who qualified as having been sexually assaulted under the first sexual assault behavior (someone put his penis into the respondent's anus, mouth, or vagina) because the UCMJ does not require abusive, humiliating, or sexual intent for this behavior to qualify as rape or sexual assault. These percentages, therefore, have the denominator as individuals who qualified as having been sexually assaulted on one of the other behaviors. See Chapter 2 for further details.

### Table C.3. Types of Sexual Assault Behaviors During Most Serious Experience, All Sexual Assault Victims by WGRA Survey Year

| | Total Active-Component Army, 2016 and 2018 Combined | By Year | | |
| --- | --- | --- | --- | --- |
| | | 2016 | 2018 | p-Value for Difference |
| Put their penis in your anus, mouth, or vagina | 33% (29%–36%) | 34% (29%–39%) | 32% (27%–37%) | 0.49 |
| Put any object or any body part other than a penis into your anus, mouth, or vagina | 20% (17%–23%) | 20% (16%–25%) | 20% (16%–24%) | 0.83 |
| Made you put any part of your body or any object into someone's mouth, vagina, or anus | 13% (10%–16%) | 14% (10%–19%) | 11% (7%–16%) | 0.32 |
| Intentionally touched private areas of your body | 80% (77%–83%) | 82% (78%–86%) | 78% (73%–83%) | 0.16 |
| Made you touch private areas of their body or someone else's body | 26% (22%–29%) | 26% (21%–31%) | 25% (21%–30%) | 0.76 |
| Attempted to put a penis, an object, or any body part into your anus, mouth, or vagina, but no penetration actually occurred | 18% (16%–21%) | 21% (17%–25%) | 16% (12%–20%) | 0.10 |

SOURCE: Authors' calculations using the 2016 and 2018 WGRA.
NOTE: Percentages are made up of only soldiers who were sexually assaulted during the year prior to WGRA administration; 95-percent CIs are shown in parentheses. Respondents were instructed to select all that apply. This table corresponds to Figure 3.2.

**Table C.4. Perpetrator Characteristics for Most Serious Experience, All Sexual Assault Victims by WGRA Survey Year**

| | Total Active-Component Army, 2016 and 2018 Combined | By Year | | |
| --- | --- | --- | --- | --- |
| | | 2016 | 2018 | *p*-Value for Difference |
| Number of perpetrators | | | | 0.62 |
| One | 63% (59%–67%) | 65% (60%–70%) | 61% (56%–67%) | |
| More than one | 33% (29%–37%) | 31% (26%–37%) | 35% (30%–41%) | |
| Not sure | 4% (2%–5%) | 4% (2%–6%) | 4% (2%–7%) | |
| In the military? | | | | 0.68 |
| All | 78% (74%–81%) | 80% (75%–84%) | 76% (71%–81%) | |
| Some but not all | 6% (5%–9%) | 6% (4%–9%) | 7% (4%–10%) | |
| None | 12% (9%–14%) | 11% (8%–15%) | 12% (8%–16%) | |
| Not sure | 4% (3%–6%) | 3% (2%–6%) | 5% (3%–8%) | |
| Gender | | | | 0.68 |
| All men | 78% (74%–81%) | 80% (74%–84%) | 76% (70%–81%) | |
| All women | 11% (9%–14%) | 11% (8%–15%) | 12% (8%–16%) | |
| Mix of men and women | 8% (5%–10%) | 7% (4%–10%) | 9% (5%–14%) | |
| Not sure | 3% (2%–5%) | 3% (1%–5%) | 4% (2%–7%) | |
| Rank, if at least one in military[a, b] | | | | |
| Enlisted/WO | 84% (81%–87%) | 86% (82%–90%) | 83% (78%–87%) | 0.27 |
| Officer | 16% (13%–19%) | 14% (10%–19%) | 18% (14%–22%) | 0.21 |
| Not sure | 8% (6%–11%) | 8% (6%–12%) | 8% (6%–12%) | 0.98 |
| Professional relationship with victim[b, c] | | | | |
| Supervisor | 12% (9%–16%) | 14% (10%–19%) | 10% (6%–15%) | 0.20 |
| Other higher-ranked member of chain of command | 16% (13%–19%) | 19% (15%–25%) | 12% (8%–17%) | 0.03 |
| Higher-ranked and outside chain of command | 23% (20%–27%) | 26% (21%–32%) | 20% (15%–25%) | 0.07 |
| Military peer of similar rank | 60% (54%–65%) | N/A | 60% (54%–65%) | N/A |

108

| | Total Active-Component Army, 2016 and 2018 Combined | By Year | | |
| --- | --- | --- | --- | --- |
| | | 2016 | 2018 | *p*-Value for Difference |
| Subordinate or someone you manage | 17% (14%–21%) | 24% (19%–29%) | 11% (7%–15%) | 0.00 |
| DoD or government civilian working for the military[d] | 5% (3%–6%) | 3% (2%–5%) | 6% (4%–9%) | 0.02 |
| Contractor[d] | 2% (1%–3%) | 2% (1%–4%) | 2% (1%–4%) | 0.60 |
| Not sure | 26% (22%–30%) | 37% (31%–42%) | 15% (11%–20%) | < 0.0001 |
| Personal relationship to victim[b] | | | | |
| Your current or former spouse[e] | 4% (3%–6%) | 6% (4%–10%) | 2% (1%–4%) | 0.00 |
| Someone you have a child with[e] | 2% (1%–3%) | 3% (1%–6%) | 1% (0%–2%) | 0.01 |
| Your significant other (boyfriend or girlfriend) who you live with[f] | 2% (1%–3%) | 3% (1%–5%) | 1% (0%–2%) | 0.06 |
| Your significant other (boyfriend or girlfriend) who you do/did not live with[f] | 6% (4%–8%) | 7% (4%–10%) | 4% (3%–7%) | 0.19 |
| Friend or acquaintance | 53% (49%–57%) | 51% (45%–56%) | 55% (50%–61%) | 0.24 |
| Family member | 1% (0%–2%) | 1% (0%–3%) | 1% (0%–2%) | 0.28 |
| Stranger | 16% (13%–19%) | 16% (12%–20%) | 15% (12%–20%) | 0.85 |
| None of the above | 27% (23%–30%) | 25% (21%–30%) | 28% (23%–33%) | 0.50 |
| Not sure | 5% (4%–7%) | 6% (4%–9%) | 5% (3%–8%) | 0.52 |

SOURCE: Authors' calculations using the 2016 and 2018 WGRA.
NOTES: Percentages are made up of only soldiers who were sexually assaulted during the year prior to WGRA administration; 95-percent CIs are shown in parentheses. This table corresponds to Figures 3.3, 3.4, and 3.5. N/A = not applicable. WO = warrant officer.
[a] This question was asked of only respondents who answered "all" or "some, but not all" to the previous question of whether the perpetrators were members of the military, and percentages should be interpreted as the percentage of victims who indicated at least one military perpetrator.
[b] Respondents were instructed to select all that apply.
[c] "Military peer of similar rank" was not an available answer choice in 2016. We therefore do not use 2016 data in other analyses using this question.
[d] Combined into "DoD/government civilian(s) working for the military/Contractor(s)" in figures.
[e] Combined into "your current or former spouse or someone you have a child with" in figures.
[f] Combined into "your significant other (boyfriend or girlfriend)" in figures.

**Table C.5. Place and Time of Most Serious Experience, All Sexual Assault Victims by WGRA Survey Year**

| | Total Active-Component Army, 2016 and 2018 Combined | By Year | | |
| --- | --- | --- | --- | --- |
| | | 2016 | 2018 | *p*-Value for Difference |
| Assault occurred during any required military activity[a] | 56% (52%–60%) | 57% (52%–63%) | 54% (48%–60%) | 0.41 |
| Place assault occurred[b] | | | | |
| Military installation | 69% (65%–72%) | 73% (68%–77%) | 64% (59%–70%) | 0.02 |
| TDY/TAD | 19% (16%–23%) | 17% (14%–22%) | 21% (16%–27%) | 0.27 |
| Deployed to a combat zone[c] | 10% (8%–13%) | 9% (6%–14%) | 11% (8%–15%) | 0.43 |
| Overseas port visit while deployed[c] | 4% (3%–6%) | 4% (2%–7%) | 5% (3%–8%) | 0.51 |
| While transitioning between operational theaters[c] | 5% (4%–8%) | 5% (3%–9%) | 5% (3%–9%) | 0.99 |
| While you were in a delayed entry program (DEP) or delayed training program (DTP)[d] | 4% (2%–7%) | 3% (1%–6%) | 5% (2%–10%) | 0.51 |
| During basic training[e] | 6% (4%–8%) | 6% (3%–9%) | 6% (3%–11%) | 0.94 |
| During any other type of military combat training | 9% (7%–12%) | 7% (4%–10%) | 12% (7%–17%) | 0.04 |
| During Officer Candidate School[e] | 4% (3%–6%) | 4% (2%–7%) | 4% (2%–7%) | 0.78 |
| During technical, MOS, advanced individual training or professional military education[e] | 10% (8%–13%) | 9% (6%–13%) | 11% (7%–16%) | 0.57 |
| While at an official military function, either on or off base | 17% (14%–21%) | 18% (14%–23%) | 16% (12%–21%) | 0.46 |
| Off base | 39% (35%–43%) | 37% (32%–43%) | 40% (35%–46%) | 0.44 |
| Time assault occurred[f] | | | | |
| At work during duty hours | 38% (34%–42%) | 38% (33%–44%) | 37% (32%–43%) | 0.78 |
| While out with friends or at a party | 36% (33%–40%) | 36% (31%–42%) | 37% (31%–42%) | 0.97 |
| On a date | 4% (3%–6%) | 5% (3%–8%) | 3% (2%–5%) | 0.18 |
| On approved leave | 7% (4%–9%) | 7% (4%–10%) | 6% (3%–11%) | 0.92 |
| In your or someone else's home or quarters | 37% (33%–41%) | 35% (30%–41%) | 39% (34%–45%) | 0.32 |

110

| | Total Active-Component Army, 2016 and 2018 Combined | By Year | | |
|---|---|---|---|---|
| | | 2016 | 2018 | *p*-Value for Difference |
| While being intimate with the person[g] | 8% (6%–12%) | 8% (6%–12%) | N/A | N/A |
| None of the above | 11% (9%–14%) | 10% (7%–13%) | 12% (8%–16%) | 0.45 |
| Do not recall | 2% (1%–4%) | 3% (2%–5%) | 2% (1%–4%) | 0.23 |

SOURCE: Authors' calculations using the 2016 and 2018 WGRA.

NOTE: Percentages are made up of only soldiers who were sexually assaulted during the year prior to WGRA administration; 95-percent CIs are shown in parentheses. This table corresponds to Figures 3.6 and 3.7. MOS = military occupational specialty. N/A = not applicable.

[a] Aggregation of the following response options: "deployed to a combat zone or transitioning between operational theaters," "basic, officer, or technical training," "while you were on TDY/TAD, at sea, or during field exercises/alerts," "while you were in any other type of military combat training," "while at an official military function (either on or off base)," and "you were at work during duty hours."

[b] Each place is a yes/no question, and multiple places could have "yes" responses.

[c] Combined into "Deployed to a combat zone or transitioning between operational theaters" for Figure 3.6.

[d] Not shown in Figure 3.6 because these assaults occurred prior to accession.

[e] Combined into "Basic, officer, or technical training" for Figure 3.6.

[f] Respondents were instructed to select all that apply.

[g] Available in 2016 only.

## Table C.6. Alcohol and Drug Involvement in Most Serious Experience, All Sexual Assault Victims by WGRA Survey Year

| | Total Active-Component Army, 2016 and 2018 Combined | By Year | | |
|---|---|---|---|---|
| | | 2016 | 2018 | *p*-Value for Difference |
| Victim was drinking alcohol | | | | 0.82 |
| Yes | 40% (36%–44%) | 40% (35%–46%) | 39% (34%–45%) | |
| No | 58% (54%–61%) | 57% (52%–63%) | 58% (52%–64%) | |
| Not sure | 3% (1%–4%) | 2% (1%–5%) | 3% (1%–6%) | |
| Perpetrator bought or gave victim alcohol | | | | 1.00 |
| Yes | 26% (22%–29%) | 26% (21%–31%) | 26% (21%–31%) | |
| No | 72% (68%–75%) | 72% (66%–77%) | 72% (67%–77%) | |
| Not sure | 3% (2%–4%) | 3% (1%–5%) | 3% (1%–4%) | |
| Perpetrator was drinking alcohol | | | | 0.03 |
| Yes | 42% (38%–46%) | 39% (33%–44%) | 45% (39%–51%) | |
| No | 39% (35%–43%) | 44% (39%–50%) | 34% (28%–39%) | |

111

| | Total Active-Component Army, 2016 and 2018 Combined | By Year | | |
|---|---|---|---|---|
| | | 2016 | 2018 | *p*-Value for Difference |
| Not sure | 19% (16%–23%) | 17% (13%–22%) | 21% (17%–26%) | |
| Victim was drugged without their knowledge or consent | | | | 0.60 |
| Yes | 7% (5%–9%) | 7% (4%–11%) | 6% (3%–10%) | |
| No | 80% (77%–83%) | 81% (76%–85%) | 79% (74%–84%) | |
| Not sure | 13% (11%–16%) | 12% (9%–16%) | 15% (10%–20%) | |

SOURCE: Authors' calculations using the 2016 and 2018 WGRA.

NOTE: Percentages are made up of only soldiers who were sexually assaulted during the year prior to WGRA administration; 95-percent CIs are shown in parentheses. This table corresponds to Figure 3.8, which presents percentages for "Yes" responses to each question.

### Table C.7. Bullying, Hazing, Sexual Harassment, and Stalking During Most Serious Experience, All Sexual Assault Victims by WGRA Survey Year

| | Total Active-Component Army, 2016 and 2018 Combined | By Year | | |
|---|---|---|---|---|
| | | 2016 | 2018 | *p*-Value of Difference |
| Victim would describe assault as hazing[a] | 17% (14%–21%) | 18% (14%–23%) | 17% (12%–22%) | 0.72 |
| Victim would describe assault as bullying[a] | 30% (26%–34%) | 36% (31%–42%) | 24% (19%–29%) | 0.00 |
| Victim was sexually harassed before assault by same perpetrator(s) | 45% (42%–49%) | 46% (41%–52%) | 45% (39%–50%) | 0.69 |
| Victim was sexually harassed after assault by same perpetrator(s) | 41% (37%–45%) | 42% (37%–48%) | 40% (34%–46%) | 0.51 |
| Victim was stalked before assault by same perpetrator(s) | 19% (16%–23%) | 20% (16%–25%) | 19% (14%–24%) | 0.64 |
| Victim was stalked after assault by same perpetrator(s) | 24% (21%–28%) | 25% (20%–30%) | 23% (19%–29%) | 0.68 |

SOURCE: Authors' calculations using the 2016 and 2018 WGRA.

NOTES: Percentages are made up of only soldiers who were sexually assaulted during the year prior to WGRA administration; 95-percent CIs are shown in parentheses. This table corresponds to Figure 3.9.

[a] Definitions of bullying and hazing changed substantially between survey years; see Table 2.3.

**Table C.8. Types of Sexual Assault Behaviors from Screener Questions, All Sexual Assault Victims by Gender**

|  | Female Victims | Male Victims | *p*-Value for Difference |
|---|---|---|---|
| Put their penis in your anus, mouth, or vagina | 40% (36%–44%) | 25% (19%–32%) | 0.00 |
| Put any object or any body part other than a penis into your anus, mouth, or vagina | 27% (23%–31%) | 20% (14%–26%) | 0.05 |
| Made you put any part of your body or any object into someone's mouth, vagina, or anus | 8% (6%–11%) | 22% (16%–28%) | < 0.0001 |
| Intentionally touched private areas of your body | 85% (82%–88%) | 84% (77%–89%) | 0.62 |
| Made you touch private areas of their body or someone else's body | 30% (27%–34%) | 27% (21%–34%) | 0.34 |
| Attempted to put a penis, an object, or any body part into your anus, mouth, or vagina, but no penetration actually occurred | 27% (23%–30%) | 14% (9%–20%) | 0.00 |

SOURCE: Authors' calculations using the 2016 and 2018 WGRA.
NOTE: Percentages are made up of only soldiers who were sexually assaulted during the year prior to WGRA administration; 95-percent CIs are shown in parentheses. This table corresponds to Figure 4.1.

**Table C.9. Perpetrator Intent and Type of Coercion from Screener Questions, All Sexual Assault Victims by Gender**

| | Female Victims | Male Victims | *p*-Value for Difference |
|---|---|---|---|
| Assaulted more than once | 62% (58%–66%) | 62% (54%–69%) | 0.91 |
| Perpetrator intent[a] | | | |
| Abusive or humiliating | 49% (44%–54%) | 59% (51%–67%) | 0.04 |
| Sexual purpose | 98% (96%–99%) | 74% (65%–81%) | < 0.0001 |
| Type of coercion | | | |
| Threatened or used physical force | 23% (20%–27%) | 22% (16%–28%) | 0.70 |
| Threatened you or someone else in another way | 23% (20%–27%) | 27% (21%–34%) | 0.19 |
| You were unconscious, asleep, or drunk, high, or drugged | 42% (38%–46%) | 32% (26%–40%) | 0.02 |
| It happened without your consent | 91% (88%–93%) | 92% (87%–95%) | 0.56 |

SOURCE: Authors' calculations using the 2016 and 2018 WGRA.

NOTE: Percentages are made up of only soldiers who were sexually assaulted during the year prior to WGRA administration and are for the behavior on which the respondent qualified as having been sexually assaulted; 95-percent CIs are shown in parentheses. This table corresponds to Figure 4.1.

[a] Perpetrator intent questions were not asked of respondents who qualified as having been sexually assaulted under the first sexual assault behavior (someone put his penis into the victim's anus, mouth, or vagina) because the UCMJ does not require abusive, humiliating, or sexual intent for this behavior to qualify as rape or sexual assault. These percentages, therefore, have the denominator as individuals who qualified as having been sexually assaulted on one of the other behaviors. See Chapter 2 for further details.

**Table C.10. Types of Sexual Assault Behaviors During Most Serious Experience, All Sexual Assault Victims by Gender**

|  | Female Victims | Male Victims | *p*-Value for Difference |
|---|---|---|---|
| Put their penis in your anus, mouth, or vagina | 39% (35%–43%) | 24% (18%–31%) | 0.00 |
| Put any object or any body part other than a penis into your anus, mouth, or vagina | 21% (18%–25%) | 18% (13%–24%) | 0.24 |
| Made you put any part of your body or any object into someone's mouth, vagina, or anus | 6% (4%–9%) | 21% (16%–28%) | < 0.0001 |
| Intentionally touched private areas of your body | 80% (77%–83%) | 81% (74%–86%) | 0.79 |
| Made you touch private areas of their body or someone else's body | 26% (22%–29%) | 25% (19%–32%) | 0.93 |
| Attempted to put a penis, an object, or any body part into your anus, mouth, or vagina, but no penetration actually occurred | 22% (19%–26%) | 13% (8%–18%) | 0.00 |

SOURCE: Authors' calculations using the 2016 and 2018 WGRA.
NOTE: Percentages are made up of only soldiers who were sexually assaulted during the year prior to WGRA administration; 95-percent CIs are shown in parentheses. Respondents were instructed to select all that apply.

**Table C.11. Perpetrator Characteristics for Most Serious Experience, All Sexual Assault Victims by Gender**

|  | Female Victims | Male Victims | *p*-Value for Difference |
|---|---|---|---|
| Number of perpetrators |  |  | 0.01 |
| One | 68% (64%–71%) | 57% (50%–65%) |  |
| More than one | 30% (27%–34%) | 37% (30%–45%) |  |
| Not sure | 2% (1%–3%) | 6% (3%–10%) |  |
| In the military? |  |  | < 0.0001 |
| All | 86% (83%–88%) | 66% (59%–73%) |  |
| Some but not all | 5% (3%–7%) | 8% (5%–13%) |  |
| None | 7% (5%–9%) | 18% (13%–24%) |  |
| Not sure | 2% (1%–3%) | 8% (4%–12%) |  |
| Gender |  |  | < 0.0001 |
| All men | 94% (92%–96%) | 54% (47%–62%) |  |

115

| | Female Victims | Male Victims | *p*-Value for Difference |
|---|---|---|---|
| All women | 1%<br>(0%–2%) | 26%<br>(20%–33%) | |
| Mix of men and women | 4%<br>(2%–6%) | 13%<br>(8%–19%) | |
| Not sure | 1%<br>(0%–2%) | 6%<br>(3%–11%) | |
| **Rank, if at least one in military**[a, b] | | | |
| Enlisted/WO | 86%<br>(83%–89%) | 81%<br>(74%–87%) | 0.12 |
| Officer | 13%<br>(10%–15%) | 21%<br>(14%–29%) | 0.01 |
| Not sure | 8%<br>(6%–11%) | 9%<br>(5%–15%) | 0.76 |
| **Professional relationship with victim**[b, c] | | | |
| Supervisor | 10%<br>(6%–14%) | 11%<br>(4%–24%) | 0.69 |
| Other higher-ranked member of chain of command | 11%<br>(7%–16%) | 14%<br>(6%–27%) | 0.52 |
| Higher-ranked and outside chain of command | 18%<br>(14%–22%) | 23%<br>(13%–36%) | 0.30 |
| Military peer of similar rank | 63%<br>(57%–68%) | 54%<br>(42%–66%) | 0.18 |
| Subordinate or someone you manage | 7%<br>(4%–10%) | 17%<br>(8%–29%) | 0.01 |
| DoD or government civilian working for the military[d] | 5%<br>(3%–9%) | 7%<br>(3%–16%) | 0.53 |
| Contractor[d] | 1%<br>(0%–3%) | 3%<br>(1%–9%) | 0.17 |
| Not sure | 12%<br>(9%–16%) | 20%<br>(11%–32%) | 0.10 |
| **Personal relationship to victim**[b] | | | |
| Your current or former spouse[e] | 5%<br>(3%–8%) | 2%<br>(1%–6%) | 0.13 |
| Someone you have a child with[e] | 2%<br>(1%–4%) | 1%<br>(0%–4%) | 0.44 |
| Your significant other (boyfriend or girlfriend) who you live with[f] | 2%<br>(1%–4%) | 2%<br>(0%–4%) | 0.68 |
| Your significant other (boyfriend or girlfriend) who you do/did not live with[f] | 6%<br>(4%–9%) | 4%<br>(2%–8%) | 0.27 |
| Friend or acquaintance | 57%<br>(53%–61%) | 46%<br>(38%–54%) | 0.01 |
| Family member | 1%<br>(0%–2%) | 1%<br>(0%–3%) | 0.49 |
| Stranger | 15% | 16% | 0.75 |

|  | Female Victims | Male Victims | p-Value for Difference |
|---|---|---|---|
|  | (12%–18%) | (11%–22%) |  |
| None of the above | 23% (19%–26%) | 32% (26%–40%) | 0.01 |
| Not sure | 3% (2%–5%) | 9% (5%–13%) | 0.00 |

SOURCE: Authors' calculations using the 2016 and 2018 WGRA.

NOTES: Percentages are made up of only soldiers who were sexually assaulted during the year prior to WGRA administration; 95-percent CIs are shown in parentheses. This table corresponds to Figures 4.2, 4.3, and 4.4. WO = warrant officer.

[a] This question was asked only of respondents who answered "all" or "some, but not all" to the previous question of whether the perpetrators were members of the military, and percentages should be interpreted as the percentage of victims who indicated at least one military perpetrator.

[b] Respondents were instructed to select all that apply.

[c] Includes data from 2018 only.

[d] Combined into "DoD/government civilian(s) working for the military/Contractor(s)" in figures.

[e] Combined into "your current or former spouse or someone you have a child with" in figures.

[f] Combined into "your significant other (boyfriend or girlfriend)" in figures.

### Table C.12. Place and Time of Most Serious Experience, All Sexual Assault Victims by Gender

|  | Female Victims | Male Victims | p-Value for Difference |
|---|---|---|---|
| Assault occurred during any required military activity[a] | 50% (45%–54%) | 65% (57%–72%) | 0.00 |
| Place assault occurred[b] |  |  |  |
| Military installation | 69% (65%–73%) | 68% (60%–74%) | 0.65 |
| TDY/TAD | 13% (11%–16%) | 28% (21%–35%) | < 0.0001 |
| Deployed to a combat zone[c] | 8% (7%–11%) | 13% (8%–19%) | 0.09 |
| Overseas port visit while deployed[c] | 2% (1%–3%) | 8% (5%–13%) | < 0.0001 |
| While transitioning between operational theaters[c] | 4% (2%–6%) | 8% (4%–12%) | 0.07 |
| While you were in a delayed entry program (DEP) or delayed training program (DTP)[d] | 1% (0%–3%) | 8% (3%–14%) | 0.00 |
| During basic training[e] | 4% (3% 6%) | 8% (4%–14%) | 0.14 |
| During any other type of military combat training | 5% (4%–8%) | 14% (9%–21%) | 0.00 |
| During Officer Candidate School[e] | 3% (2%–5%) | 5% (2%–10%) | 0.27 |
| During technical, MOS, advanced individual training or professional military education[e] | 10% (7%–12%) | 11% (6%–18%) | 0.58 |
| While at an official military function, either on or off base | 13% (10%–16%) | 23% (17%–31%) | 0.00 |

| | Female Victims | Male Victims | p-Value for Difference |
|---|---|---|---|
| Off base | 40% (36%–44%) | 37% (30%–45%) | 0.57 |
| Time assault occurred[f] | | | |
| At work during duty hours | 29% (26%–33%) | 50% (42%–57%) | < 0.0001 |
| While out with friends or at a party | 40% (36%–44%) | 32% (25%–39%) | 0.06 |
| On a date | 5% (3%–7%) | 4% (1%–8%) | 0.57 |
| On approved leave | 6% (4%–8%) | 8% (4%–14%) | 0.30 |
| In your or someone else's home or quarters | 44% (40%–48%) | 27% (20%–34%) | < 0.0001 |
| While being intimate with the person[g] | 8% (5%–11%) | 10% (4%–18%) | 0.51 |
| None of the above | 12% (10%–15%) | 9% (5%–14%) | 0.20 |
| Do not recall | 2% (1%–3%) | 4% (2%–7%) | 0.08 |

SOURCE: Authors' calculations using the 2016 and 2018 WGRA.
NOTES: Percentages are made up of only soldiers who were sexually assaulted during the year prior to WGRA administration; 95-percent CIs are shown in parentheses. This table corresponds to Figures 4.5 and 4.6. MOS = military occupational specialty.
[a] Aggregation of "deployed to a combat zone or transitioning between operational theaters," "basic, officer, or technical training," "while you were on TDY/TAD, at sea, or during field exercises/alerts," "while you were in any other type of military combat training," "while at an official military function (either on or off base)," and "you were at work during duty hours."
[b] Each place is a yes/no question, and multiple places could have "yes" responses.
[c] Combined into "Deployed to a combat zone or transitioning between operational theaters" for Figure 4.5.
[d] Not shown in Figure 4.5 because these assaults occurred prior to accession.
[e] Combined into "Basic, officer, or technical training" for Figure 4.5.
[f] Respondents were instructed to select all that apply.
[g] Includes data for 2016 only.

### Table C.13. Alcohol and Drug Involvement in Most Serious Experience, All Sexual Assault Victims by Gender

| | Female Victims | Male Victims | p-Value for Difference |
|---|---|---|---|
| Victim was drinking alcohol | | | 0.00 |
| Yes | 44% (39%–48%) | 34% (27%–42%) | |
| No | 56% (51%–60%) | 61% (53%–68%) | |
| Not sure | 1% (0%–2%) | 5% (2%–9%) | |
| Perpetrator bought or gave victim alcohol | | | 0.05 |
| Yes | 28% (24%–32%) | 22% (16%–30%) | |

|  | Female Victims | Male Victims | *p*-Value for Difference |
|---|---|---|---|
| No | 68%<br>(64%–72%) | 77%<br>(69%–83%) | |
| Not sure | 4%<br>(2%–6%) | 1%<br>(0%–4%) | |
| Perpetrator was drinking alcohol | | | < 0.0001 |
| Yes | 50%<br>(45%–54%) | 30%<br>(24%–38%) | |
| No | 36%<br>(32%–40%) | 44%<br>(36%–52%) | |
| Not sure | 15%<br>(12%–18%) | 26%<br>(20%–33%) | |
| Victim was drugged without their knowledge or consent | | | 0.55 |
| Yes | 6%<br>(4%–8%) | 8%<br>(4%–13%) | |
| No | 80%<br>(76%–83%) | 80%<br>(73%–86%) | |
| Not sure | 14%<br>(11%–17%) | 12%<br>(7%–18%) | |

SOURCE: Authors' calculations using the 2016 and 2018 WGRA.
NOTE: Percentages are made up of only soldiers who were sexually assaulted during the year prior to WGRA administration; 95-percent CIs are shown in parentheses. This table corresponds to Figure 4.7, which presents percentages for "Yes" responses to each question.

### Table C.14. Bullying, Hazing, Sexual Harassment, and Stalking During Most Serious Experience, All Sexual Assault Victims by Gender

|  | Female Victims | Male Victims | *p*-Value of Difference |
|---|---|---|---|
| Victim would describe assault as hazing[a] | 9%<br>(6%–13%) | 29%<br>(18%–41%) | < 0.0001 |
| Victim would describe assault as bullying[a] | 20%<br>(15%–25%) | 30%<br>(20%–42%) | 0.06 |
| Victim was sexually harassed before assault by same perpetrator(s) | 44%<br>(40%–48%) | 47%<br>(39%–55%) | 0.52 |
| Victim was sexually harassed after assault by same perpetrator(s) | 40%<br>(36%–44%) | 43%<br>(35%–51%) | 0.53 |
| Victim was stalked before assault by same perpetrator(s) | 18%<br>(15%–22%) | 21%<br>(15%–28%) | 0.37 |
| Victim was stalked after assault by same perpetrator(s) | 24%<br>(20%–28%) | 25%<br>(18%–32%) | 0.86 |

SOURCE: Authors' calculations using the 2016 and 2018 WGRA.
NOTES: Percentages are made up of only soldiers who were sexually assaulted during the year prior to WGRA administration; 95-percent CIs are shown in parentheses. This table corresponds to Figure 4.8.
[a] Bullying and hazing use only 2018 data because of changes in definition across the two survey years; see Table 2.3.

# Tabular Results for Chapter 5

*Female Victims by Sexual Orientation*

### Table C.15. Types of Sexual Assault Behaviors from Screener Questions, Female Sexual Assault Victims by Sexual Orientation

| | Heterosexual | LGBO | NR/PNA | *p*-Value for Difference |
|---|---|---|---|---|
| Put their penis in your anus, mouth, or vagina | 39% (34%–45%) | 39% (29%–51%) | 39% (32%–46%) | 0.99 |
| Put any object or any body part other than a penis into your anus, mouth, or vagina | 26% (22%–32%) | 32% (23%–43%) | 24% (18%–31%) | 0.37 |
| Made you put any part of your body or any object into someone's mouth, vagina, or anus | 7% (5%–11%) | 9% (4%–18%) | 8% (5%–12%) | 0.78 |
| Intentionally touched private areas of your body | 86% (82%–89%) | 84% (74%–91%) | 84% (78%–89%) | 0.84 |
| Made you touch private areas of their body or someone else's body | 34% (29%–40%) | 30% (21%–41%) | 23% (17%–29%) | 0.02 |
| Attempted to put a penis, an object, or any body part into your anus, mouth, or vagina, but no penetration actually occurred | 29% (24%–34%) | 24% (16%–35%) | 21% (15%–27%) | 0.12 |

SOURCE: Authors' calculations using the 2016 and 2018 WGRA.
NOTE: Percentages are made up of only soldiers who were sexually assaulted during the year prior to WGRA administration; 95-percent CIs are shown in parentheses. This table corresponds to Figure 5.1.

### Table C.16. Perpetrator Intent and Type of Coercion from Screener Questions, Female Sexual Assault Victims by Sexual Orientation

| | Heterosexual | LGBO | NR/PNA | *p*-Value for Difference |
|---|---|---|---|---|
| Assaulted more than once | 60% (55%–66%) | 63% (52%–73%) | 63% (55%–70%) | 0.84 |
| Perpetrator intent[a] | | | | |
|   Abusive or humiliating | 48% (40%–55%) | 37% (25%–51%) | 57% (48%–66%) | 0.04 |
|   Sexual purpose | 98% (95%–99%) | 99% (93%–100%) | 97% (92%–99%) | 0.60 |
| Type of coercion | | | | |
|   Threatened or used physical force | 21% (17%–26%) | 25% (16%–36%) | 23% (17%–30%) | 0.71 |
|   Threatened you or someone else in another way | 22% (18%–27%) | 22% (14%–33%) | 21% (16%–28%) | 0.98 |
|   You were unconscious, asleep, or drunk, high, or drugged | 42% (37%–48%) | 41% (30%–51%) | 40% (32%–47%) | 0.82 |

| | Heterosexual | LGBO | NR/PNA | p-Value for Difference |
|---|---|---|---|---|
| It happened without your consent | 91% (88%–94%) | 89% (80%–94%) | 91% (86%–95%) | 0.73 |

SOURCE: Authors' calculations using the 2016 and 2018 WGRA.
NOTES: Percentages are made up of only soldiers who were sexually assaulted during the year prior to WGRA administration and are for the behavior on which the respondent qualified as having been sexually assaulted; 95-percent CIs are shown in parentheses. This table corresponds to Figure 5.1.
[a] Perpetrator intent questions were not asked of respondents who qualified as having been sexually assaulted under the first sexual assault behavior (someone put his penis into the victim's anus, mouth, or vagina) because the UCMJ does not require abusive, humiliating, or sexual intent for this behavior to qualify as rape or sexual assault. These percentages, therefore, have the denominator as individuals who qualified as having been sexually assaulted on one of the other behaviors. See Chapter 2 for further details.

### Table C.17. Types of Sexual Assault Behaviors During Most Serious Experience, Female Sexual Assault Victims by Sexual Orientation

| | Heterosexual | LGBO | NR/PNA | p-Value for Difference |
|---|---|---|---|---|
| Put their penis in your anus, mouth, or vagina | 39% (33%–44%) | 39% (29%–51%) | 38% (31%–45%) | 0.95 |
| Put any object or any body part other than a penis into your anus, mouth, or vagina | 22% (17%–27%) | 22% (14%–32%) | 19% (14%–26%) | 0.76 |
| Made you put any part of your body or any object into someone's mouth, vagina, or anus | 5% (3%–8%) | 9% (3%–17%) | 7% (4%–11%) | 0.40 |
| Intentionally touched private areas of your body | 81% (76%–85%) | 82% (72%–89%) | 75% (69%–81%) | 0.27 |
| Made you touch private areas of their body or someone else's body | 28% (24%–34%) | 26% (17%–37%) | 19% (14%–25%) | 0.06 |
| Attempted to put a penis, an object, or any body part into your anus, mouth, or vagina, but no penetration actually occurred | 24% (19%–29%) | 23% (14%–33%) | 18% (13%–24%) | 0.34 |

SOURCE: Authors' calculations using the 2016 and 2018 WGRA.
NOTE: Percentages are made up of only soldiers who were sexually assaulted during the year prior to WGRA administration; 95-percent CIs are shown in parentheses. Respondents were instructed to select all that apply.

**Table C.18. Perpetrator Characteristics for Most Serious Experience, Female Sexual Assault Victims by Sexual Orientation**

| | Heterosexual | LGBO | NR/PNA | p-Value for Difference |
|---|---|---|---|---|
| Number of perpetrators | | | | 0.13 |
| One | 71% (66%–76%) | 73% (62%–82%) | 61% (53%–68%) | |
| More than one | 28% (23%–33%) | 25% (16%–35%) | 36% (29%–44%) | |
| Not sure | 1% (1%–3%) | 2% (0%–8%) | 3% (1%–7%) | |
| In the military? | | | | 0.17 |
| All | 84% (80%–88%) | 87% (79%–93%) | 88% (82%–92%) | |
| Some but not all | 5% (3%–8%) | 4% (1%–10%) | 6% (2%–11%) | |
| None | 9% (6%–12%) | 8% (4%–15%) | 3% (1%–7%) | |
| Not sure | 2% (1%–4%) | 0% (0%–3%) | 3% (1%–7%) | |
| Gender | | | | 0.01 |
| All men | 97% (95%–99%) | 93% (86%–97%) | 90% (84%–94%) | |
| All women | 0% (0%–2%) | 1% (0%–6%) | 2% (0%–5%) | |
| Mix of men and women | 2% (1%–4%) | 4% (1%–10%) | 6% (3%–12%) | |
| Not sure | 0% (0%–1%) | 2% (0%–7%) | 2% (0%–5%) | |
| Rank, if at least one in military[a, b] | | | | |
| Enlisted/WO | 86% (82%–89%) | 88% (79%–94%) | 87% (81%–91%) | 0.87 |
| Officer | 13% (9%–17%) | 7% (3%–14%) | 15% (10%–21%) | 0.12 |
| Not sure | 7% (5%–11%) | 10% (4%–19%) | 10% (6%–16%) | 0.62 |
| Professional relationship with victim[b, c] | | | | |
| Supervisor | 12% (6%–21%) | 7% (2%–17%) | 6% (2%–12%) | 0.20 |
| Other higher-ranked member of chain of command | 9% (5%–15%) | 8% (2%–20%) | 16% (8%–26%) | 0.23 |
| Higher-ranked and outside chain of command | 17% (12%–24%) | 14% (6%–26%) | 20% (13%–29%) | 0.63 |
| Military peer of similar rank | 63% (55%–71%) | 57% (42%–71%) | 65% (55%–75%) | 0.62 |

122

| | Heterosexual | LGBO | NR/PNA | *p*-Value for Difference |
|---|---|---|---|---|
| Subordinate or someone you manage | 6% (3%–10%) | 5% (1%–14%) | 10% (5%–17%) | 0.28 |
| DoD or government civilian working for the military[d] | 6% (3%–10%) | 2% (0%–10%) | 7% (2%–14%) | 0.49 |
| Contractor[d] | 2% (0%–5%) | 1% (0%–8%) | 1% (0%–5%) | 0.77 |
| Not sure | 10% (6%–15%) | 21% (11%–34%) | 12% (6%–20%) | 0.11 |
| Personal relationship to victim[b] | | | | |
| Your current or former spouse[e] | 4% (2%–7%) | 6% (2%–15%) | 5% (2%–9%) | 0.60 |
| Someone you have a child with[e] | 1% (0%–4%) | 4% (1%–12%) | 0% (0%–3%) | 0.06 |
| Your significant other (boyfriend or girlfriend) who you live with[f] | 1% (1%–3%) | 2% (0%–6%) | 0% (0%–3%) | 0.41 |
| Your significant other (boyfriend or girlfriend) who you do/did not live with[f] | 6% (3%–9%) | 6% (2%–13%) | 7% (3%–12%) | 0.90 |
| Friend or acquaintance | 57% (51%–62%) | 64% (53%–74%) | 53% (45%–60%) | 0.24 |
| Family member | 1% (0%–4%) | 1% (0%–5%) | 1% (0%–4%) | 0.88 |
| Stranger | 16% (12%–20%) | 9% (4%–17%) | 18% (12%–25%) | 0.19 |
| None of the above | 22% (17%–27%) | 15% (9%–23%) | 30% (24%–38%) | 0.01 |
| Not sure | 2% (1%–4%) | 7% (3%–16%) | 3% (1%–7%) | 0.05 |

SOURCE: Authors' calculations using the 2016 and 2018 WGRA.

NOTES: Percentages are made up of only soldiers who were sexually assaulted during the year prior to WGRA administration; 95-percent CIs are shown in parentheses. This table corresponds to Figures 5.2, 5.3, and 5.4. WO = warrant officer.

[a] This question was asked only of respondents who answered "all" or "some, but not all" to the previous question of whether the perpetrators were members of the military, and percentages should be interpreted as the percentage of victims who indicated at least one military perpetrator.

[b] Respondents were instructed to select all that apply.

[c] Includes data from 2018 only.

[d] Combined into "DoD/government civilian(s) working for the military/Contractor(s)" in figures.

[e] Combined into "your current or former spouse or someone you have a child with" in figures

[f] Combined into "your significant other (boyfriend or girlfriend)" in figures.

**Table C.19. Place and Time of Most Serious Experience, Female Sexual Assault Victims by Sexual Orientation**

| | Heterosexual | LGBO | NR/PNA | *p*-Value for Difference |
|---|---|---|---|---|
| Assault occurred during any required military activity[a] | 47% (42%–53%) | 46% (36%–57%) | 54% (45%–62%) | 0.35 |
| Place assault occurred[b] | | | | |
|     Military installation | 64% (59%–69%) | 78% (69%–86%) | 76% (68%–82%) | 0.00 |
|     TDY/TAD | 13% (10%–17%) | 12% (7%–20%) | 14% (9%–21%) | 0.89 |
|     Deployed to a combat zone[c] | 8% (5%–11%) | 7% (3%–13%) | 11% (7%–17%) | 0.33 |
|     Overseas port visit while deployed[c] | 1% (0%–3%) | 0% (0%–4%) | 3% (1%–7%) | 0.05 |
|     While transitioning between operational theaters[c] | 3% (1%–6%) | 2% (0%–7%) | 5% (2%–10%) | 0.35 |
|     While you were in a delayed entry program (DEP) or delayed training program (DTP)[d] | 1% (0%–2%) | 0% (0%–3%) | 4% (1%–10%) | 0.09 |
|     During basic training[e] | 4% (2%–7%) | 6% (2%–14%) | 5% (2%–10%) | 0.57 |
|     During any other type of military combat training | 5% (3%–8%) | 5% (2%–11%) | 6% (3%–11%) | 0.88 |
|     During Officer Candidate School[e] | 4% (2%–6%) | 4% (1%–9%) | 3% (1%–7%) | 1.00 |
|     During technical, MOS, advanced individual training or professional military education[e] | 10% (7%–14%) | 12% (6%–22%) | 6% (3%–11%) | 0.25 |
|     While at an official military function, either on or off base | 11% (8%–15%) | 11% (6%–19%) | 17% (11%–25%) | 0.15 |
|     Off base | 42% (37%–48%) | 36% (27%–46%) | 36% (28%–44%) | 0.28 |
| Time assault occurred[f] | | | | |
|     At work during duty hours | 27% (22%–33%) | 22% (15%–32%) | 35% (27%–44%) | 0.07 |
|     While out with friends or at a party | 41% (35%–46%) | 37% (27%–47%) | 36% (28%–45%) | 0.63 |
|     On a date | 5% (3%–8%) | 2% (0%–7%) | 5% (2%–11%) | 0.43 |
|     On approved leave | 6% (4%–10%) | 6% (2%–12%) | 4% (1%–9%) | 0.54 |
|     In your or someone else's home or quarters | 44% (39%–50%) | 55% (44%–66%) | 40% (32%–48%) | 0.07 |

| | Heterosexual | LGBO | NR/PNA | *p*-Value for Difference |
|---|---|---|---|---|
| While being intimate with the person[g] | 5% (3%–10%) | S (7%–35%) | 5% (1%–16%) | 0.02 |
| None of the above | 14% (10%–19%) | 12% (6%–21%) | 10% (6%–15%) | 0.36 |
| Do not recall | 1% (0%–3%) | 3% (1%–8%) | 2% (1%–6%) | 0.26 |

SOURCE: Authors' calculations using the 2016 and 2018 WGRA.

NOTES: Percentages are made up of only soldiers who were sexually assaulted during the year prior to WGRA administration; 95-percent CIs are shown in parentheses. This table corresponds to Figures 5.5 and 5.6. S = suppressed.

[a] Aggregation of "deployed to a combat zone or transitioning between operational theaters," "basic, officer, or technical training," "while you were on TDY/TAD, at sea, or during field exercises/alerts," "while you were in any other type of military combat training," "while at an official military function (either on or off base)," and "you were at work during duty hours."

[b] Each place is a yes/no question, and multiple places could have "yes" responses.

[c] Combined into "Deployed to a combat zone or transitioning between operational theaters" for Figure 5.5.

[d] Not shown in Figure 5.5 because these assaults occurred prior to accession.

[e] Combined into "Basic, officer, or technical training" for Figure 5.5.

[f] Respondents were instructed to select all that apply.

[g] Includes data for 2016 only.

### Table C.20. Alcohol and Drug Involvement in Most Serious Experience, Female Sexual Assault Victims by Sexual Orientation

| | Heterosexual | LGBO | NR/PNA | *p*-Value for Difference |
|---|---|---|---|---|
| Victim was drinking alcohol | | | | 0.29 |
| Yes | 44% (38%–49%) | 41% (31%–52%) | 42% (34%–50%) | |
| No | 56% (50%–61%) | 56% (46%–67%) | 56% (48%–65%) | |
| Not sure | 0% (0%–2%) | 3% (0%–8%) | 2% (0%–5%) | |
| Perpetrator bought or gave victim alcohol | | | | 0.83 |
| Yes | 28% (23%–33%) | 28% (19%–38%) | 25% (19%–32%) | |
| No | 69% (63%–73%) | 70% (60%–79%) | 71% (63%–78%) | |
| Not sure | 4% (2%–7%) | 2% (0%–7%) | 4% (2%–10%) | |
| Perpetrator was drinking alcohol | | | | 0.15 |
| Yes | 48% (42%–53%) | 59% (48%–70%) | 45% (37%–54%) | |
| No | 38% (33%–44%) | 25% (17%–36%) | 37% (29%–46%) | |
| Not sure | 14% (10%–18%) | 15% (9%–25%) | 17% (12%–24%) | |

| | Heterosexual | LGBO | NR/PNA | _p_-Value for Difference |
|---|---|---|---|---|
| Victim was drugged without their knowledge or consent | | | | 0.79 |
| Yes | 5%<br>(3%–8%) | 2%<br>(0%–7%) | 5%<br>(2%–11%) | |
| No | 80%<br>(75%–85%) | 84%<br>(75%–91%) | 80%<br>(72%–86%) | |
| Not sure | 15%<br>(11%–19%) | 14%<br>(7%–23%) | 15%<br>(10%–21%) | |

SOURCE: Authors' calculations using the 2016 and 2018 WGRA.
NOTE: Percentages are made up of only soldiers who were sexually assaulted during the year prior to WGRA administration; 95-percent CIs are shown in parentheses. This table corresponds to Figure 5.7, which presents percentages for "Yes" responses to each question.

### Table C.21. Bullying, Hazing, Sexual Harassment, and Stalking During Most Serious Experience, Female Sexual Assault Victims by Sexual Orientation

| | Heterosexual | LGBO | NR/PNA | _p_-Value of Difference |
|---|---|---|---|---|
| Victim would describe assault as hazing[a] | 9%<br>(5%–14%) | 7%<br>(2%–18%) | 11%<br>(5%–19%) | 0.77 |
| Victim would describe assault as bullying[a] | 17%<br>(11%–23%) | 13%<br>(6%–26%) | 29%<br>(20%–40%) | 0.02 |
| Victim was sexually harassed before assault by same perpetrator(s) | 45%<br>(39%–50%) | 37%<br>(27%–47%) | 46%<br>(38%–54%) | 0.33 |
| Victim was sexually harassed after assault by same perpetrator(s) | 38%<br>(33%–44%) | 42%<br>(32%–53%) | 41%<br>(33%–49%) | 0.74 |
| Victim was stalked before assault by same perpetrator(s) | 18%<br>(14%–22%) | 22%<br>(13%–33%) | 13%<br>(8%–19%) | 0.23 |
| Victim was stalked after assault by same perpetrator(s) | 23%<br>(18%–28%) | 26%<br>(17%–37%) | 23%<br>(17%–31%) | 0.79 |

SOURCE: Authors' calculations using the 2016 and 2018 WGRA.
NOTES: Percentages are made up of only soldiers who were sexually assaulted during the year prior to WGRA administration; 95-percent CIs are shown in parentheses. This table corresponds to Figure 5.8.
[a] Bullying and hazing use only 2018 data because of changes in definition across the two survey years; see Table 2.3.

**Table C.22. Types of Sexual Assault Behaviors from Screener Questions, Male Sexual Assault Victims by Sexual Orientation**

| | Heterosexual | LGBO, NR, and PNA | *p*-Value for Difference |
|---|---|---|---|
| Put their penis in your anus, mouth, or vagina | 8% (3%–16%) | 41% (31%–52%) | < 0.0001 |
| Put any object or any body part other than a penis into your anus, mouth, or vagina | 14% (8%–22%) | 26% (18%–37%) | 0.03 |
| Made you put any part of your body or any object into someone's mouth, vagina, or anus | 16% (9%–24%) | 28% (18%–38%) | 0.05 |
| Intentionally touched private areas of your body | 89% (81%–95%) | 78% (67%–86%) | 0.04 |
| Made you touch private areas of their body or someone else's body | 26% (17%–36%) | 27% (19%–37%) | 0.84 |
| Attempted to put a penis, an object, or any body part into your anus, mouth, or vagina, but no penetration actually occurred | 8% (3%–15%) | 19% (12%–29%) | 0.02 |

SOURCE: Authors' calculations using the 2016 and 2018 WGRA.
NOTE: Percentages are made up of only soldiers who were sexually assaulted during the year prior to WGRA administration; 95-percent CIs are shown in parentheses. This table corresponds to Figure 5.9.

**Table C.23. Perpetrator Intent and Type of Coercion from Screener Questions, Male Sexual Assault Victims by Sexual Orientation**

| | Heterosexual | LGBO, NR, and PNA | *p*-Value for Difference |
|---|---|---|---|
| Assaulted more than once | 62% (52%–71%) | 60% (49%–71%) | 0.83 |
| Perpetrator intent[a] | | | |
| Abusive or humiliating | 53% (43%–64%) | 65% (50%–78%) | 0.19 |
| Sexual purpose | 74% (62%–83%) | 74% (59%–85%) | 0.99 |
| Type of coercion | | | |
| Threatened or used physical force | 12% (6%–21%) | 31% (22%–41%) | 0.00 |
| Threatened you or someone else in another way | 24% (16%–34%) | 30% (21%–39%) | 0.39 |
| You were unconscious, asleep, or drunk, high, or drugged | 26% (17%–36%) | 39% (28%–50%) | 0.06 |
| It happened without your consent | 91% (83%–96%) | 93% (86%–97%) | 0.57 |

SOURCE: Authors' calculations using the 2016 and 2018 WGRA.
NOTES: Percentages are made up of only soldiers who were sexually assaulted during the year prior to WGRA administration and are for the behavior on which the respondent qualified as having been sexually assaulted; 95-percent CIs are shown in parentheses. This table corresponds to Figure 5.9.
[a] Perpetrator intent questions were not asked of respondents who qualified as having been sexually assaulted under the first sexual assault behavior (someone put his penis into the victim's anus, mouth, or vagina) because the UCMJ does not require abusive, humiliating, or sexual intent for this behavior to qualify as rape or sexual assault. These percentages, therefore, have the denominator as individuals who qualified as having been sexually assaulted on one of the other behaviors. See Chapter 2 for further details.

## Table C.24. Types of Sexual Assault Behaviors During Most Serious Experience, Male Sexual Assault Victims by Sexual Orientation

| | Heterosexual | LGBO, NR, and PNA | *p*-Value for Difference |
|---|---|---|---|
| Put their penis in your anus, mouth, or vagina | 8% (3%–16%) | 40% (30%–50%) | < 0.0001 |
| Put any object or any body part other than a penis into your anus, mouth, or vagina | 11% (5%–18%) | 25% (17%–35%) | 0.01 |
| Made you put any part of your body or any object into someone's mouth, vagina, or anus | 16% (9%–24%) | 27% (18%–38%) | 0.06 |
| Intentionally touched private areas of your body | 86% (77%–92%) | 75% (65%–84%) | 0.07 |
| Made you touch private areas of their body or someone else's body | 23% (15%–33%) | 26% (18%–36%) | 0.61 |
| Attempted to put a penis, an object, or any body part into your anus, mouth, or vagina, but no penetration actually occurred | 8% (3%–15%) | 17% (10%–26%) | 0.05 |

SOURCE: Authors' calculations using the 2016 and 2018 WGRA.
NOTE: Percentages are made up of only soldiers who were sexually assaulted during the year prior to WGRA administration; 95-percent CIs are shown in parentheses. Respondents are instructed to select all that apply.

## Table C.25. Perpetrator Characteristics for Most Serious Experience, Male Sexual Assault Victims by Sexual Orientation

| | Heterosexual | LGBO, NR, and PNA | *p*-Value for Difference |
|---|---|---|---|
| Number of perpetrators | | | 0.05 |
| One | 67% (56%–77%) | 49% (38%–60%) | |
| More than one | 29% (20%–40%) | 44% (33%–55%) | |
| Not sure | 4% (1%–10%) | 7% (3%–14%) | |
| In the military? | | | < 0.0001 |
| All | 80% (71%–86%) | 52% (40%–63%) | |
| Some but not all | 2% (0%–7%) | 14% (7%–24%) | |
| None | 14% (8%–21%) | 23% (14%–34%) | |
| Not sure | 4% (1%–10%) | 11% (6%–20%) | |
| Gender | | | < 0.0001 |
| All men | 54% (44%–64%) | 52% (41%–63%) | |
| All women | 40% (30%–50%) | 14% (7%–24%) | |

129

| | Heterosexual | LGBO, NR, and PNA | p-Value for Difference |
|---|---|---|---|
| Mix of men and women | 4% (1%–9%) | 23% (14%–34%) | |
| Not sure | 2% (0%–7%) | 11% (5%–20%) | |
| Rank, if at least one in military[a, b] | | | |
| Enlisted/WO | 86% (77%–92%) | 78% (65%–87%) | 0.16 |
| Officer | 18% (10%–30%) | 25% (15%–38%) | 0.35 |
| Not sure | 4% (1%–10%) | 12% (5%–23%) | 0.04 |
| Professional relationship with victim[b, c] | | | |
| Supervisor | 3% (0%–14%) | S (7%–44%) | 0.01 |
| Other higher-ranked member of chain of command | 5% (1%–16%) | S (9%–48%) | 0.01 |
| Higher-ranked and outside chain of command | 18% (8%–31%) | S (13%–52%) | 0.23 |
| Military peer of similar rank | S (46%–76%) | S (26%–65%) | 0.16 |
| Subordinate or someone you manage | 12% (5%–24%) | S (7%–45%) | 0.28 |
| DoD or government civilian working for the military[d] | 2% (0%–10%) | S (4%–31%) | 0.02 |
| Contractor[d] | 3% (0%–12%) | 3% (0%–15%) | 0.82 |
| Not sure | 10% (3%–22%) | S (15%–53%) | 0.01 |
| Personal relationship to victim[b] | | | |
| Your current or former spouse[e] | 3% (0%–9%) | 2% (0%–8%) | 0.96 |
| Someone you have a child with[e] | 0% (0%–3%) | 2% (0%–8%) | 0.03 |
| Your significant other (boyfriend or girlfriend) who you live with[f] | 0% (0%–3%) | 2% (0%–8%) | 0.03 |
| Your significant other (boyfriend or girlfriend) who you do/did not live with[f] | 2% (0%–7%) | 7% (2%–14%) | 0.14 |
| Friend or acquaintance | 48% (37%–59%) | 42% (31%–54%) | 0.42 |
| Family member | 0% (0%–3%) | 1% (0%–6%) | 0.16 |
| Stranger | 10% (5%–17%) | 23% (14%–34%) | 0.01 |
| None of the above | 36% (26%–46%) | 30% (20%–42%) | 0.46 |

130

| | Heterosexual | LGBO, NR, and PNA | p-Value for Difference |
|---|---|---|---|
| Not sure | 5% (2%–11%) | 13% (7%–22%) | 0.03 |

SOURCE: Authors' calculations using the 2016 and 2018 WGRA.

NOTES: Percentages are made up of only soldiers who were sexually assaulted during the year prior to WGRA administration; 95-percent CIs are shown in parentheses. This table corresponds to Figures 5.10, 5.11, and 5.12. S = suppressed. WO = warrant officer.

[a] This question was asked only of respondents who answered "all" or "some, but not all" to the previous question of whether the perpetrators were members of the military, and percentages should be interpreted as the percentage of victims who indicated at least one military perpetrator.

[b] Respondents were instructed to select all that apply.

[c] Includes data from 2018 only.

[d] Combined into "DoD/government civilian(s) working for the military/Contractor(s)" in figures.

[e] Combined into "your current or former spouse or someone you have a child with" in figures.

[f] Combined into "your significant other (boyfriend or girlfriend)" in figures.

### Table C.26. Place and Time of Most Serious Experience, Male Sexual Assault Victims by Sexual Orientation

| | Heterosexual | LGBO, NR, and PNA | p-Value for Difference |
|---|---|---|---|
| Assault occurred during any required military activity[a] | 70% (60%–78%) | 59% (47%–70%) | 0.13 |
| Place assault occurred[b] | | | |
| Military installation | 72% (63%–80%) | 63% (51%–74%) | 0.19 |
| TDY/TAD | 21% (13%–31%) | 35% (24%–47%) | 0.05 |
| Deployed to a combat zone[c] | 13% (6%–24%) | 12% (6%–20%) | 0.76 |
| Overseas port visit while deployed[c] | 3% (1%–8%) | 14% (7%–23%) | 0.00 |
| While transitioning between operational theaters[c] | 3% (1%–8%) | 12% (6%–21%) | 0.02 |
| While you were in a delayed entry program (DEP) or delayed training program (DTP)[d] | 2% (0%–7%) | 14% (6%–26%) | 0.00 |
| During basic training[e] | 2% (0%–7%) | 14% (6%–27%) | 0.00 |
| During any other type of military combat training | 9% (4%–18%) | 18% (9%–30%) | 0.12 |
| During Officer Candidate School[e] | 2% (0%–8%) | 9% (4%–17%) | 0.05 |
| During technical, MOS, advanced individual training or professional military education[e] | 4% (1%–10%) | 19% (10%–31%) | 0.00 |
| While at an official military function, either on or off base | 17% (10%–25%) | 30% (19%–42%) | 0.04 |
| Off base | 33% (24%–42%) | 43% (32%–55%) | 0.15 |

| | Heterosexual | LGBO, NR, and PNA | p-Value for Difference |
|---|---|---|---|
| Time assault occurred[f] | | | |
| At work during duty hours | 52% (42%–62%) | 47% (36%–59%) | 0.51 |
| While out with friends or at a party | 33% (24%–43%) | 33% (23%–44%) | 1.00 |
| On a date | 3% (0%–9%) | 5% (1%–12%) | 0.41 |
| On approved leave | 5% (2%–11%) | 11% (4%–24%) | 0.19 |
| In your or someone else's home or quarters | 23% (15%–32%) | 31% (20%–43%) | 0.24 |
| While being intimate with the person[g] | 6% (1%–18%) | 14% (5%–28%) | 0.21 |
| None of the above | 9% (5%–15%) | 9% (3%–20%) | 0.99 |
| Do not recall | 1% (0%–6%) | 6% (2%–13%) | 0.06 |

SOURCE: Authors' calculations using the 2016 and 2018 WGRA.
NOTES: Percentages are made up of only soldiers who were sexually assaulted during the year prior to WGRA administration; 95-percent CIs are shown in parentheses. This table corresponds to Figures 5.13 and 5.14.
[a] Aggregation of "deployed to a combat zone or transitioning between operational theaters," "basic, officer, or technical training," "while you were on TDY/TAD, at sea, or during field exercises/alerts," "while you were in any other type of military combat training," "while at an official military function (either on or off base)," and "you were at work during duty hours."
[b] Each place is a yes/no question, and multiple places could have "yes" responses.
[c] Combined into "Deployed to a combat zone or transitioning between operational theaters" for Figure 5.13.
[d] Not shown in Figure 5.13 because these assaults occurred prior to accession.
[e] Combined into "Basic, officer, or technical training" for Figure 5.13.
[f] Respondents were instructed to select all that apply.
[g] Includes data for 2016 only.

### Table C.27. Alcohol and Drug Involvement in Most Serious Experience, Male Sexual Assault Victims by Sexual Orientation

| | Heterosexual | LGBO, NR, and PNA | p-Value for Difference |
|---|---|---|---|
| Victim was drinking alcohol | | | 0.02 |
| Yes | 33% (24%–43%) | 37% (26%–49%) | |
| No | 66% (56%–75%) | 53% (41%–65%) | |
| Not sure | 1% (0%–6%) | 10% (4%–18%) | |
| Perpetrator bought or gave victim alcohol | | | 0.26 |
| Yes | 18% (11%–27%) | 28% (17%–41%) | |
| No | 81% (71%–88%) | 71% (57%–82%) | |

132

| | Heterosexual | LGBO, NR, and PNA | p-Value for Difference |
|---|---|---|---|
| Not sure | 1% (0%–5%) | 1% (0%–6%) | |
| Perpetrator was drinking alcohol | | | 0.44 |
| Yes | 28% (20%–38%) | 34% (23%–46%) | |
| No | 48% (38%–58%) | 38% (27%–50%) | |
| Not sure | 24% (16%–34%) | 28% (19%–39%) | |
| Victim was drugged without their knowledge or consent | | | 0.01 |
| Yes | 5% (1%–13%) | 12% (6%–21%) | |
| No | 90% (81%–95%) | 69% (57%–79%) | |
| Not sure | 6% (2%–12%) | 20% (11%–32%) | |

SOURCE: Authors' calculations using the 2016 and 2018 WGRA.
NOTE: Percentages are made up of only soldiers who were sexually assaulted during the year prior to WGRA administration; 95-percent CIs are shown in parentheses. This table corresponds to Figure 5.15, which presents percentages for "Yes" responses to each question.

**Table C.28. Bullying, Hazing, Sexual Harassment, and Stalking During Most Serious Experience, Male Sexual Assault Victims by Sexual Orientation**

| | Heterosexual | LGBO, NR, and PNA | p-Value of Difference |
|---|---|---|---|
| Victim would describe assault as hazing[a] | S (8%–34%) | S (23%–60%) | 0.05 |
| Victim would describe assault as bullying[a] | 15% (6%–28%) | S (30%–67%) | 0.00 |
| Victim was sexually harassed before assault by same perpetrator(s) | 42% (32%–52%) | 53% (41%–65%) | 0.13 |
| Victim was sexually harassed after assault by same perpetrator(s) | 42% (32%–53%) | 43% (32%–55%) | 0.89 |
| Victim was stalked before assault by same perpetrator(s) | 14% (8%–22%) | 30% (20%–42%) | 0.01 |
| Victim was stalked after assault by same perpetrator(s) | 15% (9%–23%) | 34% (24%–46%) | 0.00 |

SOURCE: Authors' calculations using the 2016 and 2018 WGRA.
NOTES: Percentages are made up of only soldiers who were sexually assaulted during the year prior to WGRA administration; 95-percent CIs are shown in parentheses. This table corresponds to Figure 5.16. S = suppressed.
[a] Bullying and hazing use only 2018 data because of changes in definition across the two survey years; see Table 2.3.

# Tabular Results for Chapter 6

### Table C.29. Types of Sexual Assault Behaviors from Screener Questions, All Sexual Assault Victims by Installation Risk Level

|  | High-Risk Installations | Non–High-Risk Installations | *p*-Value for Difference |
|---|---|---|---|
| Put their penis in your anus, mouth, or vagina | 33% (28%–38%) | 34% (30%–39%) | 0.67 |
| Put any object or any body part other than a penis into your anus, mouth, or vagina | 24% (20%–29%) | 24% (20%–28%) | 0.94 |
| Made you put any part of your body or any object into someone's mouth, vagina, or anus | 18% (13%–23%) | 9% (7%–13%) | 0.00 |
| Intentionally touched private areas of your body | 86% (82%–90%) | 83% (79%–86%) | 0.22 |
| Made you touch private areas of their body or someone else's body | 31% (26%–36%) | 27% (23%–32%) | 0.23 |
| Attempted to put a penis, an object, or any body part into your anus, mouth, or vagina, but no penetration actually occurred | 21% (17%–26%) | 22% (18%–26%) | 0.85 |

SOURCE: Authors' calculations using the 2016 and 2018 WGRA.
NOTE: Percentages are made up of only soldiers who were sexually assaulted during the year prior to WGRA administration; 95-percent CIs are shown in parentheses. This table corresponds to Figure 6.1.

**Table C.30. Perpetrator Intent and Type of Coercion from Screener Questions, All Sexual Assault Victims by Installation Risk Level**

| | High-Risk Installations | Non–High-Risk Installations | p-Value for Difference |
|---|---|---|---|
| Assaulted more than once | 68% (62%–73%) | 56% (51%–61%) | 0.00 |
| Perpetrator intent[a] | | | |
| Abusive or humiliating | 56% (49%–63%) | 51% (44%–57%) | 0.23 |
| Sexual purpose | 86% (80%–91%) | 87% (80%–92%) | 0.90 |
| Type of coercion | | | |
| Threatened or used physical force | 25% (21%–31%) | 20% (16%–24%) | 0.06 |
| Threatened you or someone else in another way | 28% (23%–33%) | 22% (18%–26%) | 0.09 |
| You were unconscious, asleep, or drunk, high, or drugged | 39% (33%–44%) | 37% (32%–42%) | 0.73 |
| It happened without your consent | 90% (86%–93%) | 92% (90%–94%) | 0.30 |

SOURCE: Authors' calculations using the 2016 and 2018 WGRA.

NOTES: Percentages are made up of only soldiers who were sexually assaulted during the year prior to WGRA administration and are for the behavior on which the respondent qualified as having been sexually assaulted; 95-percent CIs are shown in parentheses. This table corresponds to Figure 6.1.

[a] Perpetrator intent questions were not asked of respondents who qualified as having been sexually assaulted under the first sexual assault behavior (someone put his penis into the victim's anus, mouth, or vagina) because the UCMJ does not require abusive, humiliating, or sexual intent for this behavior to qualify as rape or sexual assault. These percentages, therefore, have the denominator as individuals who qualified as having been sexually assaulted on one of the other behaviors. See Chapter 2 for further details.

**Table C.31. Types of Sexual Assault Behaviors During Most Serious Experience, All Sexual Assault Victims by Installation Risk Level**

| | High-Risk Installations | Non–High-Risk Installations | p-Value for Difference |
|---|---|---|---|
| Put their penis in your anus, mouth, or vagina | 32% (27%–37%) | 34% (30%–39%) | 0.42 |
| Put any object or any body part other than a penis into your anus, mouth, or vagina | 20% (16%–25%) | 20% (16%–24%) | 0.94 |
| Made you put any part of your body or any object into someone's mouth, vagina, or anus | 16% (12%–22%) | 8% (6%–12%) | 0.00 |
| Intentionally touched private areas of your body | 81% (77%–86%) | 79% (75%–83%) | 0.45 |
| Made you touch private areas of their body or someone else's body | 27% (22%–32%) | 24% (20%–29%) | 0.42 |
| Attempted to put a penis, an object, or any body part into your anus, mouth, or vagina, but no penetration actually occurred | 18% (14%–22%) | 19% (15%–23%) | 0.63 |

SOURCE: Authors' calculations using the 2016 and 2018 WGRA.
NOTE: Percentages are made up of only soldiers who were sexually assaulted during the year prior to WGRA administration; 95-percent CIs are shown in parentheses. Respondents were instructed to select all that apply.

**Table C.32. Perpetrator Characteristics for Most Serious Experience, All Sexual Assault Victims by Installation Risk Level**

| | High-Risk Installations | Non–High-Risk Installations | p-Value for Difference |
|---|---|---|---|
| Number of perpetrators | | | 0.01 |
| One | 58% (52%–64%) | 69% (63%–74%) | |
| More than one | 37% (32%–43%) | 29% (24%–34%) | |
| Not sure | 5% (2%–8%) | 2% (1%–4%) | |
| In the military? | | | 0.30 |
| All | 79% (73%–83%) | 77% (72%–81%) | |
| Some but not all | 8% (5%–11%) | 5% (3%–8%) | |
| None | 9% (6%–14%) | 14% (10%–18%) | |
| Not sure | 4% (2%–7%) | 4% (2%–7%) | |
| Gender | | | 0.17 |
| All men | 74% (69%–80%) | 81% (76%–86%) | |
| All women | 14% (9%–19%) | 9% (6%–13%) | |

| | High-Risk Installations | Non–High-Risk Installations | *p*-Value for Difference |
|---|---|---|---|
| Mix of men and women | 8% (5%–12%) | 8% (4%–12%) | |
| Not sure | 4% (2%–8%) | 2% (1%–4%) | |
| Rank, if at least one in military[a, b] | | | |
| Enlisted/WO | 85% (80%–89%) | 84% (80%–88%) | 0.78 |
| Officer | 16% (12%–22%) | 15% (12%–19%) | 0.70 |
| Not sure | 8% (5%–12%) | 9% (6%–12%) | 0.94 |
| Professional relationship with victim[b, c] | | | |
| Supervisor | 7% (4%–12%) | 14% (7%–24%) | 0.06 |
| Other higher-ranked member of chain of command | 10% (6%–17%) | 14% (8%–24%) | 0.35 |
| Higher-ranked and outside chain of command | 17% (12%–24%) | 23% (15%–32%) | 0.27 |
| Military peer of similar rank | 63% (55%–71%) | 55% (47%–63%) | 0.16 |
| Subordinate or someone you manage | 10% (6%–16%) | 11% (5%–20%) | 0.76 |
| DoD or government civilian working for the military[d] | 7% (3%–12%) | 6% (3%–10%) | 0.69 |
| Contractor[d] | 1% (0%–4%) | 2% (1%–5%) | 0.41 |
| Not sure | 15% (9%–23%) | 15% (10%–21%) | 0.99 |
| Personal relationship to victim[b] | | | |
| Your current or former spouse[e] | 4% (2%–7%) | 4% (2%–7%) | 0.80 |
| Someone you have a child with[e] | 1% (0%–4%) | 2% (1%–4%) | 0.70 |
| Your significant other (boyfriend or girlfriend) who you live with[f] | 2% (1%–5%) | 2% (1%–3%) | 0.70 |
| Your significant other (boyfriend or girlfriend) who you do/did not live with[f] | 6% (4%–9%) | 5% (3%–8%) | 0.64 |
| Friend or acquaintance | 55% (49%–60%) | 51% (46%–56%) | 0.35 |
| Family member | 1% (0%–2%) | 1% (0%–3%) | 0.65 |
| Stranger | 16% (12%–21%) | 15% (12%–19%) | 0.84 |
| None of the above | 26% (21%–31%) | 27% (22%–32%) | 0.74 |

137

| | High-Risk Installations | Non–High-Risk Installations | *p*-Value for Difference |
|---|---|---|---|
| Not sure | 6%<br>(3%–9%) | 5%<br>(3%–8%) | 0.83 |

SOURCE: Authors' calculations using the 2016 and 2018 WGRA.
NOTES: Percentages are made up of only soldiers who were sexually assaulted during the year prior to WGRA administration; 95-percent CIs are shown in parentheses. This table corresponds to Figures 6.2, 6.3, and 6.4.
[a] This question was asked only of respondents who answered "all" or "some, but not all" to the previous question of whether the perpetrators were members of the military, and percentages should be interpreted as the percentage of victims who indicated at least one military perpetrator.
[b] Respondents were instructed to select all that apply.
[c] Includes data from 2018 only.
[d] Combined into "DoD/government civilian(s) working for the military/Contractor(s)" in figures.
[e] Combined into "your current or former spouse or someone you have a child with" in figures.
[f] Combined into "your significant other (boyfriend or girlfriend)" in figures.

### Table C.33. Place and Time of Most Serious Experience, All Sexual Assault Victims by Installation Risk Level

| | High-Risk Installations | Non–High-Risk Installations | *p*-Value for Difference |
|---|---|---|---|
| Assault occurred during any required military activity[a] | 58%<br>(52%–64%) | 53%<br>(48%–59%) | 0.24 |
| Place assault occurred[b] | | | |
| Military installation | 71%<br>(65%–76%) | 67%<br>(62%–71%) | 0.28 |
| TDY/TAD | 21%<br>(17%–27%) | 17%<br>(13%–22%) | 0.16 |
| Deployed to a combat zone[c] | 13%<br>(9%–18%) | 7%<br>(5%–10%) | 0.02 |
| Overseas port visit while deployed[c] | 5%<br>(3%–9%) | 3%<br>(2%–6%) | 0.22 |
| While transitioning between operational theaters[c] | 7%<br>(4%–11%) | 4%<br>(2%–7%) | 0.10 |
| While you were in a delayed entry program (DEP) or delayed training program (DTP)[d] | 4%<br>(2%–7%) | 4%<br>(1%–9%) | 0.94 |
| During basic training[e] | 6%<br>(3%–9%) | 6%<br>(3%–11%) | 0.85 |
| During any other type of military combat training | 10%<br>(7%–15%) | 8%<br>(5%–12%) | 0.38 |
| During Officer Candidate School[e] | 4%<br>(2%–7%) | 4%<br>(2%–7%) | 0.84 |
| During technical, MOS, advanced individual training or professional military education[e] | 8%<br>(5%–11%) | 13%<br>(9%–17%) | 0.06 |
| While at an official military function, either on or off base | 15%<br>(11%–20%) | 19%<br>(15%–24%) | 0.19 |
| Off base | 36%<br>(31%–42%) | 41%<br>(36%–46%) | 0.23 |

| | High-Risk Installations | Non–High-Risk Installations | p-Value for Difference |
|---|---|---|---|
| Time assault occurred[f] | | | |
| At work during duty hours | 41% (36%–47%) | 34% (29%–39%) | 0.05 |
| While out with friends or at a party | 35% (29%–40%) | 38% (33%–43%) | 0.35 |
| On a date | 5% (3%–9%) | 3% (2%–5%) | 0.15 |
| On approved leave | 6% (4%–9%) | 7% (4%–12%) | 0.63 |
| In your or someone else's home or quarters | 35% (30%–41%) | 39% (34%–45%) | 0.24 |
| While being intimate with the person[g] | 7% (4%–13%) | 9% (5%–15%) | 0.53 |
| None of the above | 9% (6%–14%) | 12% (9%–16%) | 0.23 |
| Do not recall | 3% (2%–6%) | 2% (1%–3%) | 0.20 |

SOURCE: Authors' calculations using the 2016 and 2018 WGRA.

NOTE: Percentages are made up of only soldiers who were sexually assaulted during the year prior to WGRA administration; 95-percent CIs are shown in parentheses. Table corresponds to Figures 6.5 and 6.6.

[a] Aggregation of "deployed to a combat zone or transitioning between operational theaters," "basic, officer, or technical training," "while you were on TDY/TAD, at sea, or during field exercises/alerts," "while you were in any other type of military combat training," "while at an official military function (either on or off base)," and "you were at work during duty hours."

[b] Each place is a yes/no question, and multiple places could have "yes" responses.

[c] Combined into "Deployed to a combat zone or transitioning between operational theaters" for Figure 6.5.

[d] Not shown in Figure 4.5 because these assaults occurred prior to accession.

[e] Combined into "Basic, officer, or technical training" for Figure 6.5.

[f] Respondents were instructed to select all that apply.

[g] Includes data for 2016 only.

**Table C.34. Alcohol and Drug Involvement in Most Serious Experience, All Sexual Assault Victims by Installation Risk Level**

|  | High-Risk Installations | Non–High-Risk Installations | p-Value for Difference |
|---|---|---|---|
| Victim was drinking alcohol |  |  | 0.04 |
| Yes | 37% (32%–43%) | 42% (37%–48%) |  |
| No | 59% (53%–65%) | 56% (51%–62%) |  |
| Not sure | 4% (2%–8%) | 1% (0%–3%) |  |
| Perpetrator bought or gave victim alcohol |  |  | 0.67 |
| Yes | 25% (20%–31%) | 26% (22%–31%) |  |
| No | 73% (67%–78%) | 71% (66%–76%) |  |
| Not sure | 2% (1%–4%) | 3% (2%–6%) |  |
| Perpetrator was drinking alcohol |  |  | 0.36 |
| Yes | 40% (34%–46%) | 44% (38%–49%) |  |
| No | 39% (33%–45%) | 39% (34%–45%) |  |
| Not sure | 21% (17%–27%) | 17% (14%–21%) |  |
| Victim was drugged without their knowledge or consent |  |  | 0.78 |
| Yes | 7% (4%–11%) | 6% (4%–9%) |  |
| No | 80% (75%–85%) | 80% (75%–84%) |  |
| Not sure | 12% (9%–17%) | 14% (10%–19%) |  |

SOURCE: Authors' calculations using the 2016 and 2018 WGRA.
NOTE: Percentages are made up of only soldiers who were sexually assaulted during the year prior to WGRA administration; 95-percent CIs are shown in parentheses. This table corresponds to Figure 6.7, which presents percentages for "Yes" responses to each question.

**Table C.35. Bullying, Hazing, Sexual Harassment, and Stalking During Most Serious Experience, All Sexual Assault Victims by Installation Risk Level**

|  | High-Risk Installations | Non–High-Risk Installations | *p*-Value of Difference |
|---|---|---|---|
| Victim would describe assault as hazing[a] | 19% (13%–27%) | 14% (7%–23%) | 0.29 |
| Victim would describe assault as bullying[a] | 25% (19%–33%) | 22% (15%–30%) | 0.54 |
| Victim was sexually harassed before assault by same perpetrator(s) | 49% (43%–55%) | 42% (37%–48%) | 0.10 |
| Victim was sexually harassed after assault by same perpetrator(s) | 44% (38%–50%) | 38% (33%–44%) | 0.16 |
| Victim was stalked before assault by same perpetrator(s) | 21% (16%–26%) | 18% (14%–23%) | 0.41 |
| Victim was stalked after assault by same perpetrator(s) | 25% (21%–31%) | 23% (18%–28%) | 0.50 |

SOURCE: Authors' calculations using the 2016 and 2018 WGRA.

NOTES: Percentages are made up of only soldiers who were sexually assaulted during the year prior to WGRA administration; 95-percent CIs are shown in parentheses. This table corresponds to Figure 6.8.

[a] Bullying and hazing use only 2018 data because of changes in definition across the two survey years; see Table 2.3.

# Appendix D. Tabular Results by Gender and Survey Year

In Tables D.1–D.7, we provide results organized by gender and survey year.

**Table D.1. Types of Sexual Assault Behaviors from Screener Questions, All Sexual Assault Victims by Gender and WGRA Survey Year**

| | Female Victims | | | Male Victims | | |
|---|---|---|---|---|---|---|
| | 2016 | 2018 | *p*-Value for Difference | 2016 | 2018 | *p*-Value for Difference |
| Put their penis in your anus, mouth, or vagina | 41% (35%–47%) | 39% (34%–44%) | 0.60 | 27% (19%–37%) | 22% (14%–33%) | 0.43 |
| Put any object or any body part other than a penis into your anus, mouth, or vagina | 27% (22%–33%) | 26% (22%–31%) | 0.78 | 19% (12%–27%) | 21% (13%–31%) | 0.69 |
| Made you put any part of your body or any object into someone's mouth, vagina, or anus | 9% (5%–13%) | 8% (5%–11%) | 0.68 | 24% (16%–33%) | 19% (11%–30%) | 0.48 |
| Intentionally touched private areas of your body | 85% (80%–89%) | 86% (81%–89%) | 0.84 | 89% (82%–94%) | 77% (66%–86%) | 0.02 |
| Made you touch private areas of their body or someone else's body | 31% (26%–37%) | 29% (25%–35%) | 0.59 | 26% (18%–35%) | 28% (19%–39%) | 0.77 |
| Attempted to put a penis, an object, or any body part into your anus, mouth, or vagina, but no penetration actually occurred | 31% (26%–37%) | 22% (18%–27%) | 0.02 | 15% (9%–23%) | 13% (6%–22%) | 0.66 |

SOURCE: Authors' calculations using the 2016 and 2018 WGRA.
NOTE: Percentages are made up of only soldiers who were sexually assaulted during the year prior to WGRA administration; 95-percent CIs are shown in parentheses.

**Table D.2. Perpetrator Intent and Type of Coercion from Screener Questions, All Sexual Assault Victims by Gender and WGRA Survey Year**

| | Female Victims | | | Male Victims | | |
|---|---|---|---|---|---|---|
| | **2016** | **2018** | **_p_-Value for Difference** | **2016** | **2018** | **_p_-Value for Difference** |
| Assaulted more than once | 64% (59%–70%) | 60% (55%–66%) | 0.30 | 68% (58%–77%) | 55% (43%–66%) | 0.08 |
| Perpetrator intent[a] | | | | | | |
| Abusive or humiliating | 51% (43%–58%) | 47% (40%–55%) | 0.54 | 63% (52%–73%) | 55% (42%–68%) | 0.37 |
| Sexual purpose | 97% (95%–99%) | 98% (95%–99%) | 0.76 | 69% (57%–79%) | 79% (66%–89%) | 0.17 |
| Type of coercion | | | | | | |
| Threatened or used physical force | 26% (20%–31%) | 21% (17%–25%) | 0.14 | 20% (13%–28%) | 24% (15%–35%) | 0.53 |
| Threatened you or someone else in another way | 25% (20%–30%) | 21% (17%–26%) | 0.32 | 28% (20%–37%) | 26% (18%–37%) | 0.78 |
| You were unconscious, asleep, or drunk, high, or drugged | 43% (37%–49%) | 41% (35%–46%) | 0.48 | 30% (21%–39%) | 35% (25%–47%) | 0.42 |
| It happened without your consent | 89% (85%–93%) | 92% (88%–94%) | 0.32 | 94% (88%–97%) | 90% (81%–96%) | 0.31 |

SOURCE: Authors' calculations using the 2016 and 2018 WGRA.
NOTES: Percentages are made up of only soldiers who were sexually assaulted during the year prior to WGRA administration and are for the behavior on which the respondent qualified as having been sexually assaulted; 95-percent CIs are shown in parentheses.
[a] Perpetrator intent questions were not asked of respondents who qualified as having been sexually assaulted under the first sexual assault behavior (someone put his penis into the victim's anus, mouth, or vagina) because the UCMJ does not require abusive, humiliating, or sexual intent for this behavior to qualify as rape or sexual assault. These percentages, therefore, have the denominator as individuals who qualified as having been sexually assaulted on one of the other behaviors. See Chapter 2 for further details.

**Table D.3. Types of Sexual Assault Behaviors During Most Serious Experience, All Sexual Assault Victims by Gender and WGRA Survey Year**

| | Female Victims | | | Male Victims | | |
|---|---|---|---|---|---|---|
| | **2016** | **2018** | **_p_-Value for Difference** | **2016** | **2018** | **_p_-Value for Difference** |
| Put his penis in your anus, mouth, or vagina | 40% (35%–46%) | 38% (33%–43%) | 0.48 | 26% (18%–35%) | 22% (14%–33%) | 0.57 |
| Put any object or any body part other than a penis into your anus, mouth, or vagina | 21% (16%–27%) | 22% (17%–26%) | 0.93 | 19% (12%–27%) | 16% (9%–26%) | 0.65 |
| Made you put any body part or object into someone's mouth, vagina, or anus | 7% (4%–11%) | 6% (4%–9%) | 0.63 | 23% (16%–32%) | 19% (11%–30%) | 0.53 |

| | Female Victims | | | Male Victims | | |
|---|---|---|---|---|---|---|
| | 2016 | 2018 | *p*-Value for Difference | 2016 | 2018 | *p*-Value for Difference |
| Intentionally touched private areas of your body | 79% (74%–84%) | 80% (76%–84%) | 0.72 | 86% (79%–92%) | 75% (63%–84%) | 0.04 |
| Made you touch private areas of their or someone else's body | 27% (22%–33%) | 24% (20%–29%) | 0.44 | 25% (17%–34%) | 26% (17%–37%) | 0.81 |
| Attempted to put a penis, object, or any body part into your anus, mouth, or vagina, but no penetration occurred | 26% (20%–31%) | 19% (15%–24%) | 0.06 | 14% (8%–22%) | 11% (5%–20%) | 0.50 |

SOURCE: Authors' calculations using the 2016 and 2018 WGRA.
NOTE: Percentages are made up of only soldiers who were sexually assaulted during the year prior to WGRA administration; 95-percent CIs are shown in parentheses. Respondents were instructed to select all that apply.

### Table D.4. Perpetrator Characteristics for Most Serious Experience, All Sexual Assault Victims by Gender and WGRA Survey Year

| | Female Victims | | | Male Victims | | |
|---|---|---|---|---|---|---|
| | 2016 | 2018 | *p*-Value for Difference | 2016 | 2018 | *p*-Value for Difference |
| Number of perpetrators | | | 1.00 | | | 0.37 |
| One | 68% (62%–73%) | 68% (62%–73%) | | 62% (52%–72%) | 52% (40%–63%) | |
| More than one | 30% (25%–36%) | 30% (25%–36%) | | 32% (23%–43%) | 42% (31%–54%) | |
| Not sure | 2% (1%–4%) | 2% (1%–4%) | | 5% (2%–11%) | 6% (2%–14%) | |
| In the military? | | | 0.49 | | | 0.65 |
| All | 87% (83%–91%) | 85% (80%–88%) | | 70% (60%–78%) | 62% (50%–73%) | |
| Some but not all | 5% (3%–9%) | 5% (3%–8%) | | 7% (3%–14%) | 10% (5%–18%) | |
| None | 6% (4%–9%) | 8% (5%–11%) | | 17% (11%–25%) | 19% (11%–30%) | |
| Not sure | 1% (0%–3%) | 3% (1%–5%) | | 6% (3%–13%) | 9% (4%–17%) | |
| Gender | | | 0.08 | | | 0.62 |
| All men | 96% (93%–98%) | 93% (89%–95%) | | 58% (49%–68%) | 49% (38%–61%) | |
| All women | 1% (0%–2%) | 1% (0%–3%) | | 25% (17%–34%) | 28% (19%–39%) | |
| Mix of men and women | 3% (1%–6%) | 5% (2%–8%) | | 11% (6%–18%) | 16% (8%–27%) | |
| Not sure | 0% (0%–1%) | 2% (0%–4%) | | 6% (2%–12%) | 7% (2%–16%) | |

144

| | **Female Victims** | | | **Male Victims** | | |
|---|---|---|---|---|---|---|
| | **2016** | **2018** | **_p_-Value for Difference** | **2016** | **2018** | **_p_-Value for Difference** |
| Rank, if at least one in military[a, b] | | | | | | |
|   Enlisted/WO | 89% (85%–92%) | 84% (80%–88%) | 0.08 | 82% (72%–89%) | 81% (68%–89%) | 0.82 |
|   Officer | 9% (6%–12%) | 16% (13%–21%) | 0.00 | 22% (12%–34%) | 20% (12%–32%) | 0.87 |
|   Not sure | 7% (4%–11%) | 9% (6%–13%) | 0.36 | 10% (5%–18%) | 7% (2%–17%) | 0.46 |
| Professional relationship with victim[b, c] | | | | | | |
|   Supervisor | 14% (9%–19%) | 10% (6%–14%) | 0.22 | 15% (9%–24%) | 11% (4%–24%) | 0.54 |
|   Other higher-ranked member of chain of command | 18% (13%–24%) | 11% (7%–16%) | 0.04 | 22% (14%–31%) | 14% (6%–27%) | 0.28 |
|   Higher-ranked and outside chain of command | 29% (23%–35%) | 18% (14%–22%) | 0.00 | 23% (15%–33%) | 23% (13%–36%) | 0.98 |
|   Military peer of similar rank | N/A | 63% (57%–68%) | N/A | N/A | 54% (42%–66%) | N/A |
|   Subordinate or someone you manage | 21% (16%–27%) | 7% (4%–10%) | < 0.0001 | 27% (18%–38%) | 17% (8%–29%) | 0.16 |
|   DoD or government civilian working for the military[d] | 3% (1%–5%) | 5% (3%–9%) | 0.05 | 3% (1%–8%) | 7% (3%–16%) | 0.16 |
|   Contractor[d] | 1% (0%–2%) | 1% (0%–3%) | 0.36 | 5% (2%–10%) | 3% (1%–9%) | 0.45 |
|   Not sure | 35% (29%–42%) | 12% (9%–16%) | < 0.0001 | 38% (28%–49%) | 20% (11%–32%) | 0.02 |
| Personal relationship to victim[b] | | | | | | |
|   Your current or former spouse[e] | 7% (4%–12%) | 3% (1%–5%) | 0.02 | 4% (1%–10%) | 0% (0%–4%) | 0.00 |
|   Someone you have a child with[e] | 3% (1%–8%) | 1% (0%–2%) | 0.08 | 2% (0%–6%) | 0% (0%–4%) | 0.05 |
|   Your significant other (boyfriend or girlfriend) who you live with[f] | 2% (1%–7%) | 2% (1%–3%) | 0.50 | 3% (1%–7%) | 0% (0%–4%) | 0.02 |
|   Your significant other (boyfriend or girlfriend) who you do/did not live with[f] | 7% (4%–12%) | 6% (3%–9%) | 0.46 | 6% (2%–12%) | 2% (0%–8%) | 0.20 |
|   Friend or acquaintance | 55% (49%–61%) | 60% (54%–66%) | 0.17 | 45% (35%–56%) | 47% (35%–59%) | 0.83 |
|   Family member | 1% (0%–4%) | 1% (0%–3%) | 0.69 | 1% (0%–5%) | 0% (0%–4%) | 0.22 |
|   Stranger | 16% (12%–21%) | 15% (11%–19%) | 0.67 | 16% (10%–24%) | 17% (9%–26%) | 0.90 |

| | Female Victims | | | Male Victims | | |
|---|---|---|---|---|---|---|
| | 2016 | 2018 | *p*-Value for Difference | 2016 | 2018 | *p*-Value for Difference |
| None of the above | 22% (17%–26%) | 24% (19%–29%) | 0.51 | 31% (22%–40%) | 34% (24%–47%) | 0.58 |
| Not sure | 3% (1%–7%) | 3% (1%–5%) | 0.66 | 9% (5%–16%) | 8% (4%–16%) | 0.79 |

SOURCE: Authors' calculations using the 2016 and 2018 WGRA.
NOTES: Percentages are made up of only soldiers who were sexually assaulted during the year prior to WGRA administration; 95-percent CIs are shown in parentheses. N/A = not applicable. WO = warrant officer.
[a] This question was asked only of respondents who answered "all" or "some, but not all" to the previous question of whether the perpetrators were members of the military, and percentages should be interpreted as the percentage of victims who indicated at least one military perpetrator.
[b] Respondents were instructed to select all that apply.
[c] "Military peer of similar rank" was not an available answer choice in 2016. We therefore do not use 2016 data in other analyses using this question.
[d] Combined into "DoD/government civilian(s) working for the military/Contractor(s)" in figures.
[e] Combined into "your current or former spouse or someone you have a child with" in figures.
[f] Combined into "your significant other (boyfriend or girlfriend)" in figures.

### Table D.5. Place and Time of Most Serious Experience, All Sexual Assault Victims by Gender and WGRA Survey Year

| | Female Victims | | | Male Victims | | |
|---|---|---|---|---|---|---|
| | 2016 | 2018 | *p*-Value for Difference | 2016 | 2018 | *p*-Value for Difference |
| Assault occurred during any required military activity[a] | 52% (46%–58%) | 47% (42%–53%) | 0.24 | 64% (54%–73%) | 65% (53%–76%) | 0.91 |
| Place assault occurred[b] | | | | | | |
| Military installation | 73% (67%–78%) | 66% (60%–71%) | 0.07 | 73% (63%–81%) | 62% (50%–73%) | 0.11 |
| TDY/TAD | 13% (9%–17%) | 14% (10%–18%) | 0.64 | 24% (16%–33%) | 33% (22%–45%) | 0.20 |
| Deployed to a combat zone[c] | 6% (4%–9%) | 11% (8%–14%) | 0.04 | 13% (6%–23%) | 12% (7%–21%) | 0.87 |
| Overseas port visit while deployed[c] | 1% (0%–2%) | 2% (1%–4%) | 0.15 | 8% (3%–14%) | 9% (4%–18%) | 0.69 |
| While transitioning between operational theaters[c] | 4% (1%–9%) | 4% (2%–7%) | 0.92 | 7% (3%–14%) | 8% (3%–16%) | 0.86 |
| While you were in a delayed entry program (DEP) or delayed training program (DTP)[d] | 1% (0%–5%) | 1% (0%–3%) | 0.99 | 6% (2%–12%) | 10% (3%–22%) | 0.37 |
| During basic training[e] | 5% (3%–8%) | 4% (2%–7%) | 0.47 | 6% (3%–13%) | 9% (2%–22%) | 0.60 |
| During any other type of military combat training | 3% (1%–6%) | 8% (5%–12%) | 0.01 | 11% (6%–19%) | 18% (8%–31%) | 0.26 |

| | Female Victims | | | Male Victims | | |
|---|---|---|---|---|---|---|
| | **2016** | **2018** | ***p*-Value for Difference** | **2016** | **2018** | ***p*-Value for Difference** |
| During Officer Candidate School[e] | 3% (1%–6%) | 4% (2%–6%) | 0.67 | 5% (2%–12%) | 5% (2%–13%) | 0.91 |
| During technical, MOS, advanced individual training or professional military education[e] | 10% (6%–14%) | 9% (6%–13%) | 0.86 | 9% (4%–17%) | 14% (6%–26%) | 0.39 |
| While at an official military function, either on or off base | 12% (9%–17%) | 13% (9%–18%) | 0.76 | 26% (18%–36%) | 20% (11%–32%) | 0.37 |
| Off base | 39% (33%–45%) | 41% (35%–46%) | 0.62 | 35% (26%–45%) | 39% (29%–51%) | 0.58 |
| Time assault occurred[f] | | | | | | |
| At work during duty hours | 30% (24%–36%) | 29% (24%–35%) | 0.91 | 50% (39%–60%) | 50% (38%–61%) | 0.98 |
| While out with friends or at a party | 40% (34%–46%) | 39% (34%–45%) | 0.90 | 32% (23%–42%) | 32% (22%–43%) | 0.97 |
| On a date | 5% (2%–8%) | 5% (3%–7%) | 0.98 | 6% (2%–13%) | 1% (0%–6%) | 0.07 |
| On approved leave | 5% (3%–9%) | 6% (4%–9%) | 0.70 | 9% (4%–16%) | 7% (2%–20%) | 0.79 |
| In your or someone else's home or quarters | 45% (39%–51%) | 44% (38%–49%) | 0.76 | 23% (15%–33%) | 32% (22%–44%) | 0.18 |
| While being intimate with the person[g] | 8% (5%–11%) | N/A | N/A | 10% (4%–18%) | N/A | N/A |
| None of the above | 12% (8%–16%) | 13% (9%–17%) | 0.77 | 7% (4%–13%) | 10% (4%–21%) | 0.49 |
| Do not recall | 2% (1%–3%) | 2% (1%–4%) | 0.83 | 5% (2%–10%) | 2% (0%–7%) | 0.19 |

SOURCE: Authors' calculations using the 2016 and 2018 WGRA.
NOTES: Percentages are made up of only soldiers who were sexually assaulted during the year prior to WGRA administration; 95-percent CIs are shown in parentheses. MOS = military occupational specialty. N/A = not applicable.
[a] Aggregation of "deployed to a combat zone or transitioning between operational theaters," "basic, officer, or technical training," "while you were on TDY/TAD, at sea, or during field exercises/alerts," "while you were in any other type of military combat training," "while at an official military function (either on or off base)," and "you were at work during duty hours."
[b] Each place is a yes/no question, and multiple places could have "yes" responses.
[c] Combined into "Deployed to a combat zone or transitioning between operational theaters" for figures.
[d] Not shown in figures because these assaults occurred prior to accession.
[e] Combined into "Basic, officer, or technical training" for figures.
[f] Respondents were instructed to select all that apply.
[g] Available in 2016 only.

147

**Table D.6. Alcohol and Drug Involvement in Most Serious Experience, All Sexual Assault Victims by Gender and WGRA Survey Year**

| | Female Victims | | | Male Victims | | |
|---|---|---|---|---|---|---|
| | 2016 | 2018 | *p*-Value for Difference | 2016 | 2018 | *p*-Value for Difference |
| Victim was drinking alcohol | | | 0.02 | | | 0.98 |
| Yes | 46% (40%–52%) | 42% (36%–47%) | | 34% (24%–44%) | 35% (24%–47%) | |
| No | 54% (48%–60%) | 57% (51%–62%) | | 61% (51%–71%) | 60% (48%–71%) | |
| Not sure | 0% (0%–1%) | 2% (1%–4%) | | 5% (2%–11%) | 5% (1%–13%) | |
| Perpetrator bought or gave victim alcohol | | | 0.9 | | | 0.75 |
| Yes | 27% (22%–33%) | 29% (24%–34%) | | 24% (15%–34%) | 20% (11%–32%) | |
| No | 69% (63%–75%) | 67% (62%–73%) | | 75% (64%–83%) | 79% (67%–88%) | |
| Not sure | 3% (1%–7%) | 4% (2%–6%) | | 2% (0%–6%) | 1% (0%–5%) | |
| Perpetrator was drinking alcohol | | | 0.17 | | | 0.16 |
| Yes | 48% (41%–54%) | 52% (46%–57%) | | 27% (18%–36%) | 35% (24%–47%) | |
| No | 39% (33%–45%) | 32% (27%–38%) | | 50% (40%–61%) | 36% (25%–48%) | |
| Not sure | 13% (9%–18%) | 16% (13%–21%) | | 23% (15%–32%) | 29% (20%–40%) | |
| Victim was drugged without their knowledge or consent | | | 0.34 | | | 0.32 |
| Yes | 7% (4%–12%) | 4% (2%–7%) | | 7% (3%–14%) | 9% (3%–18%) | |
| No | 78% (72%–83%) | 82% (77%–86%) | | 84% (76%–91%) | 75% (63%–86%) | |
| Not sure | 14% (10%–20%) | 14% (10%–18%) | | 9% (4%–15%) | 16% (7%–28%) | |

SOURCE: Authors' calculations using the 2016 and 2018 WGRA.
NOTE: Percentages are made up of only soldiers who were sexually assaulted during the year prior to WGRA administration; 95-percent CIs are shown in parentheses.

**Table D.7. Bullying, Hazing, Sexual Harassment, and Stalking During Most Serious Experience, All Sexual Assault Victims by Gender and WGRA Survey Year**

| | Female Victims | | | Male Victims | | |
|---|---|---|---|---|---|---|
| | **2016** | **2018** | ***p*-Value of Difference** | **2016** | **2018** | ***p*-Value of Difference** |
| Victim would describe assault as hazing[a] | 11% (7%–16%) | 9% (6%–13%) | 0.45 | 27% (19%–37%) | 29% (18%–41%) | 0.82 |
| Victim would describe assault as bullying[a] | 28% (22%–34%) | 20% (15%–25%) | 0.03 | 47% (37%–58%) | 30% (20%–42%) | 0.02 |
| Victim was sexually harassed before assault by same perpetrator(s) | 45% (39%–51%) | 44% (38%–50%) | 0.85 | 48% (38%–59%) | 46% (34%–58%) | 0.75 |
| Victim was sexually harassed after assault by same perpetrator(s) | 41% (35%–47%) | 39% (34%–45%) | 0.66 | 44% (34%–55%) | 41% (30%–53%) | 0.65 |
| Victim was stalked before assault by same perpetrator(s) | 19% (14%–25%) | 17% (13%–21%) | 0.46 | 21% (14%–30%) | 21% (12%–33%) | 0.98 |
| Victim was stalked after assault by same perpetrator(s) | 24% (19%–30%) | 24% (19%–29%) | 0.98 | 26% (18%–36%) | 23% (13%–35%) | 0.62 |

SOURCE: Authors' calculations using the 2016 and 2018 WGRA.
NOTES: Percentages are made up of only soldiers who were sexually assaulted during the year prior to WGRA administration; 95-percent CIs are shown in parentheses.
[a] Bullying and hazing use only 2018 data because of changes in definition across the two survey years; see Table 2.3.

# Appendix E. Tabular Results by Gender and Installation Risk Level

In Tables E.1–E.7, we provide results organized by gender and installation risk level.

**Table E.1. Types of Sexual Assault Behaviors from Screener Questions, All Sexual Assault Victims by Gender and Installation Risk Level**

| | Female Victims | | | Male Victims | | |
|---|---|---|---|---|---|---|
| | High-Risk Installations | Non–High-Risk Installations | p-Value for Difference | High-Risk Installations | Non–High-Risk Installations | p-Value for Difference |
| Put their penis in your anus, mouth, or vagina | 43% (37%–49%) | 38% (33%–43%) | 0.22 | 23% (16%–32%) | 28% (18%–39%) | 0.47 |
| Put any object or any body part other than a penis into your anus, mouth, or vagina | 27% (22%–33%) | 27% (22%–32%) | 0.84 | 21% (14%–29%) | 18% (10%–28%) | 0.65 |
| Made you put any part of your body or any object into someone's mouth, vagina, or anus | 10% (7%–15%) | 6% (4%–10%) | 0.09 | 26% (17%–35%) | 15% (9%–25%) | 0.08 |
| Intentionally touched private areas of your body | 87% (83%–91%) | 84% (80%–87%) | 0.19 | 85% (77%–92%) | 81% (71%–89%) | 0.45 |
| Made you touch private areas of their body or someone else's body | 35% (29%–41%) | 27% (22%–32%) | 0.05 | 27% (19%–36%) | 26% (17%–37%) | 0.89 |
| Attempted to put a penis, an object, or any body part into your anus, mouth, or vagina, but no penetration actually occurred | 28% (22%–34%) | 26% (21%–31%) | 0.60 | 14% (8%–22%) | 13% (7%–22%) | 0.82 |

SOURCE: Authors' calculations using the 2016 and 2018 WGRA.
NOTE: Percentages are made up of only soldiers who were sexually assaulted during the year prior to WGRA administration; 95-percent CIs are shown in parentheses.

**Table E.2. Perpetrator Intent and Type of Coercion from Screener Questions, All Sexual Assault Victims by Gender and Installation Risk Level**

| | Female Victims | | | Male Victims | | |
|---|---|---|---|---|---|---|
| | High-Risk Installations | Non–High-Risk Installations | p-Value for Difference | High-Risk Installations | Non–High-Risk Installations | p-Value for Difference |
| Assaulted more than once | 67% (62%–73%) | 58% (53%–64%) | 0.02 | 68% (58%–78%) | 52% (40%–63%) | 0.03 |
| Perpetrator intent[a] | | | | | | |
|   Abusive or humiliating | 52% (44%–60%) | 47% (40%–54%) | 0.38 | 60% (49%–70%) | 57% (44%–70%) | 0.74 |
|   Sexual purpose | 99% (96%–100%) | 97% (94%–99%) | 0.28 | 77% (66%–86%) | 69% (54%–81%) | 0.29 |
| Type of coercion | | | | | | |
|   Threatened or used physical force | 27% (21%–33%) | 20% (16%–25%) | 0.08 | 24% (17%–33%) | 18% (10%–28%) | 0.29 |
|   Threatened you or someone else in another way | 27% (21%–33%) | 20% (16%–25%) | 0.06 | 28% (21%–37%) | 26% (17%–36%) | 0.68 |
|   You were unconscious, asleep, or drunk, high, or drugged | 42% (36%–48%) | 42% (37%–47%) | 0.99 | 35% (26%–45%) | 28% (18%–39%) | 0.29 |
|   It happened without your consent | 91% (86%–94%) | 91% (87%–93%) | 0.98 | 90% (82%–95%) | 96% (90%–99%) | 0.08 |

SOURCE: Authors' calculations using the 2016 and 2018 WGRA.
NOTES: Percentages are made up of only soldiers who were sexually assaulted during the year prior to WGRA administration and are for the behavior on which the respondent qualified as having been sexually assaulted; 95-percent CIs are shown in parentheses.
[a] Perpetrator intent questions were not asked of respondents who qualified as having been sexually assaulted under the first sexual assault behavior (someone put his penis into the victim's anus, mouth, or vagina) because the UCMJ does not require abusive, humiliating, or sexual intent for this behavior to qualify as rape or sexual assault. These percentages, therefore, have the denominator as individuals who qualified as having been sexually assaulted on one of the other behaviors. See Chapter 2 for further details.

151

**Table E.3. Types of Sexual Assault Behaviors During Most Serious Experience, All Sexual Assault Victims by Gender and Installation Risk Level**

| | Female Victims | | | Male Victims | | |
|---|---|---|---|---|---|---|
| | High-Risk Installations | Non–High-Risk Installations | p-Value for Difference | High-Risk Installations | Non–High-Risk Installations | p-Value for Difference |
| Put their penis in your anus, mouth, or vagina | 41% (35%–47%) | 38% (32%–43%) | 0.38 | 22% (15%–31%) | 28% (18%–39%) | 0.35 |
| Put any object or any body part other than a penis into your anus, mouth, or vagina | 21% (16%–27%) | 22% (17%–27%) | 0.87 | 18% (12%–27%) | 16% (9%–26%) | 0.72 |
| Made you put any part of your body or any object into someone's mouth, vagina, or anus | 8% (5%–13%) | 5% (3%–8%) | 0.20 | 25% (17%–35%) | 15% (9%–25%) | 0.10 |
| Intentionally touched private areas of your body | 80% (75%–85%) | 79% (75%–83%) | 0.74 | 82% (73%–89%) | 78% (68%–87%) | 0.50 |
| Made you touch private areas of their body or someone else's body | 28% (22%–33%) | 24% (20%–29%) | 0.35 | 26% (18%–35%) | 24% (15%–35%) | 0.76 |
| Attempted to put a penis, an object, or any body part into your anus, mouth, or vagina, but no penetration actually occurred | 22% (17%–28%) | 22% (18%–27%) | 0.97 | 13% (7%–21%) | 12% (6%–21%) | 0.85 |

SOURCE: Authors' calculations using the 2016 and 2018 WGRA.
NOTE: Percentages are made up of only soldiers who were sexually assaulted during the year prior to WGRA administration; 95-percent CIs are shown in parentheses. Respondents were instructed to select all that apply.

**Table E.4. Perpetrator Characteristics for Most Serious Experience, All Sexual Assault Victims by Gender and Installation Risk Level**

| | Female Victims | | | Male Victims | | |
|---|---|---|---|---|---|---|
| | High-Risk Installations | Non–High-Risk Installations | p-Value for Difference | High-Risk Installations | Non–High-Risk Installations | p-Value for Difference |
| Number of perpetrators | | | 0.24 | | | 0.05 |
| One | 65% (58%–71%) | 70% (64%–75%) | | 51% (42%–61%) | 67% (54%–78%) | |
| More than one | 34% (28%–40%) | 28% (23%–33%) | | 41% (31%–51%) | 31% (20%–43%) | |
| Not sure | 2% (0%–4%) | 2% (1%–5%) | | 8% (4%–14%) | 2% (0%–8%) | |
| In the military? | | | 0.08 | | | 0.35 |
| All | 89% (84%–92%) | 84% (80%–87%) | | 68% (59%–77%) | 63% (52%–73%) | |
| Some but not all | 5% | 5% | | 10% | 5% | |

| | Female Victims | | | Male Victims | | |
|---|---|---|---|---|---|---|
| | **High-Risk Installations** | **Non–High-Risk Installations** | *p*-Value for **Difference** | **High-Risk Installations** | **Non–High-Risk Installations** | *p*-Value for **Difference** |
| | (3%–9%) | (3%–8%) | | (5%–17%) | (2%–12%) | |
| None | 4%<br>(2%–7%) | 9%<br>(7%–12%) | | 15%<br>(9%–23%) | 23%<br>(14%–33%) | |
| Not sure | 2%<br>(1%–4%) | 2%<br>(1%–4%) | | 7%<br>(3%–13%) | 9%<br>(4%–18%) | |
| Gender | | | 0.62 | | | 0.62 |
| All men | 94%<br>(91%–97%) | 94%<br>(91%–96%) | | 54%<br>(44%–64%) | 54%<br>(43%–66%) | |
| All women | 1%<br>(0%–3%) | 1%<br>(0%–2%) | | 26%<br>(18%–35%) | 27%<br>(18%–37%) | |
| Mix of men and women | 4%<br>(2%–7%) | 4%<br>(2%–6%) | | 12%<br>(7%–19%) | 15%<br>(7%–28%) | |
| Not sure | 0%<br>(0%–2%) | 1%<br>(0%–3%) | | 8%<br>(4%–15%) | 4%<br>(1%–11%) | |
| Rank, if at least one in military[a, b] | | | | | | |
| Enlisted/WO | 88%<br>(83%–91%) | 85%<br>(81%–89%) | 0.29 | 81%<br>(72%–88%) | 82%<br>(69%–91%) | 0.96 |
| Officer | 13%<br>(9%–17%) | 12%<br>(9%–16%) | 0.85 | 20%<br>(12%–31%) | 22%<br>(12%–35%) | 0.79 |
| Not sure | 8%<br>(5%–12%) | 8%<br>(5%–12%) | 0.95 | 9%<br>(4%–16%) | 9%<br>(3%–20%) | 0.90 |
| Professional relationship with victim[b, c] | | | | | | |
| Supervisor | 7%<br>(3%–12%) | 12%<br>(6%–21%) | 0.16 | 7%<br>(2%–18%) | S<br>(4%–48%) | 0.15 |
| Other higher-ranked member of chain of command | 9%<br>(5%–17%) | 12%<br>(8%–19%) | 0.46 | 11%<br>(4%–24%) | S<br>(4%–48%) | 0.44 |
| Higher-ranked and outside chain of command | 16%<br>(11%–23%) | 19%<br>(13%–26%) | 0.45 | 19%<br>(9%–33%) | S<br>(12%–55%) | 0.29 |
| Military peer of similar rank | 72%<br>(64%–79%) | 54%<br>(46%–62%) | 0.00 | S<br>(36%–67%) | S<br>(38%–76%) | 0.58 |
| Subordinate or someone you manage | 6%<br>(3%–11%) | 7%<br>(4%–12%) | 0.69 | 15%<br>(6%–27%) | S<br>(5%–48%) | 0.58 |
| DoD or government civilian working for the military[d] | 5%<br>(2%–10%) | 6%<br>(3%–11%) | 0.50 | 9%<br>(3%–22%) | 4%<br>(0%–16%) | 0.31 |
| Contractor[d] | 1%<br>(0%–4%) | 1%<br>(0%–4%) | 0.61 | 2%<br>(0%–10%) | 5%<br>(0%–17%) | 0.36 |

153

| | Female Victims | | | Male Victims | | |
|---|---|---|---|---|---|---|
| | High-Risk Installations | Non–High-Risk Installations | *p*-Value for Difference | High-Risk Installations | Non–High-Risk Installations | *p*-Value for Difference |
| Not sure | 9% (5%–14%) | 15% (10%–21%) | 0.07 | S (11%–40%) | S (5%–31%) | 0.35 |
| Personal relationship to victim[b] | | | | | | |
| Your current or former spouse[e] | 6% (3%–11%) | 4% (2%–7%) | 0.28 | 1% (0%–5%) | 4% (1%–13%) | 0.05 |
| Someone you have a child with[e] | 2% (0%–8%) | 2% (0%–5%) | 0.68 | 0% (0%–3%) | 2% (0%–8%) | 0.09 |
| Your significant other (boyfriend or girlfriend) who you live with[f] | 3% (1%–8%) | 1% (0%–3%) | 0.20 | 1% (0%–5%) | 2% (0%–8%) | 0.42 |
| Your significant other (boyfriend or girlfriend) who you do/did not live with[f] | 9% (5%–13%) | 5% (3%–8%) | 0.10 | 3% (1%–8%) | 6% (2%–14%) | 0.37 |
| Friend or acquaintance | 58% (51%–64%) | 57% (52%–63%) | 0.88 | 51% (41%–61%) | 38% (28%–50%) | 0.08 |
| Family member | 1% (0%–3%) | 1% (0%–3%) | 0.87 | 0% (0%–3%) | 1% (0%–6%) | 0.40 |
| Stranger | 16% (12%–22%) | 14% (11%–19%) | 0.51 | 15% (9%–24%) | 17% (10%–27%) | 0.73 |
| None of the above | 22% (18%–28%) | 23% (18%–28%) | 0.89 | 30% (21%–39%) | 36% (25%–48%) | 0.39 |
| Not sure | 3% (1%–6%) | 3% (2%–6%) | 0.67 | 9% (4%–15%) | 9% (4%–17%) | 0.93 |

SOURCE: Authors' calculations using the 2016 and 2018 WGRA.
NOTES: Percentages are made up of only soldiers who were sexually assaulted during the year prior to WGRA administration; 95-percent CIs are shown in parentheses. S = suppressed
[a] This question was asked only of respondents who answered "all" or "some, but not all" to the previous question of whether the perpetrators were members of the military, and percentages should be interpreted as the percentage of victims who indicated at least one military perpetrator.
[b] Respondents were instructed to select all that apply.
[c] Includes data from 2018 only.
[d] Combined into "DoD/government civilian(s) working for the military/Contractor(s)" in figures.
[e] Combined into "your current or former spouse or someone you have a child with" in figures.
[f] Combined into "your significant other (boyfriend or girlfriend)" in figures.

**Table E.5. Place and Time of Most Serious Experience, All Sexual Assault Victims by Gender and Installation Risk Level**

| | Female Victims | | | Male Victims | | |
|---|---|---|---|---|---|---|
| | High-Risk Installations | Non–High-Risk Installations | p-Value for Difference | High-Risk Installations | Non–High-Risk Installations | p-Value for Difference |
| Assault occurred during any required military activity[a] | 51% (44%–57%) | 49% (43%–54%) | 0.61 | 66% (55%–75%) | 63% (51%–74%) | 0.72 |
| Place assault occurred[b] | | | | | | |
| Military installation | 70% (64%–76%) | 69% (63%–74%) | 0.66 | 71% (61%–80%) | 63% (51%–73%) | 0.24 |
| TDY/TAD | 12% (9%–17%) | 14% (11%–18%) | 0.53 | 31% (22%–41%) | 23% (13%–35%) | 0.25 |
| Deployed to a combat zone[c] | 9% (6%–13%) | 8% (5%–11%) | 0.44 | 17% (10%–26%) | 7% (3%–14%) | 0.04 |
| Overseas port visit while deployed[c] | 1% (0%–3%) | 2% (1%–4%) | 0.69 | 10% (5%–17%) | 7% (2%–14%) | 0.46 |
| While transitioning between operational theaters[c] | 5% (2%–10%) | 3% (1%–6%) | 0.27 | 9% (4%–16%) | 6% (2%–13%) | 0.37 |
| While you were in a delayed entry program or delayed training program[d] | 2% (0%–5%) | 1% (0%–3%) | 0.43 | 6% (2%–13%) | 10% (3%–24%) | 0.38 |
| During basic training[e] | 6% (3%–9%) | 4% (2%–6%) | 0.26 | 6% (2%–12%) | 11% (3%–24%) | 0.27 |
| During any other type of military combat training | 5% (3%–9%) | 5% (3%–8%) | 0.99 | 15% (9%–24%) | 13% (5%–26%) | 0.70 |
| During Officer Candidate School[e] | 4% (2%–6%) | 3% (2%–6%) | 0.92 | 5% (2%–12%) | 5% (2%–12%) | 0.97 |
| During technical, MOS, advanced individual training or professional military education[e] | 8% (5%–12%) | 11% (8%–15%) | 0.17 | 8% (3%–15%) | 16% (7%–29%) | 0.13 |
| While at an official military function, either on or off base | 12% (8%–17%) | 13% (10%–17%) | 0.61 | 18% (12%–27%) | 31% (20%–44%) | 0.05 |
| Off base | 38% (32%–45%) | 41% (35%–46%) | 0.59 | 34% (25%–44%) | 42% (31%–54%) | 0.30 |
| Time assault occurred[f] | | | | | | |
| At work during duty hours | 32% (26%–38%) | 28% (23%–33%) | 0.31 | 52% (42%–62%) | 46% (35%–58%) | 0.48 |
| While out with friends or at a party | 41% (34%–47%) | 39% (34%–45%) | 0.73 | 29% (20%–38%) | 37% (26%–48%) | 0.26 |
| On a date | 6% (3%–10%) | 4% (2%–6%) | 0.26 | 5% (2%–11%) | 2% (0%–7%) | 0.27 |

155

| | Female Victims | | | Male Victims | | |
|---|---|---|---|---|---|---|
| | High-Risk Installations | Non–High-Risk Installations | p-Value for Difference | High-Risk Installations | Non–High-Risk Installations | p-Value for Difference |
| On approved leave | 7% (4%–10%) | 5% (3%–8%) | 0.35 | 5% (2%–12%) | 12% (4%–25%) | 0.16 |
| In your or someone else's home or quarters | 44% (38%–50%) | 44% (39%–50%) | 0.89 | 26% (18%–35%) | 29% (18%–42%) | 0.62 |
| While being intimate with the person[g] | 8% (4%–15%) | 7% (4%–12%) | 0.78 | 7% (2%–16%) | S (4%–30%) | 0.24 |
| None of the above | 9% (6%–13%) | 15% (11%–20%) | 0.02 | 10% (4%–19%) | 7% (3%–14%) | 0.45 |
| Do not recall | 2% (1%–4%) | 2% (1%–3%) | 0.95 | 5% (2%–10%) | 2% (0%–7%) | 0.23 |

SOURCE: Authors' calculations using the 2016 and 2018 WGRA.
NOTES: Percentages are made up of only soldiers who were sexually assaulted during the year prior to WGRA administration; 95-percent CIs are shown in parentheses.
[a] Aggregation of "deployed to a combat zone or transitioning between operational theaters," "basic, officer, or technical training," "while you were on TDY/TAD, at sea, or during field exercises/alerts," "while you were in any other type of military combat training," "while at an official military function (either on or off base)," and "you were at work during duty hours."
[b] Each place is a yes/no question, and multiple places could have "yes" responses.
[c] Combined into "Deployed to a combat zone or transitioning between operational theaters" for figures.
[d] Not shown in Figure 4.5 because these assaults occurred prior to accession.
[e] Combined into "Basic, officer, or technical training" for figures.
[f] Respondents were instructed to select all that apply.
[g] Includes data for 2016 only.

**Table E.6. Alcohol and Drug Involvement in Most Serious Experience, All Sexual Assault Victims by Gender and Installation Risk Level**

| | Female Victims | | | Male Victims | | |
|---|---|---|---|---|---|---|
| | High-Risk Installations | Non–High-Risk Installations | p-Value for Difference | High-Risk Installations | Non–High-Risk Installations | p-Value for Difference |
| Victim was drinking alcohol | | | 0.97 | | | 0.14 |
| Yes | 43% (37%–50%) | 44% (38%–49%) | | 31% (22%–41%) | 39% (28%–51%) | |
| No | 56% (49%–62%) | 55% (50%–61%) | | 62% (52%–72%) | 59% (47%–70%) | |
| Not sure | 1% (0%–3%) | 1% (0%–2%) | | 7% (3%–14%) | 2% (0%–7%) | |
| Perpetrator bought or gave victim alcohol | | | 0.93 | | | 0.83 |
| Yes | 28% (23%–34%) | 28% (23%–33%) | | 22% (13%–32%) | 23% (13%–34%) | |
| No | 68% (62%–74%) | 68% (63%–73%) | | 77% (67%–86%) | 76% (64%–85%) | |

| | Female Victims | | | Male Victims | | |
|---|---|---|---|---|---|---|
| | High-Risk Installations | Non–High-Risk Installations | p-Value for Difference | High-Risk Installations | Non–High-Risk Installations | p-Value for Difference |
| Not sure | 3% (1%–6%) | 4% (2%–7%) | | 1% (0%–5%) | 2% (0%–7%) | |
| Perpetrator was drinking alcohol | | | 0.33 | | | 0.46 |
| Yes | 52% (46%–59%) | 48% (42%–53%) | | 27% (18%–37%) | 35% (25%–47%) | |
| No | 32% (26%–38%) | 38% (33%–44%) | | 45% (35%–56%) | 41% (30%–54%) | |
| Not sure | 16% (11%–21%) | 14% (11%–18%) | | 28% (19%–37%) | 23% (15%–33%) | |
| Victim was drugged without their knowledge or consent | | | 0.22 | | | 0.81 |
| Yes | 7% (4%–12%) | 5% (3%–8%) | | 7% (3%–15%) | 9% (4%–18%) | |
| No | 81% (75%–86%) | 79% (74%–84%) | | 80% (70%–87%) | 81% (68%–90%) | |
| Not sure | 12% (8%–16%) | 16% (12%–21%) | | 13% (7%–21%) | 10% (3%–23%) | |

SOURCE: Authors' calculations using the 2016 and 2018 WGRA.
NOTE: Percentages are made up of only soldiers who were sexually assaulted during the year prior to WGRA administration; 95-percent CIs are shown in parentheses.

157

**Table E.7. Bullying, Hazing, Sexual Harassment, and Stalking During Most Serious Experience, All Sexual Assault Victims by Gender and Installation Risk Level**

| | Female Victims | | | Male Victims | | |
|---|---|---|---|---|---|---|
| | High-Risk Installations | Non–High-Risk Installations | *p*-Value of Difference | High-Risk Installations | Non–High-Risk Installations | *p*-Value of Difference |
| Victim would describe assault as hazing[a] | 11% (6%–17%) | 8% (4%–13%) | 0.36 | S (17%–46%) | S (10%–49%) | 0.74 |
| Victim would describe assault as bullying[a] | 22% (15%–30%) | 18% (12%–24%) | 0.35 | S (17%–44%) | S (14%–52%) | 0.88 |
| Victim was sexually harassed before assault by same perpetrator(s) | 48% (41%–54%) | 42% (36%–47%) | 0.17 | 50% (40%–60%) | 43% (31%–55%) | 0.38 |
| Victim was sexually harassed after assault by same perpetrator(s) | 44% (37%–50%) | 38% (32%–43%) | 0.16 | 45% (35%–55%) | 40% (29%–52%) | 0.57 |
| Victim was stalked before assault by same perpetrator(s) | 21% (16%–27%) | 16% (12%–20%) | 0.12 | 20% (13%–29%) | 22% (13%–34%) | 0.73 |
| Victim was stalked after assault by same perpetrator(s) | 27% (21%–33%) | 22% (17%–26%) | 0.14 | 24% (16%–33%) | 26% (16%–38%) | 0.74 |

SOURCE: Authors' calculations using the 2016 and 2018 WGRA.
NOTES: Percentages are made up of only soldiers who were sexually assaulted during the year prior to WGRA administration; 95-percent CIs are shown in parentheses. S = suppressed.
[a] Bullying and hazing use only 2018 data because of changes in definition across the two survey years; see Table 2.3.

# Abbreviations

| | |
|---|---|
| CI | confidence interval |
| DMDC | Defense Manpower Data Center |
| DoD | U.S. Department of Defense |
| LGBO | lesbian, gay, bisexual, or other |
| NR | no response |
| OPA | Office of People Analytics |
| PNA | prefer not to answer |
| S | suppressed |
| TDY | temporary duty |
| UCMJ | Uniform Code of Military Justice |
| WGRA | Workplace and Gender Relations Survey of Active Duty Members |

# References

Breslin, Rachel A., Lisa Davis, Kimberly Hylton, Ariel Hill, William Klauberg, Mark Petusky, and Ashlea Klahr, *2018 Workplace and Gender Relations Survey of Active Duty Members: Overview Report*, Alexandria, Va.: Office of People Analytics, U.S. Department of Defense, OPA Report No. 2019-027, May 2019.

Breslin, Rachel A., Ashlea Klahr, and Adon Neria, *The Continuum of Harm: Examining the Correlates of Sexual Assault Victimization*, Alexandria, Va.: Office of People Analytics, U.S. Department of Defense, September 2020.

Calkins, Avery, Matthew Cefalu, Terry L. Schell, Linda Cottrell, Sarah O. Meadows, and Rebecca L. Collins, *Sexual Harassment and Gender Discrimination in the Active-Component Army: Variation in Most Serious Event Characteristics by Gender and Installation Risk*, Santa Monica, Calif.: RAND Corporation, RR-A1385-1, 2021. As of October 29, 2021: https://www.rand.org/pubs/research_reports/RRA1385-1.html

Clopper, C. J., and E. S. Pearson, "The Use of Confidence or Fiducial Limits Illustrated in the Case of the Binomial," *Biometrika*, Vol. 26, No. 4, 1934, pp. 404–413.

Davis, Lisa, Amanda Grifka, Kristin Williams, and Margaret Coffey, eds., *2016 Workplace and Gender Relations Survey of Active Duty Members: Overview Report*, Alexandria, Va.: Office of People Analytics, OPA Report No. 2016-050, May 2017.

Davis, Lisa, William Klauberg, Natalie Namrow, Mark Petusky, Yvette Claros, Kimberly Hylton, Alisha Creel, and Ashlea Klahr, *2018 Service Academy Gender Relations Survey: Overview Report*, Alexandria, Va.: Office of People Analytics, U.S. Department of Defense, OPA Report No. 2018-075, January 2019.

Department of Defense Instruction 1020.03, *Harassment Prevention and Response in the Armed Forces*, Washington, D.C.: U.S. Department of Defense, incorporating change 1, December 29, 2020.

DoD—*See* U.S. Department of Defense.

Farrell, Brenda S., *Military Personnel: Actions Needed to Address Sexual Assaults of Male Servicemembers*, Washington, D.C.: U.S. Government Accountability Office, GAO-15-284, March 2015.

Farrell, Brenda S., *Sexual Violence: Actions Needed to Improve DOD's Efforts to Address the Continuum of Unwanted Sexual Behaviors*, Washington, D.C.: U.S. Government Accountability Office, GAO-18-33, December 2017.

Hanley, James A., and Abby Lippman-Hand, "If Nothing Goes Wrong, Is Everything All Right? Interpreting Zero Numerators," *JAMA*, Vol. 249, No. 13, 1983, pp. 1743–1745.

Independent Review Commission on Sexual Assault in the Military, *Hard Truths and the Duty to Change: Recommendations from the Independent Review Commission on Sexual Assault in the Military*, Washington, D.C.: U.S. Department of Defense, 2021.

Kish, Leslie, *Survey Sampling*, New York: Wiley, 1965.

Matthews, Miriam, Andrew R. Morral, Terry L. Schell, Matthew Cefalu, Joshua Snoke, and R. J. Briggs, *Organizational Characteristics Associated with Risk of Sexual Assault and Sexual Harassment in the U.S. Army*, Santa Monica, Calif.: RAND Corporation, RR-A1013-1, 2021. As of October 29, 2021:
https://www.rand.org/pubs/research_reports/RRA1013-1.html

Morral, Andrew R., Kristie L. Gore, and Terry L. Schell, eds., *Sexual Assault and Sexual Harassment in the U.S. Military,* Vol. 1, *Design of the 2014 RAND Military Workplace Study*, Santa Monica, Calif.: RAND Corporation, RR-870/1-OSD, 2014. As of October 29, 2021:
https://www.rand.org/pubs/research_reports/RR870z1.html

Morral, Andrew R., Miriam Matthews, Matthew Cefalu, Terry L. Schell, and Linda Cottrell, *Effects of Sexual Assault and Sexual Harassment on Separation from the U.S. Military: Findings from the 2014 RAND Military Workplace Study*, Santa Monica, Calif.: RAND Corporation, RR-870/10-OSD, 2021. As of October 29, 2021:
https://www.rand.org/pubs/research_reports/RR870z10.html

Morral, Andrew R., and Terry L. Schell, *Sexual Assault of Sexual Minorities in the U.S. Military*, Santa Monica, Calif.: RAND Corporation, RR-A1390-1, 2021. As of October 28, 2021:
https://www.rand.org/pubs/research_reports/RRA1390-1.html

National Defense Research Institute, *Sexual Assault and Sexual Harassment in the U.S. Military: Top-Line Estimates for Active-Duty Service Members from the 2014 RAND Military Workplace Study*, Santa Monica, Calif.: RAND Corporation, RR-870-OSD, 2014. As of November 22, 2021:
https://www.rand.org/pubs/research_reports/RR870.html

Office of People Analytics, *2018 Workplace and Gender Relations Survey of Active Duty Members: Statistical Methodology Report*, Ft. Belvoir, Va.: U.S. Department of Defense, OPA Report No. 2019-026, May 2019.

OPA—*See* Office of People Analytics.

Schell, Terry L., Matthew Cefalu, Coreen Farris, and Andrew R. Morral, *The Relationship Between Sexual Assault and Sexual Harassment in the U.S. Military: Findings from the RAND Military Workplace Study*, Santa Monica, Calif.: RAND Corporation, RR-3162-OSD, 2021. As of October 31, 2021:
https://www.rand.org/pubs/research_reports/RR3162.html

Schell, Terry L., Andrew R. Morral, Matthew Cefalu, Coreen Farris, and Miriam Matthews, *Risk Factors for Sexual Assault and Sexual Harassment in the U.S. Military: Findings from the 2014 RAND Military Workplace Study*, Santa Monica, Calif.: RAND Corporation, RR-870/9-OSD, 2021. As of November 22, 2021:
https://www.rand.org/pubs/research_reports/RR870z9.html

Trump-Steele, Rachel, Samantha Daniel, Tina DeMarco, Surya Sampath, Laura Severance, and Ashlea Klahr, *Experiences of Sexual Minority Active Duty Service Members with Sexual Harassment and Sexual Assault*, Alexandria, Va.: Office of People Analytics, OPA Report No. 2021-23, June 2021.

Under Secretary of Defense for Personnel and Readiness Clifford L. Stanley, "Repeal of 'Don't Ask, Don't Tell,'" memorandum, Washington, D.C., September 20, 2011.

U.S. Code, Title 10, Armed Forces, Section 920, Rape and Sexual Assault Generally.

U.S. Department of Defense, *Manual for Courts-Martial United States*, Washington, D.C., 2019.

U.S. Secretary of Defense, "Immediate Actions to Counter Sexual Assault and Harrassment and the Establishment of a 90-Day Independent Review Commission on Sexual Assault in the Military," memorandum for senior Pentagon leadership, commanders of the combatant commands, defense agency and DoD field activity directors, Washington, D.C. February 26, 2021.